AFRICAN HISTORICAL DICTIONARIES
Edited by Jon Woronoff

1. *Cameroon*, by Victor T. LeVine and Roger P. Nye. 1974. *Out of print. See No. 48.*
2. *The Congo*, 2nd ed., by Virginia Thompson and Richard Adloff. 1984. *Out of print. See No. 69.*
3. *Swaziland*, by John J. Grotpeter. 1975.
4. *The Gambia*, 2nd ed., by Harry A. Gailey. 1987. *See No. 79.*
5. *Botswana*, by Richard P. Stevens. 1975. *Out of print. See No. 70.*
6. *Somalia*, by Margaret F. Castagno. 1975.
7. *Benin [Dahomey]*, 2nd ed., by Samuel Decalo. 1987. *Out of print. See No. 61.*
8. *Burundi*, by Warren Weinstein. 1976. *Out of print. See No. 73.*
9. *Togo*, 3rd ed., by Samuel Decalo. 1996.
10. *Lesotho*, by Gordon Haliburton. 1977.
11. *Mali*, 3rd ed., by Pascal James Imperato. 1996.
12. *Sierra Leone*, by Cyril Patrick Foray. 1977.
13. *Chad*, 3rd ed., by Samuel Decalo. 1997.
14. *Upper Volta*, by Daniel Miles McFarland. 1978.
15. *Tanzania*, by Laura S. Kurtz. 1978.
16. *Guinea*, 3rd ed., by Thomas O'Toole with Ibrahima Bah-Lalya. 1995.
17. *Sudan*, by John Voll. 1978. *Out of print. See No. 53.*
18. *Rhodesia/Zimbabwe*, by R. Kent Rasmussen. 1979. *Out of print. See No. 46.*
19. *Zambia*, by John J. Grotpeter. 1979.
20. *Niger*, 3rd ed., by Samuel Decalo. 1996.
21. *Equatorial Guinea*, 2nd ed., by Max Liniger-Goumaz. 1988.
22. *Guinea-Bissau*, 3rd ed., by Richard Lobban and Joshua Forrest. 1996.
23. *Senegal*, by Lucie G. Colvin. 1981. *Out of print. See No. 65.*
24. *Morocco*, by William Spencer. 1980. *Out of print. See No. 71.*
25. *Malawi*, by Cynthia A. Crosby. 1980. *Out of print. See No. 54.*
26. *Angola*, by Phyllis Martin. 1980. *Out of print. See No. 52.*
27. *The Central African Republic*, by Pierre Kalck. 1980. *Out of print. See No. 51.*
28. *Algeria*, by Alf Andrew Heggoy. 1981. *Out of print. See No. 66.*
29. *Kenya*, by Bethwell A. Ogot. 1981.
30. *Gabon*, by David E. Gardinier. 1981. *Out of print. See No. 58.*
31. *Mauritania*, by Alfred G. Gerteiny. 1981. *Out of print. See No. 68.*
32. *Ethiopia*, by Chris Prouty and Eugene Rosenfeld. 1981. *Out of print. See No. 56.*
33. *Libya*, 2nd ed., by Ronald Bruce St. John. 1991.
34. *Mauritius*, by Lindsay Rivire. 1982. *Out of print. See No. 49.*
35. *Western Sahara*, by Tony Hodges. 1982. *Out of print. See No. 55.*

68. *Mauritania*, 2nd ed., by Anthony G. Pazzanita. 1996.
69. *Congo*, 3rd ed., by Samuel Decalo, Virginia Thompson, and Richard Adloff. 1996.
70. *Botswana*, 3rd ed., by Jeff Ramsay, Barry Morton, and Fred Morton. 1996.
71. *Morocco*, 2nd ed., by Thomas K. Park. 1996.
72. *Tanzania*, 2nd ed., by Thomas P. Ofcansky and Rodger Yeager. 1997.
73. *Burundi*, 2nd ed., by Ellen K. Eggers. 1997.
74. *Burkina Faso*, 2nd ed., by Daniel Miles McFarland and Lawrence Rupley. 1998.
75. *Eritrea*, by Tom Killion. 1998.
76. *Democratic Republic of Congo (Zaire)*, by F. Scott Bobb. 1998. (Revised edition of *Historical Dictionary of Zaire*, No. 43)
77. *Kenya*, 2nd ed., by Robert M. Maxon and Thomas P. Ofcansky. 1999.
78. *South Africa*, 2nd ed., by Christopher Saunders and Nicholas Southey. 1999.
79. *The Gambia*, 3rd ed., by Arnold Hughes and Harry A. Gailey. 1999.

Historical Dictionary of The Gambia

Third Edition

Arnold Hughes and
Harry A. Gailey

African Historical Dictionaries, No. 79

The Scarecrow Press, Inc.
Lanham, Maryland, and London
1999

SCARECROW PRESS, INC.

Published in the United States of America
by Scarecrow Press, Inc.
4720 Boston Way, Lanham, Maryland 20706
http://www.scarecrowpress.com

4 Pleydell Gardens, Folkestone
Kent CT20 2DN, England

Copyright © 1999 by Arnold Hughes

First edition, by Harry A. Gailey, published in 1975 by Scarecrow Press,
Metuchen, N. J.

Second edition, by Harry A. Gailey, published in 1987 by Scarecrow Press,
Metuchen, N. J.

British Library Cataloguing in Publication Information Available

Library of Congress Cataloging-in-Publication Data

Hughes, Arnold.
    Historical dictionary of the Gambia / Arnold Hughes, Harry A. Gailey. —
3rd ed.
       p.   cm. — (African historical dictionaries ; no. 79)
    Rev. ed. of: Historical dictionary of the Gambia / Harry A. Gailey. 2nd ed.
1987.
    Includes bibliographical references.
    ISBN 0-8108-3660-2 (cloth : alk. paper)
    1. Gambia—History Dictionaries.   I. Gailey, Harry A. II. Gailey, Harry A.
Historical dictionary of the Gambia.   III. Title.   IV. Series.
DT509.5.G34   1999
966.51'003—dc21   99-30681
                                             CIP

For
Diana

Contents

Editor's Foreword

Of all Africa's artificial boundaries, none is more artificial than that surrounding The Gambia. Just a narrow sliver of land along the river that gives it sustenance, it was already assumed in colonial times that the Gambia would be absorbed into surrounding French possessions. But Great Britain held on to it, and the new state was born in 1965. Again, following domestic upheavals, it appeared that it might, this time, be swallowed up by neighboring Senegal. However, that did not happen and is unlikely with the demise of the Senegambia Confederation. Thus, after more than three decades, The Gambia is still charting its own course. Its record compares favorably with that of larger and better-endowed African countries. For some time it was one of Africa's few multiparty states with a relative degree of democracy. Although this was cut off by a military coup, movement is now grudgingly in the right direction. The economy, never strong, is also gaining strength. While there are many causes for concern, there is also some room for hope.

The Gambia's very resilience, despite its small size, makes it worthy of greater notice. Certainly, after more than a decade, it merits a revised edition of the *Historical Dictionary of The Gambia*. Like its two predecessors, this volume looks at The Gambia's history from precolonial and colonial times to the present. It includes entries on significant persons, places and events, institutions and parties, and various political, economic and social topics. Naturally, the book has grown. The chronology is longer, the introduction probes more deeply, and the dictionary entries are more numerous. In particular, the bibliography has been extended to take into account new scholarship and publications.

The first two editions were written by Harry A. Gailey Jr. Professor Gailey, who was Coordinator of African Studies at San Jose University, has been a pioneering historian of The Gambia and author of numerous articles about the country, as well as *A History of The Gambia*, the standard text on its history up to independence. The third edition has been expanded by another leading authority, Arnold Hughes. Professor Hughes, until recently

Director of the Centre of West African Studies at the University of Birmingham, U.K., has specialized in the study of the more recent political history of The Gambia. A frequent visitor to The Gambia, he has written numerous articles and book chapters both on its domestic politics and its external relations, as well as editing *The Gambia: Studies in Society and Politics*. Between them they have provided an extended and up-to-date record of The Gambia.

Jon Woronoff
Series Editor

Acronyms and Abbreviations

AFPRC	Armed Forces Provisional Ruling Council
APRC	Alliance for Patriotic Re-orientation and Construction
BOAC	British Overseas Airways Corporation
BRPA	Bathurst Rate Payers Association
BTU	Bathurst Trade Union
BYMS	Bathurst Young Muslim Society
CDC	Colonial/Commonwealth Development Corporation
CD & WA	Colonial Development and Welfare Acts
CMS	Church Missionary Society
DCA	Democratic Congress Alliance
ECOWAS	Economic Community of West African States
ERP	Economic Recovery Programme
GATU	Gambia Amalgamated Trade Union
GCP	Gambia Congress Party
GDP	Gambia Democratic Party
GDP	Gross Domestic Product
GFF	Gambia Field Force
GLU	Gambia Labour Union
GMC	Gambia Muslim Congress
GMDMU	Gambia Motor Drivers and Mechanics Union
GNA	Gambia National Army
GNG	Gambia National Gendarmerie
GNP	Gambia National Party
GNU	Gambia National Union
GOMB	Groundnut Oilseeds Marketing Board
GPMB	Gambia Produce Marketing Board (formerly GOMB)
GPP	Gambia People's Party
GSRP	Gambia Socialist Revolutionary Party
GWC	Gambia Workers Confederation
GWU	Gambia Workers Union
ICFTU	International Confederation of Free Trade Unions

IMF	International Monetary Fund
MFDC	Movement of Democratic Forces of the Casamance/Mouvement des Forces Démocratiques de la Casamance
MOJA-G	Movement for Justice in Africa-Gambia
MP	Member of Parliament
MRC	Medical Research Council
NCBWA	National Congress of British West Africa
NCP	National Convention Party
NGO	Nongovernmental Organization
NLP	National Liberation Party
NRP	National Reconciliation Party
OAU	Organization of African Unity
OMVG	Organisation for the Development of the Gambia River Basin
PDOIS (DOI)	People's Democratic Organisation for Independence and Socialism
PDP	People's Democratic Party
PPA	People's Progressive Alliance
PPP	People's Progressive Party (originally Protectorate People's Party)
PS	Parti Socialiste
PSD	Programme for Sustainable Development
RAC	Royal African Corps
RAMC	Royal Army Medical Corps
RWAFF	Royal West African Frontier Force
UDP	United Democratic Party
UP	United Party

THE GAMBIA

Km
0 10 20 30

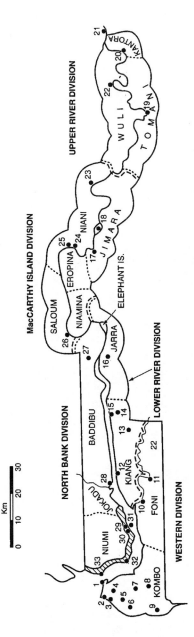

NORTH BANK DIVISION

MacCARTHY ISLAND DIVISION

UPPER RIVER DIVISION

WESTERN DIVISION

LOWER RIVER DIVISION

JOKADU

NIUMI

BADDIBU

SALOUM

NIAMINA

EROPINA

NIANI

WULI

KANTORA

TOMANI

JIMARA

ELEPHANT IS.

JARRA

KIANG

FONI

KOMBO

- - - - - Pre-colonial boundaries
- - - Colonial divisional boundaries
▨▨▨ The ceded mile

Map Key

1. Banjul (Bathurst)—St. Mary's Island
2. Cape Point
3. Bakau
4. Serekunda
5. Sukuta (Sabaji)
6. Brufut
7. Yundum
8. Brikama
9. Gunjur
10. Bintang
11. Bwiam (Geregia)
12. Tankular
13. Sankandi
14. Tendaba
15. Mansakonko
16. Kwinella
17. Wallikunda
18. Georgetown (Janjangbure)
19. Basse Santa So
20. Kristikunda
21. Barrakunda
22. Fatatenda
23. Karantaba (Pisania)
24. Kuntaur
25. Wassu
26. Joar
27. Farafenni
28. Kerewan
29. Juffure (San Domingo)
30. Albreda
31. James Island (St. Andrew's Island)
32. Dog Island (James Island)
33. Barra/Fort Bullen

Chronology

7th to 9th Centuries.   Estimated date of construction of stone circles, possibly by ancestors of Jola people. First southeastward migrations of significant numbers of Fulbe probably took place during this time.

13th to 15th Centuries.   Period of Malian hegemony over the western Sudan. Gambian Mandinka kingdoms were the westernmost extension of that empire. Large numbers of Muslim converts appeared in the Senegambia.

16th to 17th Centuries.   Period of state building among the Wolof in Senegal. Development of Jolof, Walo, Baol, and Cayor. Serer kingdoms of Sine and Saloum also developed in this period. First permanent European settlements in Senegambia during this time. Gradual acceleration of the slave trade.

18th Century.   Creation of Islamic theocracy in the Futa Toro and continued conversion of large numbers of Gambians, particularly Fulbe, to Islam. Century-long French-British conflicts in Senegambia which disrupted trade and helped keep the slave trade to a minimal level.

1455 and 1456   First two Portuguese voyages (Cadamosto and Usidimare) to the Gambia River.

1458   Diego Gomez explored the Gambia River.

1553   First English voyages to the Gambia.

1588   First English monopoly company for West African trade.

1618   Royal charter given to the Company of Adventurers of London trading into Africa.

1620   Richard Jobson sent to the Gambia as company factor.

1621   Dutch West Indies Company established at Goree.

1651   Courlanders in the Gambia; built fort on St. Andrews (James) Island. Commonwealth Guinea Company formed.

1652 Prince Rupert in the Gambia.

1661 English captured James Island on March 19.

1662 Royal Adventurers Company formed.

1668 Gambia Adventurers Company established.

1672 French Senegal Company formed.

1672–1752 Royal African Company.

1677 French captured Goree.

1681 French established Albreda.

1689–1783 Trade wars in Senegambia between France and Great Britain.

1696 French Royal Senegal Company established.

1730 Francis Moore, factor for Royal African Company,
arrived in the Gambia.

1750 Company of Merchants Trading in Africa formed.

1758 French bases in Senegal captured.

1765–1783 British Province of the Senegambia.

1779 James Fort destroyed for last time.

1783–1821 Gambia again controlled by Company of Merchants.

1790 Major Houghton left the Gambia for Timbuktu.

1795–1798 Mungo Park's explorations from the Gambia.

1805 Beginning of Mungo Park's second expedition.

1807 British decision to abolish the slave trade. British settlement of the Gambia formed.

1816 Purchase of St. Mary's Island from King of Kombo and beginnings of Bathurst (Banjul). British abandoned James Fort.

1821 Gambia placed under jurisdiction of Sierra Leone.

1823 First British establishment in April at MacCarthy Island. Arrival of first contingent of Christian missionaries.

1826 The King of Barra (Niumi) granted the Ceded Mile to Great Britain.

1830   First recorded shipment of groundnuts from the Gambia.

1831–1832   The Barra or Anglo-Niumi War between the British and the King of Barra.

1843   Gambia created a separate Colony with Executive and Legislative Councils.

1851   Beginnings of Soninke-Marabout Wars in Kombo.

1853   The King of Kombo ceded a portion of Kombo to the British.

1855   Marabout attack upon British Kombo and Bathurst.

1857   French surrendered Albreda to British.

1860–1867   Ma Bah attempted to create a Senegambia Islamic empire.

1861–1881   Alfa and Musa Molloh created the Fulbe state of Fuladu.

1862   Marabouts invaded Barra.

1864   Amer Faal's operations in Niumi. Fodi Kabba attacked Yundum.

1865   Report of Parliamentary Committee on West Africa.

1866   Gambia placed under jurisdiction of Sierra Leone again.

1866–1870   First negotiations for exchange of the Gambia between Great Britain and France.

1873–1875   Fodi Silla destroyed remaining Soninke power in Kombo.

1875–1876   Second period of negotiations for exchange of the Gambia between Great Britain and France.

1877–1887   Civil war in Baddibu between forces of Biram Cisse, Sait Maty, and Mamadou N'Dare.

1888   Gambia became a separate colony; reinstatement of Legislative and Executive Councils.

1889   Anglo-French agreement which fixed the present boundaries of the Gambia.

1891   International Boundary Commission sent to the Gambia.

1892   Following threats to the work of the Anglo-French boundary commission, Fodi Kabba was driven into Casamance by British forces.

1894   Fodi Silla captured by the French and exiled. First comprehensive Ordinance for governing the Protectorate.

1900   Travelling Commissioner Sitwell's party ambushed at Sankandi.

1901   British-French punitive expedition and death of Fodi Kabba. Office of Administrator upgraded to Governor.

1904   Anglo-French Convention began the entente and granted the French the right to a mid-river port.

1913   General revision of Ordinance for the governing of the Protectorate.

1914–1918   World War I. Gambia Company, Royal West African Frontier Force (RWAFF), saw service in the Cameroon and East Africa.

1915   Enlargement of Legislative Council.

1919–1922   Redemption of French five-franc piece.

1923   Opening of Armitage School, Georgetown.

1929   Bathurst Trade Union formed.

1931   Bathurst Urban District Council created.

1933   A third African member of Legislative Council nominated by the Bathurst Urban District Council.

1933   General reorganization of Protectorate government and courts system.

1935   Name of Bathurst Urban District Council changed to Bathurst Advisory Town Council.

1939–1945   World War II. Gambian troops of RWAFF active in China-Burma-India theatre. Yundum airfield constructed as Allied transit base.

1940   First British Colonial Development and Welfare Act.

1943   K. W. Blackburne's report on immediate and long-range economic needs of the Gambia.

1945–1950   Reconstruction of port, street, and sewer facilities of Bathurst with Colonial Development and Welfare funds.

1947   Reorganization and enlargement of Legislative Council.

1948–1951   Yundum egg project fiasco.

1949–1954   Wallikunda rice scheme.

1951   New Constitution. Reorganization of the Legislative Council which provided for two elected members from Bathurst, and one from Kombo St. Mary. Gambia Democratic Party (GDP) formed.

1952   Gambia Muslim Congress (GMC) formed. United Party (UP) formed. First class at Yundum College for teachers.

1953   Meeting of 34 Gambian representatives to revise the Constitution.

1954   New Constitution allowing direct elective principle for seven members of the Legislative Council.

1956   Gambia Workers Union created.

1957   Sinking of Barra ferry in May with loss of over 50 lives.

1959   Protectorate People's Party formed; later renamed People's Progressive Party (PPP).

1960   New Constitution. Legislative Council became House of Representatives with 19 directly elected seats. First national elections held. PPP largest single party in the House. Democratic Congress Alliance (DCA) created.

1961   P. S. N'Jie appointed the first Gambian Chief Minister.

1962   New Constitution allowing full internal self government and a 36-member House of Representatives with ministerial government. Second national elections. PPP won overall majority and D. K. Jawara became Prime Minister.

1963   First major comprehensive census of the Gambia.

1965   The Gambia achieved independence from Great Britain on February 18. Voters rejected proposal for a republic in November referendum.

1970   Voters approved proposal for a republic in a second referendum in April. Sir Dawda Jawara became the first President of The Gambia.

1972   Elections. PPP further increased parliamentary majority, 28 seats to UP's three. President Jawara reelected President.

1975–1979   First Sahel drought period.

1976   Formation of National Convention Party (NCP).

1977   Parliamentary elections. PPP again won, 27 seats to NCP's five. NCP replaced UP as main opposition party. President Jawara reelected.

1981   Attempted coup d'etat on July 30 in Banjul by disaffected paramilitary police and radical political opponents of PPP government. Senegalese army intervened to restore President Jawara to power. State of Emergency declared and estimated 600 persons killed. Uprising led to creation of Senegambia Confederation in December.

1982   Senegambia Confederation officially inaugurated February 1. Parliamentary and presidential elections. PPP returned to power with 27 out of 35 seats and Sir Dawda reelected President.

1986   Formation of Gambia People's Party (GPP) and People's Democratic Organisation for Independence and Socialism (PDOIS).

1987   Parliamentary and presidential elections. PPP won 31 of 36 seats and Sir Dawda returned to power.

1989   Dissolution of Senegambia Confederation in December.

1992   Presidential and parliamentary elections. Formation of the new People's Democratic Party (PDP). PPP won 25 of 36 seats and Sir Dawda returned to power.

1994   Successful military coup on July 22. Constitution suspended, political parties abolished, and Jawara exiled to United Kingdom. Lieutenant Yahya Jammeh headed military junta—Armed Forces Provisional Ruling Council (AFPRC).

1994   November. Unsuccessful attempt by disaffected junior officers to overthrow AFPRC.

1995   January. Second unsuccessful attempt to overthrow Jammeh. Two junta leaders, Lieutenants Sana Sabally and Sadibou Hydara, jailed for their part in organizing plot.

1996   Following national consultations and a referendum, a new constitution was introduced and presidential elections held in September. Old political parties still banned. Jammeh, candidate of army-backed Alliance for Patriotic Re-orientation and Construction (APRC), defeated Ousainu Darboe of the United Democratic Party (UDP) and two other challengers.

1997   Parliamentary elections held in January. APRC won 33 seats to seven for UDP in five-party contest for 45 seats in renamed National Assembly.

Introduction

The tiny Republic of The Gambia is situated in the extreme western part of the African continent, surrounded on three sides by Senegal. The boundaries of The Gambia are completely artificial, having nothing to do with natural ethnic or geographic lines of demarcation. They were first drawn in 1889 during a meeting of French and British delegates in Paris and were only slightly modified by later survey parties. The boundaries thus agreed upon satisfied both European governments and were meant to be only temporary since both parties were convinced that eventually there would be an exchange of the territory. For a variety of reasons, no transfer ever took place, and thus 1,038,145 (1993) Gambians are constrained to live in a country whose limits are six miles distant from either side of the Gambia River, save at the river's estuary where the country is 30 miles wide, and about 200 miles in length; making a total land area of 4,361 square miles (11,295 square kilometers), approximately the size of the Lebanon or Jamaica. These boundaries exclude The Gambia from free access to its natural hinterland and divide the Gambian Wolof, Jola, Mandinka, and Fulbe people from their kinsmen in Senegal.

The present-day boundaries of The Gambia present specific problems for the historian. Much of its history was not confined to the narrow serpentine state, but extended over the broad savannah and sahel areas that today compose Senegal. This is particularly true of the period extending from the 13th to the 16th centuries when the Gambia Valley was being populated by a series of complex migrations. Although little detailed information is available, the Wolof, Mandinka, and Fulbe people established themselves in different parts of the Senegambia and there created first village- or clan-based polities and finally large kingdoms. These state-building processes were still going on when the first European traders came to the Senegambian coast. By the beginning of the 17th century, however, large complex states had been created throughout the region with kings, advisors, bureaucracies, and armed forces. The economic basis of each of these states was village-oriented agriculture, although trade was important, particularly for those living near the rivers or close to a hinterland trade route.

EUROPEAN PRESENCE ON THE GAMBIA

European contact with the Gambia region dates to 1455, when the Portuguese first entered the estuary of the river. For over a century they maintained intermittent contacts with the area, unchallenged by any European rival. During this period a number of Portuguese chose to settle in the Gambia, and the Portuguese government and Catholic Church sponsored missionary activities among the Mandinka. However, the Gambia was never an important trading entrepot, and the Portuguese had decided to concentrate their efforts elsewhere along the west coast even before their trading monopoly was attacked by other European states. During the early 17th century, few Portuguese traders came to the Gambia on a regular basis. By the 18th century, the Portuguese interlude was only dimly remembered by the people of the Gambia and the Portuguese left behind nothing of permanence.

The latter half of the 16th century witnessed continental rivalries of European states that were invariably transformed into worldwide conflicts. During the next two centuries, England, France, and Holland vied with one another for dominance in the world's mercantile trade. Transferred to the Senegambia region, these European quarrels disturbed the general peace, lowered profits, and ultimately prevented any one state from gaining a monopoly of the area's trade. At this juncture it is important to note that the Senegambia was not an area possessing great amounts of ivory, timber, pepper, or gold, and thus was bypassed by the major thrust of European trade in favor of more lucrative areas such as the Gold Coast. Nevertheless, trading companies were active in the Gambia from 1588 onward.

As the slave trade became more important, European investment in ships, fixed goods, and trading materials also increased in the Gambia. The trading pattern for all European states was dictated by mercantilism. Companies would be formed by stockholders, who would receive a charter from a European monarch giving them sole privileges to trade in a specific area. These companies would then attempt to exploit their grant by sending out to West Africa a wide variety of trade products to exchange for African goods. In some areas the company men would be forced to trade directly from their ships; in others, they would be allowed by the African rulers to build temporary trading stations and, in a few instances, including the Gold Coast, the Europeans manned a series of permanent fortified trading posts.

Although British trade in the Senegambia dates to 1553 and French to 1560, the first permanent trading post in the Gambia was erected by the tiny Baltic Duchy of Courland (Latvia) in 1651. It purchased an island in the Gambia River called St. Andrew's Island and there constructed a fort. In 1661, the Courlanders were driven out by the English, who renamed the tiny island after James, Duke of York. James Island continued to be the center of English trading activities in the Gambia for over a century, first for the Royal Adventurers of England Trading into Africa, then the Royal African Company and, lastly, independent merchants.

French companies meanwhile had carved out a trading sphere further to the north, at the mouth of the Senegal River, and also opposite Cape Verde. St. Louis was founded in 1638, the island of Goree was taken from the Dutch in 1677, and the French established a station at Albreda opposite James Island in 1681. The 18th-century history of the French in the Senegambia is one of continual conflict with British elements on the Gambia River. For a brief period after 1760, the British controlled all French territory and created the Province of the Senegambia, only to return it all to France after the Treaty of Versailles in 1783. During the last stages of the American Revolution, a French force so completely destroyed the fort on James Island that it was never occupied again. The British presence on the Gambia River in the last two decades of the 18th century was maintained by private traders without any definite official support for their activities.

All was changed by the 1807 British decision to abolish the slave trade as of January 1, 1808. It then became necessary to attempt to control the activities of British nationals along the western coast of Africa. For this purpose a squadron of the Royal Navy was despatched to patrol the coastline. The force needed harbor facilities, which involved the British government directly in the administration of the Freetown Colony, and in 1816, Captain Alexander Grant was authorized to establish a base on the Gambia River.

He rejected the old site of British authority, James Island, and instead negotiated the cession, by the King of Kombo, of Banjul Island (which he renamed St. Mary's Island), adjacent to the south bank near the mouth of the river. In the next four years, Grant and his small garrison of a few hundred troops constructed administration buildings, harbor facilities, and barracks on the island. Within months of its foundation, the new town of Bathurst (today Banjul) had attracted considerable numbers of neighboring Africans. In the 1820s and 1830s, the population of the area was greatly augmented by Wolof merchants from the Cape Verde area and by Africans liberated from captured slave ships. In 1821, the administration of the new Colony was taken from the Company of Merchants and vested in the Governor of

Freetown. Affairs in the Gambia were handled directly by an Administrator subordinate to the Governor. The size of the Colony was increased in 1823 by the acquisition of MacCarthy Island and in 1826 by the ruler of Barra's cession of what was known as the Ceded Mile.

AFRICAN SOCIETIES BEFORE EUROPEAN INTERVENTION

European trade rivalry and the change in the fortunes of one state or another had little to do with the lives of the majority of Africans in the Senegambia. They, of course, were affected by the volume, type, and direction of trade, but direct relations with Europeans were not typical in the Gambia. There were no revolutionary economic changes in any of the kingdoms, since the area was never a major center for the slave trade and there were few other products that the Europeans wanted. Thus the Mandinka polities along the river and the Serer and Wolof states to the north continued to evolve slowly with little outside interference.

In the early 19th century, there were nine Mandinka kingdoms on the south side of the Gambia River: Kombo, Foni, Kiang, Jarra, Niamina, Eropina, Jimara, Tomani, and Kantora. Along the north bank there were five kingdoms: Niumi, Baddibu, Upper and Lower Niami, and Wuli. Although each state was separate, and customs and polities differed to a certain extent in each, all of them shared certain commonalities. Each society was divided into three endogamous castes: the freeborn, the artisans and praise singers, and the slaves. Each state had a king (*mansa*) chosen from a specific royal lineage. Each king had his council of advisors and an armed force to defend the state; if necessary, he could use this force to impose his will upon the state. Each kingdom was subdivided into the territorial units of the village, ward, and family compound. Each village area was governed by a *satee-tiyo,* a representative of the senior lineage of the village, and his council. The ward leaders, or *kabilo-tiyos,* administered their areas with the help of advisors. Thus each state was held together by a combination of tradition, kinship patterns, and force. The population of many of these kingdoms was relatively homogeneous, but some of the kings ruled over large non-Mandinka minorities. There were Wolof and Serer in Niumi and Baddibu, the Jola were located in Kombo and Foni, and there were many Serahuli in the upriver kingdom of Wuli. Large numbers of Fulbe had traditionally migrated from the Futa Toro to the Futa Jallon through some of the Mandinka states. By the mid-19th century the Fulbe had become a significant factor in the affairs of Eropina, Jimara, Tomani, and Kantora.

To the north of the Gambia River were the larger, more powerful polities of the Serer and Wolof. Each of the Wolof states had evolved from the earlier kingdom of Jolof in the 16th century. The Serer kingdoms of Sine and Saloum had evolved in the same period with a mixed population. The Wolof and Serer states, like those of the Mandinka, were of the Sudanic type with a king representing a particular lineage, nobles who controlled much of the land made up the king's councils, and commanded the armies, and peasants, artisans, and slaves. Each polity maintained a large army, and there was incessant diplomatic maneuvering and open warfare between the states because each king was jealous of his prerogatives and wanted to dominate his neighbors.

In the 19th century all the Senegambian kingdoms were subjected to new pressures and the intensification of old cleavages. After the mid-century, the French became much more active in the hinterland of the Senegambia. The forward policy of Governor Louis Faidherbe effectively converted much of the coastal region of Senegal into a French protectorate. Groundnuts had become an important item of trade, particularly in Sine and Saloum, and French traders there demanded protection. Attempts to provide this embroiled the French in the internal affairs of all the kingdoms north of the Gambia River. The British government, although disavowing territorial ambitions, nevertheless interfered continually in the affairs of the Gambian kingdoms. From their base at Bathurst they mounted a number of punitive expeditions against both the traditional rulers and their Marabout challengers.

THE SONINKE-MARABOUT WARS

The most fundamental changes in the 19th century were introduced by proselytizing Muslim teachers, known as Marabouts. Islam had made slow but steady progress among the peoples of the Senegambia during the previous two centuries. The religious revival that had wrought such great reforms in the societies of Futa Toro, Macina, Futa Jallon, and northern Nigeria reached the Senegambia by the 1850s. Seeking basic religious, social, and political reforms, the Marabouts and their growing number of followers attacked the traditional Mandinka—Soninke—systems of rule in the kingdoms of the Gambia. Thus began the half-century of internecine conflicts known as the Soninke-Marabout Wars.

The first major test between the old order and the new religious beliefs occurred in the south bank kingdoms of Kombo and Foni. In Kombo, Fodi Kabba of Gunjur, operating with the followers of Omar of Sabaji from 1853 to 1855, conquered a large area of the western section of the kingdom. When the British Administrator, Colonel O'Connor, appeared to favor the Soninke rulers, the Marabouts began planning for the total removal of British power. In June 1855, the Marabouts overwhelmed the advance elements of the British garrison in an ambush, forcing O'Connor to retreat to Bathurst, having sustained casualties of over one-quarter of his force. Only with extreme difficulty and considerable numbers of reinforcements was he able to defeat the Marabouts. Although O'Connor's final victory stabilized the British position, it ultimately did little to protect the traditional rulers, as yet more people pledged their loyalties to Fodi Kabba, Fodi Silla, and their lieutenants. The British would give no physical support to the traditional rulers, contenting themselves with intervening from time to time to arrange a truce between the antagonists. The last of these interludes lasted for seven years after the truce of 1864. The final test of strength of the two factions in Kombo occurred between 1871 and 1875. In the latter year, the king, Tomani Bojang, surrendered his last fortified town, accepted the peace terms of Fodi Silla, and became a Muslim.

During the 1860s, Fodi Kabba shifted the area of his activities to Foni and Kiang. Except in Jola country, he and the other Marabouts were generally successful in imposing their will upon the people. The Jola, however, remained stubbornly independent and "pagan." Fodi Kabba's forces did not receive a serious check in other parts of the south bank kingdoms until they encountered the westward moving elements of the Fulbe armies loyal to Alfa and Musa Molloh. Eastern Kiang and western Jarra became for the rest of the century the rough dividing line between the territories controlled by Fodi Kabba and those controlled by his enemies, the Mollohs.

The reforms demanded by the early Marabouts related specifically to the spread of Islam. They wanted to eradicate "pagan" influences and substitute for them a well-ordered Muslim society. However, even at the beginning the movement drew to it a wide spectrum of protesters, many of whom were little concerned with the advancement of Islam. Throughout the Gambia the initial Marabout successes were tied to the military or political skill of a few men. As these men supplanted their Soninke enemies, they tended to lose their religious fervor, and much of the warfare after 1870 was motivated primarily by personal or economic considerations rather than religion. Although this shift of emphasis is quite noticeable in the careers of Fodi Kabba and Fodi Silla, the best illustration of the secular nature of revolt against traditional authority is the career of the Mollohs in their state of Fuladu.

During the first half of the 19th century, there was an increasing influx of Fulbe into the south bank kingdoms of Tomani, Jimara, and Eropina. A Fulbe elephant hunter of Jimara, who later took the name Alfa Molloh and was renowned for his ability with arms, quarrelled with his Mandinka overlord in the late 1860s. This began a revolt that, within five years, swept away the old system of government. In this phase as well as in later wars, Alfa Molloh counted heavily on the support of his fellow Fulbe rulers in the theocracies of Futa Toro and Futa Jallon. It was believed that he had taken the Tijaniyya oath and had been made a deputy of Al Hajj Umar, the leading religious warrior in the middle Niger at this time. Such rumors did not damage his image and were important in gaining Muslim adherents. However, the mantle of religious reformer rested lightly upon Alfa, and his son, Musa, was even less committed to the spread of Islam. They ranged themselves against Fodi Kabba and, in the 1880s, Musa consistently allied his state against the expansion of Ma Bah's successors. Both the Mollohs were more concerned with the preservation of Fuladu, which they had created, than with advancing the cause of their religion against traditional "pagan" beliefs.

After Alfa's death in 1881, Fuladu was divided into two parts since, by the Fulbe law of succession, the kingship was inherited by Musa's uncle, Bakari Dembel. Musa, who had led his father's armies, refused to accept this situation. He led his followers southward and established a fortified base in Hamdallai. He continued to pay nominal allegiance to his uncle, but it was Musa who was the real power in Fuladu. Finally, in 1892, he moved against Bakari and proclaimed himself king of Fuladu. Long before this, Musa had created the best-organized state in the Gambia. The highly centralized bureaucracy of the state placed almost absolute civil power in his hands. His control of the military forces assured Musa that his authority over his section of Fuladu was complete. This Fulbe autocracy would be altered only by the actions of the French and British.

The only serious attempt during the Soninke-Marabout Wars to establish a true theocracy of the type successfully achieved by Al Hajj Umar and Usuman dan Fodio elsewhere in West Africa was that of Ma Bah, the ruler of Baddibu. Ma Bah, a religious teacher, puritan, and Tijaniyya reformer, seized power in Baddibu in 1861, driving out the traditional rulers. Very soon he had gathered around him a significant number of believers, and with this force he attempted to expand his control over Niumi. Here he encountered active opposition from the British and personally abandoned the forceful incorporation of Niumi into his kingdom. However, his lieutenant, Amer Faal, continued the Marabout conquests there, and by the 1880s, the bulk of Niumi was controlled by the Muslims.

Ma Bah differed from most of his contemporaries because he always saw himself as a religious teacher and leader who was merely working out God's will in destroying the pagan kingdoms of the Senegambia. His armies were led by subordinates. Only once did his forces seriously attempt to gain a foothold on the south bank of the Gambia. In 1863, Ma Bah authorized a large segment of his army to cross the river and attack the Soninkes in Kiang. In one of the major battles of the Soninke-Marabout Wars, Ma Bah's forces were decisively beaten at Kwinella. After this, Ma Bah turned his full attention toward the overthrow of the Serer and Wolof states to the north.

In his attempt to create a large Senegambian theocracy, Ma Bah was aided by the ex-rulers of Cayor, Macadou and Lat Dior, and their followers. By early 1865, the bulk of Saloum was under his control, and that summer his forces conquered Jolof. At this juncture his schemes were foiled by the French. They had at first welcomed Ma Bah since it appeared that he was weakening the power of the traditional rulers in Senegal. However, he had succeeded too well. The French, who considered the entire Senegal as their trading sphere, did not want a large powerful unified polity to take the place of the divided, weaker traditional states. Governor Pinet Laprade of Senegal decided to halt Ma Bah's advance and proceeded to Kaolack with approximately 5,000 men. At the battle of Pathebadiane in November 1865, the French and their allies were narrowly defeated and forced to retreat. Ma Bah, however, was attempting too much with his limited forces. He was supporting Lat Dior in southern Cayor and Amer Faal in Niumi, as well as maintaining forces in Saloum and Jolof. In 1867, Ma Bah decided to end the potential threat of the Serer state of Sine and accompanied his army in its invasion. In the most crucial conflict of the Soninke-Marabout Wars, the Sine forces defeated those of Ma Bah, and the prophet-teacher himself was killed.

The practical realization of the dream of a united Senegambia ended with Ma Bah's death. Within a brief period, Saloum and Jolof became independent, and Baddibu itself was rent by civil war. The chiefs of Baddibu selected Ma Bah's brother, Mamadou N'Dare, as the ruler, but within a decade his rule was disputed by one of his lieutenants, Biram Cisse. Soon afterward, Ma Bah's son, Sait Maty, also claimed the throne. In the armed conflicts which followed, Mamadou lost most of his power and the kingdom was ruled by Biram Cisse and Sait Maty. This state of affairs greatly reduced Baddibu's power and made its absorption by the French and British easy.

EUROPEAN INTERVENTION

The continuing disturbances of the Soninke-Marabout Wars interfered with trade and made the British possessions on the Gambia River appear worthless to Parliament and to a ministry devoted to saving money. All the Administrators of the Gambia were under orders to do nothing that would involve the British in a major conflict in the hinterland. Thus they acted against the Soninkes or Marabouts only when it was impossible to avoid some kind of definite action and when the chances of precipitating a larger conflict appeared minimal. Otherwise, the British were content to act as arbiters in the conflicts. The Parliamentary Report of 1865 entitled "Report on the conditions of the British settlements on the West Coast of Africa" confirmed the no-expansion policy in the Gambia.

The French, however, since the governorship of Faidherbe, had been pursuing an aggressive trade policy in the independent Wolof and Serer states. The increasing value of the groundnut crop aided the few, but ardent, French imperialists in Senegal and in France. These men saw a potentially great future for France in West Africa. Thus the Governors of Senegal used what military forces they had to upset Wolof governments in Baol, Walo, and Cayor, in order to blunt the westward ambitions of Al Hajj Umar and his son, Ahmadu; to build forts in Sine, Saloum, and Jolof; and to help defeat Ma Bah's ambitions.

It is not surprising, therefore, that the French government should approach the British concerning an exchange of some French territory in return for the British possession on the Gambia River. The idea of such a trade-off was first suggested by the French in 1866. After four years of negotiations, almost all the details for an exchange had been completed when the onset of the Franco-Prussian War stopped all discussions. Internal difficulties in France postponed the resumption of negotiations until 1875. The French Foreign Ministry again found the British government receptive to their proposals. However, a combination of parliamentary and commercial opposition from British and Gambian merchants halted the exchange. Despite this failure, the French government was convinced that, in time, Britain would cede the unwanted territory and France would be in possession of the Gambia River, the most economical highway to the interior of West Africa.

The "scramble" for Africa became a reality in the 1880s, and the French began to occupy coastal areas that had long been considered British spheres. In Senegal they absorbed the coastal Wolof states and began in the late 1880s to interfere in the quarrels in Baddibu and Fuladu. The British government, spurred on by the urging of the Gambian Administrators, who believed that Britain was about to lose the Gambia by default, finally authorized the establishment of a Protectorate. In 1888, the Gambia was separated from the administrative control of Sierra Leone. In the following year, British and French representatives met in Paris to allocate spheres of influence in West Africa. The British delegation was prepared to cede the

Gambia, provided the French would be more flexible in their demands elsewhere. When it became apparent that the French delegates were not prepared to compromise, the British demanded control of the river. British lack of interest in territorial acquisition in the Senegambia can be seen in their refusal to demand more territory than the narrow riverine strip that the French were willing to admit was a British sphere. However, neither power considered that the boundaries drawn by the Anglo-French Convention of 1889 were to be permanent.

Administrator Sir Robert Llewelyn had seen British policy change in the space of a few months from non-expansionist to expansionist. After the 1889 Convention, he was charged with developing some suitable method of bringing law and order to the new Protectorate and devising a permanent system of government for the area. At first he could do little but announce the Protectorate and enter into generalized agreements with various Gambian chiefs. His first use of the military, in 1891, was to protect the Anglo-French Boundary Commissioners from possible attack by Fodi Kabba and Fodi Silla. In January 1893, he assigned two Travelling Commissioners, one for the north bank and the other for the south, to convey his orders and requests to the Gambian rulers. In the following year the Gambian government issued the first comprehensive Protectorate Ordinance. Although the full implications of this Ordinance were not felt for some time, it established the form of government for most of the Gambia, which was to continue until just prior to independence. Later called "indirect rule," this system had the advantage of disturbing the Protectorate Gambians to a very limited extent, and yet the British authorities at Bathurst could control overall political activities in the Protectorate by ordinances which were then enforced by their Commissioners.

The Anglo-French Convention of 1889 presented many of the Gambian rulers in the Senegambia with almost insoluble problems. The accord meant for some the division of their kingdoms, forcing them to make a choice of which European government to accept as their overlord. To others, the establishment of European authority meant the abandonment of a lifestyle which had been established for over a generation. Fodi Silla was the first to feel the changed nature of European activity. After he had been overawed by British gunboats in 1891, he remained quiescent until 1893, recognized by the British as the ruler of western Kombo. Then problems related to trade, particularly his participation in the slave trade, prompted the British to invade his territory. In February 1894, his main base of Gunjur was taken, and he was forced to flee to the Casamance. There he was arrested by French authorities and deported to St. Louis.

Fodi Kabba was driven into the Casamance in 1892, and from there he continued to support those Gambians dissatisfied with British rule. Periodically his followers would go on raids into the Gambia and retreat to French territory before effective pursuit could be organized. In 1900, at Sankandi, Travelling Commissioner F. C. Sitwell and other members of his party were killed. The town was known to be allied to Fodi Kabba, and the British and French decided to end his power permanently. A joint military expedition was mounted in 1901, and in March of that year Fodi Kabba was killed. Musa Molloh of Fuladu had decided in the early 1890s to live in peace with his neighbors and the Europeans. He chose to continue to live at Hamdallai in the Casamance and cooperated with the French. In 1901, he took part in the expedition against his old enemy, Fodi Kabba. However, his freedom from direct control had ended, and, when the French decided to build a military post at Hamdallai, he burned the town and retreated with many of his followers to British Fuladu. There he was recognized as chief, received a stipend, and was generally left alone until after World War I. Then, reacting to rumors of his cruel and arbitrary actions, the British deposed him and sent him into exile. Four years later, in 1923, he was allowed to return, but he was almost completely stripped of power in the small territory which the British allotted to him.

GAMBIA UNDER COLONIAL RULE

The British assumption of power in the Gambia was largely without incident. Most Gambians were obviously exhausted by the half-century of wars, and many welcomed peace. The system of "indirect rule" as developed in the 20th century permitted a considerable degree of continuity in the political and social systems which had existed prior to 1889. During the first 35 years of the 20th century, a series of Protectorate Ordinances was enacted, fixing the responsibilities of the state-supported chiefs, the Travelling Commissioners (District Officers), and the central administration. In very general terms, the central government, which was also that of the Colony area, comprised the Governor, the appointive Legislative and Executive Councils, the Secretariat, and the various departments such as Agriculture, Marine and Public Works. The central government made all laws and regulations for the Protectorate, and the departments were responsible for work undertaken in the areas of their jurisdiction in the Protectorate. Government in the Protectorate was carried on by a minimal number of Travelling Commissioners, subsequently renamed Divisional Commissioners (there were never more than five), who supervised the work of the 35 recognized chiefs and who saw that the laws enacted by the central government were carried out.

The key to social and economic development in the British system of rule in all Africa was the amount of money the Treasury would make available. The British Colonial Office followed a general rule that all territories had to live within their budgets. This meant that more economically viable territories such as Nigeria could expect considerable development of roads, transport, agriculture, and even education. A small, poor area such as the Gambia was hard pressed just to meet its recurrent budget. Another facet of British financial administration was its conservatism. Although the Gambia had acquired considerable cash reserves by 1918, these funds normally were not used for development. Thus few improvements were made in the Protectorate until after World War II, when Colonial Development and Welfare Acts funds became available for the first time. The Colony area, basically the capital Bathurst and its surrounding territory, was more fortunate. In Bathurst, the port facilities were improved, some streets were paved, a hospital was established, and missionary groups maintained elementary and secondary schools.

The Gambia in the first half of the 20th century progressed very little. It was sustained by a single export crop, groundnuts, whose taxable value was just enough to keep the government functioning. Beginning in 1942, the British government held out promises of a better future for the Gambia, when Colonial Development and Welfare Funds would become available. These promises were never fully realized, although some of the funds allocated allowed for improvements in the water supply, streets, and harbor facilities of the capital city. Measures such as these served to remind the colonial territories of the advantages of fighting alongside Britain and were an earnest of British commitment to improving the well-being of their dependencies. By 1947, it was apparent that the funds promised for improving Bathurst, building a new government center, and modernizing the airport would not be forthcoming. The British government's decision not to improve Yundum airport meant that the worldwide air transport system would not have a major base in the Gambia. The major airlines instead chose Dakar where the French were more willing to invest in the necessary facilities. The Colonial Development Corporation wasted over £2 million between 1947 and 1954 in two schemes—the Yundum Egg Project and the Rice Farm at Wallikunda. Both of these failed more because of administrative error than any other factor. Nevertheless, the failures inhibited the British from undertaking any further major development projects in the Gambia.

Thus in the 1950s, the Gambia was still dependent upon one crop, and its communication and transport infrastructure was still primitive. In the Protectorate there were no all-weather roads, only one secondary school, and one hospital for over a quarter of a million people. Government river steamers, plying from Bathurst to Basse, calling at numerous wharf-towns en route, and a large fleet of privately-owned groundnut cutters, played a vital part in trade and in keeping communications open during the wet season.

THE NATIONALIST AWAKENING

The post–World War II years elsewhere in British Africa witnessed the rise of nationalist movements seeking greater African participation in government and eventual independence. This nationalism, combined with the desire of the British government to be rid of unprofitable territories, wrought a revolution in Africa within a decade. The British began by making concessions to the Western-educated, middle-class Africans, recognized African political parties, and eventually negotiated for the independence of their African territories. In 1957, the Gold Coast became independent as Ghana, in 1960, Nigeria, and, in 1961, Sierra Leone, leaving the Gambia as the only area in West Africa still under British control. Although the earliest stirrings of political consciousness dated back to the interwar years, with the formation of a Gambia section of the inter-territorial National Congress of British West Africa, a Rate Payers Association in Bathurst, and the first trade union, the Bathurst Trade Union, it was only after World War II that political parties emerged to contest the opportunities created by constitutional developments.

In 1947, 1952, and 1954, there were changes in the size and composition of the Legislative and Executive Councils. The first direct elections to the Legislative Council, for Bathurst and Kombo St. Mary only, were held in 1951. These were sufficient to encourage the formation of political parties in the Colony, although the Protectorate remained unaffected until 1960, when the first national elections were held. Between 1947 and 1960, Protectorate interests in the Legislative Council were served through nominated members, mainly chiefs and European officials. Further reforms in 1954 introduced quasi-ministerial posts, again for the leaders of Bathurst-based political parties only. By the late 1950s, political awareness had extended to the Protectorate, and a new rural-based political movement emerged.

Political parties were formed very late in the Gambia and tended to reflect Colony interests and serve the interests of politically ambitious members of the Bathurst elite at the time when electoral politics were first introduced in 1951. Rev. John C. Faye was instrumental in creating the Gambia Democratic

Party (GDP) in 1951, and I. M. Garba-Jahumpa formed the Gambia Muslim Congress (GMC) early in 1952. In the same year, supporters of P. S. N'Jie set up the United Party (UP). These parties debated local Colony issues and were prevented by law from campaigning in the Protectorate.

One of the major reasons for the lack of a national policy was the confusion in almost every quarter about the Gambia's future. It appeared that the territory was too small and poor for independence to be considered as a viable goal. As other British West African territories progressed toward independence, several alternative arrangements were proposed for the Gambia. There was the "Malta Plan," which envisaged the Gambia obtaining limited self-government, while at the same time sending representatives to the British Parliament. After Malta opted for full independence, this approach was abandoned. Governor Sir Percy Wyn-Harris favored a "Channel Islands" solution, whereby the Gambia would achieve internal self-government but continue to rely on Britain in such matters as defense, foreign representation, and economic development. This too was abandoned, as was the even more controversial proposal, favored by Wyn-Harris's successor, Sir Edward Windley, to encourage a union of the Gambia with the neighboring French colony of Senegal, which achieved its independence in 1960. In the end most Gambians preferred independence as a sovereign state, in keeping with the rest of British Africa.

The devolution of power to Africans in British territories represented a reversal of the philosophy of government that had been dominant throughout the century. Traditional rulers, and the system of indirect rule they loyally operated on behalf of the imperial power, were abandoned in favor of Westminster parliamentary institutions based on political parties and directly elected legislatures. Given that few traditional rulers had a Western education, it was inevitable that the previously despised Western-educated Africans would inherit power from the British. In the Gambia, this process was particularly difficult for the Colonial Office since it had always supported the chiefs in governing the Protectorate. Educated, Colony-based Gambians had been specifically prohibited from any type of political activity in the Protectorate. However, with the grant of independence to other West African territories, the British could not refuse the demands of Gambian political parties that the elective principle be extended to the Protectorate. The Constitution of 1960 provided for direct elections for the seven Colony and 12 Protectorate seats in the House. The chiefs' powers to influence central policy were severely curtailed, since they had the right to elect among themselves only eight members to the House of Assembly, the renamed Legislative Council.

A new political party, the Protectorate People's Party, was formed in 1959 by a small group of educated provincials, anxious to ensure that political power would not be transferred to the urban elite. A senior veterinary officer from the Protectorate, David (who later reverted to his earlier name of Dawda) Jawara, was selected as leader of the new party. The party appealed most directly to the Protectorate, since its leaders were primarily Mandinka and they stressed how much the Protectorate had been ignored in the past. The UP, led by P. S. N'Jie, a Wolof Bathurst lawyer, also expected to do well in the elections of 1960. N'Jie had gained a considerable reputation in the 1950s as an opponent of the policies of the British administration. The leaders of the other major parties, I. M. Garba Jahumpa and John C. Faye, joined their two parties together just before the election to form the Democratic Congress Alliance (DCA). All parties campaigned vigorously throughout the Protectorate and, despite the newness of the electoral system, there was very heavy voter participation in the elections of 1960.

Owing to the nature of the Constitution, the elections produced a veritable stalemate. The Protectorate People's Party, renamed the People's Progressive Party (PPP) to demonstrate its national and modern credentials, won eight Protectorate seats; the UP gained five Colony seats and one Protectorate seat; and the Democratic Congress Alliance won only three seats. The eight chiefs, selected by means of a separate election among the 35 chiefs, thus became very important, not only for the composition of the House and the selection of the Ministers, but for the appointment of a Gambian Chief Minister. In 1961 the Governor made his choice. Since the chiefs would not support Jawara, and the PPP refused to consider a chief for this position, the Governor appointed P. S. N'Jie of the UP as the Gambia's first Chief Minister. Jawara and the other PPP ministers immediately resigned from the government in protest.

It was very soon apparent that the 1960 Constitution was not satisfactory to any of the Gambian parties. Two Constitutional Conferences were held, in May and July 1961, resulting in a new instrument which provided for responsible government. The new Constitution further marginalized the Protectorate chiefs; in the 36-strong House, the chiefs were reduced to only four indirectly elected representatives while 25 members were to be directly elected from the Protectorate. New elections were held in 1962, and the results were a vindication of the PPP's claim that the previous government was not representative. They gained over 64 percent of all votes cast and won 18 seats, while the UP managed only 13. Dawda Jawara became the Prime Minister, and the PPP became the government. Even before the election of 1962, it was apparent that within a short period the Gambia would receive its independence, although there were still serious doubts in Britain about the ability of the territory to afford that status. In 1963, the Gambia received the grant of full self-government, and discussions were soon begun on the mechanisms of achieving independence and its date. Despite protests from the UP, the British government agreed with Jawara that there was no need for new elections before the transfer of power. On February 18, 1965, The Gambia became an independent nation within the Commonwealth, barely four years since the Governor had agonized over the decision to appoint a Chief Minister with very circumscribed powers.

INDEPENDENCE

Despite widespread scepticism expressed about the ability of such a tiny country to survive as an independent state, The Gambia both retained its sovereignty in the face of persistent Senegal advances for union between the two countries and was able to dispense with British financial subvention in the years after independence. Fears of ethnic-regional clashes, which occurred so frequently in other former African colonies, were assuaged by Jawara's deliberate policy of converting the PPP from a Mandinka-Protectorate revanchist organization into a nationwide party. This was achieved by a combination of measures: key opposition MPs were wooed to the ruling party through promises of ministerial appointments and development resources for their home areas; government and party policy statements and development programs stressed the national character of the new administration; and the lack of trained personnel among the Protectorate elite now swept to office ensured a continuing place for the better-educated Bathurst elite in the administrative and legal branches of the state, even if the Cabinet was now dominated by provincials.

The effects of this policy of reconciling historic divisions between capital and country and between the various ethnic communities were to be seen in the collapse of the UP within a decade. In 1962, the UP had eight seats to the PPP's 13. A decade later, the UP's parliamentary strength had shrunk to three and its rural following had been permanently lost through a steady stream of defections by its MPs to the PPP and a series of election defeats. Political and economic patronage, combined with the lack of a credible leadership and program on the part of the UP, rather than state repression, led to this situation.

By 1972, the PPP appeared to be on the verge of becoming a one-party state. Following overwhelming approval in a national referendum on April

24, 1970 (an earlier attempt in November 1965 had been narrowly defeated), The Gambia became a republic with an executive President. This, and the near-annihilation of the UP in the general elections in 1972—it was now reduced to three seats in its original stronghold, Bathurst—suggested that The Gambia would rapidly become a single-party state under an authoritarian presidency. This failed to happen for two principal reasons. Firstly, President Jawara personally remained committed to multiparty democracy and, secondly, the PPP itself faced internal upheavals, which led to the formation of a new opposition party in the mid-1970s to challenge its political hegemony.

The 1972 elections had thrown up a large number of disaffected independent candidates, who had been passed over as PPP candidates, but these were too unimpressive and disorganized to pose a serious challenge. However in 1975, former Vice President and founder member of the PPP, Sheriff Dibba, clashed with Jawara and was expelled from the PPP. Supported principally by fellow-Mandinka from his home area in the Baddibus, alienated by Jawara's policy of opening up the PPP and government office to defectors from rival parties and ethnic groups, Dibba formed his own National Convention Party (NCP), in order to contest the general elections due the following year. In the event, neither Dibba nor the NCP could present themselves as a credible alternative to Jawara and the PPP or as a replacement for the near-extinct UP. Jawara continued to enjoy a widespread national following, whereas Dibba found it hard to shake off the negative image of being a disgruntled tribalist. His party's manifesto offered little that was not already PPP policy, and he had to face the double humiliation of losing his own seat and of the NCP winning only five seats in the elections, all in areas with strong Baddibu Mandinka voters.

Defeat in 1977 did not diminish Dibba's hopes of winning subsequent elections. He fared no better in the 1982 elections, mainly because he was in detention (though later to be released) for alleged involvement in the abortive coup of July 1981 and the NCP was smeared by government supporters. Though Dibba won back his own seat, Central Baddibu, in the 1987 elections, the NCP could not increase its parliamentary strength. In 1982, the strongest challenge to the PPP came once again from independent candidates, mainly frustrated party members as before. On this occasion, five independents won, but most crossed over to the PPP in due course. In the last election before the 1994 military coup, the NCP managed to increase its seats to six, but it was still hopelessly outnumbered by the PPP. Neither could Dibba dent Jawara's strong majority in the presidential elections of these years.

A new opposition party, formed in 1986 to offer a fresh challenge to the

PPP, fared even worse. Three former PPP ministers, headed by another former Vice President, Assan Musa Camara, set up the Gambia People's Party (GPP) in opposition both to the PPP and to the NCP. Not only did it fail to win a single seat in the 1987 elections, but Camara lost in his own parliamentary constituency, Kantora. He also trailed a poor third in the presidential election, despite his personal reputation as an honest politician. The GPP did little better in the 1992 elections; although it won two seats, Camara failed to regain his lost seat and again came in third in the presidential election.

It was clear in the postindependence period that as long as the PPP remained united, there was little hope of any rival party defeating it. Jawara's own standing as the bringer of independence and the powerful political and economic patronage enjoyed by the PPP, together with a steady, if modest, growth in the economy and the distribution of social and economic benefits, ensured the government's success. However, the repeated successes of the PPP contributed to its eventual demise. Patronage politics led to an unacceptable toleration of corruption and misuse of office by leading politicians, plus their reluctance to share office with younger contenders or allow rival political parties any chance of success through electoral politics, bred alienation and hostility among young people, particularly among educated and semi-educated elements in the Banjul area. Such elements turned to revolutionary ideologies — a mixture of marxism and radical pan-Africanism — and turned their backs on parliamentary politics. Instead, they intensified a tradition of urban militancy dating back to late colonial days; this time denouncing the Jawara government for a variety of defects, both real and invented, including corruption and mismanagement, despotism on Jawara's part, and excessive subservience to the West in economic and foreign policy. New radical organizations appeared or lurked beneath the surface of politics — the National Liberation Party (NLP), the Movement for Justice in Africa-Gambia (MOJA-G), the Gambia Socialist Revolutionary Party (GSRP), and the clandestine publishers of the *Voice of the Future*. Acts of political vandalism took place, and there was open talk of political change having to come about through violent means. A sharp decline in the Gambian economy in the early 1980s, compounded by drought and poor harvests, as well as several financial scandals, eroded the standing of the government and provided additional grievances among frustrated youths in the urban centers. The political explosion that followed was not confined to civilian malcontents, however; it brought into politics for the first, but not last, time elements of the security forces.

The Gambian army, such as it was, was abolished as an economy measure in 1958 when the Gambia Regiment of the old Royal West African

Frontier Force (RWAFF) was replaced by a smaller and cheaper Gambia Field Force. A paramilitary force of a few hundred men, it was deployed periodically to deal with urban disorder and to police elections, but it was not considered as having any political aspirations or capacity to overthrow the state. In 1980–1981, serious disaffection, based more on internal rivalries than ideology, broke out in the Field Force. Good government intelligence and prompt assistance from Senegal prevented a coup taking place in October 1980, though a senior Field Force commander was murdered. On July 30, 1981, another plot came to fruition, this time between disaffected Field Force elements and members of the banned GSRP, headed by a rejected political aspirant, Kukoi Samba Sanyang. Subscribing to an ill-formed marxist agenda, as well as pursuing personal grievances, the plotters almost succeeded in overthrowing the Gambian government during President Jawara's absence overseas. It was only the resistance of a small band of loyal police and a much larger Senegalese military intervention that caused the insurrection to fail, but only after a week of fighting, the loss of hundreds of lives in the Banjul area, and considerable economic damage.

Secure in their mutual defense alliance with Senegal, Jawara and the PPP sought to rebuild their partially shattered reputations. Mass arrests and trials, and a lengthy state of emergency, together with the need to put right the damage caused by the rebellion, preoccupied the government for the next couple of years. In time, normality was restored, and general elections were even held in 1982, despite the emergency. While the PPP went on to win overwhelming electoral victories in two further elections, the economic situation continued to deteriorate, and The Gambia was forced to accept an Economic Recovery Programme (ERP) devised by the World Bank and International Monetary Fund (IMF). By the early 1990s the economy had achieved measurable improvement, and the ERP was replaced by a Programme for Sustainable Development (PSD). On the security side, the Field Force was disbanded and two carefully vetted new defense units formed— a para-military Gambia National Gendarmerie (GNG), trained by the Senegalese, and a Gambia National Army (GNA), set up with British assistance (later to be replaced by Nigerian assistance). A Treaty of Confederation with Senegal (effective 1982–1989) also legitimized the presence of Senegalese forces on Gambian soil on a long-term basis. Public pledges by the PPP leadership to put its house in order lent further credibility to the belief that The Gambia was back on course for democratic governance and economic development. These expectations were exploded in a new military insurrection in July 1994.

MILITARY INTERVENTION AND APRC GOVERNMENT

Despite its small size, deliberate bifurcation, and political vetting, the Gambian military reemerged as political arbiter on July 22, 1994, when a group of disaffected junior army officers seized power in a brief and bloodless coup. President Jawara and his immediate entourage were allowed safe passage to Senegal in a visiting American warship, but other members of government and senior officials fared less well. The self-declared Armed Forces Provisional Ruling Council (AFPRC), headed by Lieutenant Yahya Jammeh, abolished the Constitution, outlawed political parties, and arrested those members of government still in the country. A purge of the civil service also took place. The army takeover was inspired by a number of factors — members of the junta accepted the radicals' critique of PPP rule and denounced its alleged tyranny, corruption and failure to develop the country over the past two decades; but there appeared to be elements of personal dissatisfaction on the part of the rebellious soldiers as well, and even criticism of the dominance of seconded Nigerian personnel in the higher echelons of the army.

On this occasion, the Senegalese government refused to intervene militarily; and neither was the United States government prepared to instruct the crew of the visiting warship, *Lamoure County,* to put down the insurrection. Relations with Senegal had soured since the early days of confederation, mainly because the two countries could not agree on the future of the Senegambia Confederation, which had been ushered in with proclamations of a common destiny in February 1982. Clearly, the Senegalese had hoped to exploit the dependence of the Gambian government on Senegal and had sought to convert what, initially, had been a deliberately loosely constructed association into a full-blown union of the two countries. Historical Gambian antipathy to a loss of political autonomy and fear of the economic consequences of merger with a much larger neighbor, were reinforced by a growing belief in the 1980s that the country was now capable of managing its own affairs. The continued Senegalese military presence in The Gambia was an embarrassment to the government, and each attempt by the Dakar government to forge closer ties only led to further disenchantment with the relationship. Finally, in mid-1989, the Senegalese government, under the pretext of a military crisis on its border with Mauritania, unilaterally withdrew its forces from The Gambia and placed the confederation on hold. The confederation was formally wound up the same December, leaving the Senegalese government embittered and unwilling to provide any further military support to the Jawara government.

Despite its international reputation as one of the few democratic regimes in Africa, the Jawara government was abandoned. All that its friends abroad were prepared to do was to cut off aid to the military junta, until such a time as elected government was restored or conclusive evidence of a transfer of power was provided. As events would reveal, this no longer meant the restoration of former President Jawara and the PPP.

Initially the AFPRC enjoyed a great deal of popularity, particularly among the young. Other groups in society—the press and labor and professional associations—were more cautious. To win support, the junta courted the Gambian public with promises of root and branch reform of government and a program of economic rehabilitation. Civilians representative of a broad spectrum of opinion were co-opted into the government, and a number of commissions of enquiry were set up to punish corrupt politicians and officials and recover stolen public assets. The junta also sought to capitalize on a sense of national indignation arising from the severe economic disruption, particularly to the vital tourist industry, resulting from the sanctions policy imposed by major Western trading partners and aid providers.

While pro-junta elements argued for an unspecified spell of military government in order to bring about a complete transformation of political life, most Gambians wanted a return to elected civilian rule in as short a time as possible. Bowing to domestic and international pressure, as well as to fears about its own internal cohesion—there had been attempts to overthrow Jammeh in November 1994 and January 1995 (on the latter occasion by two members of the junta itself—Lieutenants Sana Sabally and Sadibou Hydara, respectively Vice Chairman of the AFPRC and Interior Minister)—the AFPRC established a National Consultative Commission in December 1995 to sound out national opinion on the duration of the transition period. In a less than ideal situation, the Commission reported that most Gambians favored a maximum transition period of two years, rather than the four years favored by the junta. Consequently, AFPRC Chairman, Jammeh, announced a new transition program to be completed in 1996. In the event, the process was not completed until January 1997 when general elections were held to a new parliament, renamed the National Assembly.

The process of transition was not without controversy. The AFPRC pushed through the new Constitution, disregarding some key recommendations made by its panel of constitutional experts, and put it to a national referendum on August 8, 1996, in which it was approved by 70.35 percent of voters. Chairman Jammeh, who, initially had stated he would give up politics, allowed himself to be named head of a new party, the Alliance for Patriotic Re-orientation and Construction (APRC), and to stand as its presidential candidate (having had the minimum age requirement reduced to allow him to contest). A pro-junta civil organization, the July 22 Movement, ostensibly formed to promote civic education, served very effectively as a propaganda instrument for the APRC and Jammeh. Presidential and parliamentary elections held in September 1996 and January 1997 produced an all too familiar result, a substantial personal victory for Jammeh and an overwhelming majority for the APRC; Jammeh won 56 percent of the vote, and the APRC won 33 out of 45 seats. Both the referendum and the elections aroused a great deal of controversy, with all opposition parties claiming that the APRC had won by a combination of rigging the new Constitution and the elections and improper use of state resources; charges reminiscent of those made in past elections about the PPP. The PPP itself and its leaders, together with the NCP and GPP and their leaders, were not allowed to contest.

The Jammeh government has continued to face accusations of misrule. Domestic opposition groups, supported by external bodies, such as Amnesty International, which, in December 1997, released a damning report on human rights abuses in The Gambia, persist in claiming violations of the Constitution with regard to their political activities. The APRC has also had to contend with accusations of financial irregularities. Finally, the security situation is not entirely untroubled, despite the activities of the National Intelligence Agency and the absence of further plotting within the ranks of the armed forces. In November 1996, armed men, allegedly followers of Kukoi Samba Sanyang, leader of the abortive coup of 1981, caused a number of deaths in an attack, from across the Senegalese border, on an army barracks at Farafenni. There was also an attack on a police post at Kartong, near the border with Casamance, in July 1997, carried out by former soldiers who had taken part in the 1994 attempted coup. Such incidents, and continuing problems with neighboring Senegal over transit rights for the Gambian re-export trade, provide continuing evidence of the vulnerability of small states such as The Gambia, not only to internal pressures but also to destabilizing forces outside their territorial boundaries.

The economic situation has made some recovery from the difficult period of late 1994, when Western aid donors sharply reduced their assistance programs in retaliation for the overthrow of the elected Gambian government, and the British government advised British visitors, the mainstay of the tourist industry, itself a major element of the economy, to stay away from The Gambia, owing to the volatile political situation at the time. Jammeh initially chose an intransigent line—claiming that Allah would be the government's World Bank and that the public commissions enquiring into the theft of government resources by former ministers and officials would generate sufficient revenue to offset the financial boycott. At the same time, he turned to other sources of financial assistance, principally Taiwan, which offered him a timely and substantial loan, which itself would become the subject of accusations of impropriety on the part of his government.

More importantly, the AFPRC made concessions on the political front and, by agreeing to a timetable for a return to civilian rule and implementing its stages during 1995–1997, was able to persuade Western donor countries to lift their sanctions. It was also noticeable that the AFPRC, notwithstanding its radical rhetoric, retained the recovery program, the Programme for Sustainable Recovery (PSD), which the deposed PPP had agreed upon with the World Bank. By 1996, Jammeh felt confident enough to launch the "Vision 2020" program, which reinforced and extended a market-driven approach to Gambian economic development. Ahead of the elections of 1996–1997, the AFPRC launched a number of major projects aimed at winning over the new electorate and foreign trading partners—among these a national television station and an enlarged and modernized airport at Yundum. Hopes of turning The Gambia into the "Singapore" of West Africa in the early 21st century, first envisaged by the PPP and retained as a centerpiece of the APRC's economic vision, would still depend on a number of imponderables—the ability of the government to complete the internal economic and administrative reforms, which would provide foreign investors with the financial climate and human resources necessary to wish to invest in The Gambia, and the resolution of wider problems in the subregion, which would enable Banjul to emerge as its financial and commercial center.

Please note cross-references in the text are indicated in bold type.

The Dictionary

-A-

AFRICAN-WEST INDIAN SOCIETY. A "friendly" society set up by former West Indian soldiers, retired from the employ of the British, who had chosen to stay in the **Colony,** and other local Africans in **Bathurst** in the 1860s. Although concerned with issues of a general welfare nature, the society also represented its members in their dealings with government. Its leader was a discharged soldier of the West India Regiment, Thomas King, and the society can be regarded as the first modern political association in the Gambia.

AGRICULTURE. The Gambia is predominantly an agricultural society with over 70 percent of the population dependent on farming. Farming in The Gambia is overwhelmingly based on small family holdings, centered on over 1,000 small villages, cultivating crops for immediate consumption and for cash. Land is generally owned by the local community and vested in individual families according to customary law. Though farming is based on family labor, some activities are carried out using communal labor organized through age grade associations (*kafos*). A division of labor occurs, with men clearing the ground for cultivation and women being responsible for food crops, such as rice, sorghum, maize, millet, and vegetables. The major cash crop is **groundnuts,** cultivated by men, and accounting for 50 percent of cultivated land. Animal husbandry plays an important part in the rural economy as well.

Traditionally, Fula (**Fulbe**) have predominated in cattle raising, tending the herds of other groups as well as their own. Goats, sheep, and poultry are also found in large numbers, but pigs are rare, owing to The Gambia being a predominantly Muslim country. Farm production is very dependent on the vagaries of rainfall, as most crops are rain fed, notwithstanding the close proximity of the **Gambia River,** which tends to be cut off by mangrove swamps from the principal farming land. Additionally, Gambian farmers suffer from poor soils and a lack of capital, fertilizers, and technical inputs. Government attempts to introduce agricultural

25

extension services and several large-scale agricultural schemes have not met with great success, and an Agricultural Development Bank had to be wound up because of large-scale fraud. Cooperative societies, organized nationally through a government Cooperatives Department, have played an important part in the production and sale of groundnuts since colonial times, but have also suffered considerably from corruption on the part of national and local officials.

In recent years some success has been achieved by expatriate non-governmental organizations (NGOs) in promoting village "vegetable farms," to improve diet and provide women with surpluses to sell in local markets. There is very little large-scale commercial farming in The Gambia, though there has been interest, on the fringes of the Greater **Banjul** area, in supplying horticultural produce for the urban market and the tourist industry, and for exporting by air to overseas markets.

AHMADIYYA. A Pakistan-based Islamic sect founded in the 19th century by Hazrat Mirza Ahmad. Its major theme is the reconciliation of Islam and Christianity. In the last four decades, active proselytizing by missionary teachers has converted many Africans, particularly in coastal towns, to this belief. Despite their record in the provision of schools and medical facilities, non-Gambian Ahmadis were excluded from the country in 1997.

AKU. A name initially given to Yoruba **recaptives** rescued by the Royal Navy from slave ships. It was subsequently extended to mean all the recaptives' Westernized descendants in the **Colony** area. In the Gambia, the Akus in the late 19th and 20th centuries came to exercise an influence far beyond their numbers. They adopted Western modes of living, accepted Christianity, and educated their children in Sierra Leone and Great Britain. The Aku became successful traders, entered the professions, and, in the period between 1945 and independence, came to dominate many important government positions in the Gambia. Muslim members of the Aku community were known as Aku-Marabout. **Wolof** who converted to Protestantism were known as Aku-Wolof. Thought at one time to be dying out as a unique community because of intermarriage with surrounding peoples and a low fertility rate, the Aku have made something of a comeback in numbers in recent years, increasing from 4,386 in 1973 to 16,556 in 1993, although this increase may be due to changes in the census definition of the community.

ALBREDA. Today a small river-port village located in upper **Niumi.** it was for a long time the trading center for the French in their efforts to dominate the **Gambia River** trade. The French **Senegal Company** first obtained trading rights to that portion of the north bank area in 1679, and Albreda was established two years later opposite the English post on **James Island.** During the century-long period of wars between England and France, Albreda was looted and abandoned many times. The French retained their proprietary rights to the area until the Convention of 1857 with Britain gave them exclusive rights to **Portendic** in return for relinquishing their claims to Albreda. Runaway slaves who reached the flag post at Albreda, from which the British Union Jack flew, were granted political sanctuary.

ALFA MOLLOH (1820s–1881). The creator of the state of **Fuladu** and one of the main participants in the **Soninke-Marabout Wars** in the upper river during the 1870s. A member of the **Fulbe Firdu,** he was born Molloh Egue in the old **Mandinka** kingdom of **Jimara,** probably in the 1820s. He was an elephant hunter and had gained a great reputation for his prowess before a disagreement with the ruler of Jimara caused him to lead a revolt of the **Fulbe** against the traditional rulers. It was rumored that he had met with **Al Hajj Umar Tall** and had taken the **Tijaniyya** oath before 1867. His devotion to **Islam,** however, appears to have been more a matter of expediency than of true devotion. It did gain him support from the Islamic states of **Futa Jallon** and **Futa Toro.** His forces in a five-year period conquered **Jimara, Tomani,** and a number of smaller chieftaincies southward to the **Casamance** and then laid the foundations for the centralized state of Fuladu, constructed largely with the conquests of his son **Musa Molloh.** Molloh Egue, soon after his initial conquest, assumed the name of Alfa Molloh. He did not hesitate to use force to subdue potential rivals, and his chief agent in establishing control over the Fulbe was Musa and his army. After the Alfa's death in 1881, Fuladu was torn by internecine strife because, according to the matrilineal system of succession, Alfa's brother, Bakari Dembel, inherited the throne.

ALKAALOO (ALKALO, pl. ALKAALOOLU). A title given to an African ruler's representative to a European trading area. In time, it came to mean to the **Mandinka** the same as *satee-tiyo,* or village head.

ALLIANCE FOR PATRIOTIC RE-ORIENTATION AND CONSTRUCTION (APRC). Formed in mid-1996 by the military junta, the

Armed Forces Provisional Ruling Council (AFPRC), to contest forth-coming presidential and parliamentary elections. The new party brought together supporters of the military coup and defectors from banned opposition parties. The APRC won the disputed general elections of January 1997 with a large majority, 33 out of 45 seats (51.12 percent of the vote, but with five candidates returned unopposed) on a platform of "Empowerment of the People," stressing national unity, transparency and probity in government, and economic and social development. President **Yahya Jammeh** is the APRC's Party Chairman and Saihou Sanyang its General Secretary.

ALMAMY. The spiritual leader in Muslim societies, concerned with prayer, education, and general religious rule-making. In many **Mandinka** villages there was a type of dual control shared between the religious leader and the *alkaaloo,* the secular leader.

AMER FAAL. One of the chief lieutenants of **Ma Bah** in the **Kombo** and **Ceded Mile** areas between 1864 and 1866. The difficulties there were precipitated by the British decision to allow refugees from the wars in Saloum to settle in the Ceded Mile area. In 1866, Amer Faal's continual raids reopened the question of British supremacy along the lower north bank territory and led, the same year, to a large British-led expedition being mounted against him and his **Marabout** allies. **Albreda** was taken without casualties, but Amer Faal's main stockaded base, Tubab Kolon, had to be taken by force.

ANGLICAN MISSION. Its activities in the Gambia date from 1821 when, at the request of **Sir Charles MacCarthy,** the Church Missionary Society in London sent a chaplain, Robert Hughes, to provide for the spiritual needs of the **Bathurst** garrison. Hughes and his wife died within six months and, due to high mortality rates, there was no Anglican representative in Bathurst for much of the first half of the 19th century.

The **Wesleyan mission** had to supply the garrison with a chaplain. In 1836, the government allowed Anglicans to use the former officers' mess for church services. No permanent church in Bathurst was erected until the present structure was built in 1901, on land provided by the government near MacCarthy Square. In 1855, missionary work was begun by the Anglican Church of the West Indies among the Susus along the Rio Pongas. In 1935, this area was combined with that of the Gambia to form the diocese of the Gambia and Rio Pongas, with Rev. John Charles Sydney

Daly as its first Bishop. Although not as active in the education field as the Wesleyans, the Anglicans did open a church school in Bathurst as early as 1869, and from the 1920s they maintained one small elementary school at Kristikunda, in the Upper River Division. The diocese of The Gambia today also includes Senegal and the Cape Verde Republic. There are an estimated 1,500 Anglican communicants in the Gambia.

ANGLO-FRENCH CONVENTION (1882). The culmination of over three years' effort by the British Foreign Office, which wanted a clear demarcation of British and French spheres of influence in West Africa. The Convention granted most of the French claims along the coast between Conakry and Freetown and called for both Britain and France to maintain the status quo. Implicit in the terms of the Convention was the desire to rectify spheres of influence, and this very clearly meant an exchange of the Gambia for some suitable French territory elsewhere. Although the British Foreign Office continued for some time to recognize the status quo, the Convention never became effective because the French Chamber of Deputies refused to ratify it.

ANGLO-FRENCH CONVENTION (1889). British pressures, by 1887, led to a specific understanding with the French government on delimitation of territory in Senegambia. By the close of 1888, the French were present in a number of places along the banks of the **Gambia River,** and British authorities in the Gambia had begun to sign treaties with riverine rulers. In April 1889, a series of high-level meetings were initiated in Paris with the object of warding off any possible conflict between the agents of the two powers in the Gambia, Sierra Leone, the Gold Coast, and Nigeria. The Convention established coastal boundary lines between the spheres of influence of the two powers in all these areas, but the agreement had more far-reaching ramifications for the Gambia than for any of the other territories. E. H. Egerton of the Foreign Office and Augustus Hemming of the Colonial Office represented Britain, while the French delegates were M. Nisard, Director of Protectorates of the Foreign Ministry, and M. Bayol, Governor of Senegal.

The British delegates at first tried to obtain a clear-cut demarcation of spheres of influence in western Africa. Failing in this, they decided to force the French to recognize their claims to both banks of the Gambia River, effectively conceding the hinterland of the Gambia to French control. At the third general session, this limited British objective was gained when the French delegates admitted in principle that the Gambia was a

British river. M. Bayol drew two lines upon a map from the mouth of the river to **Yarbutenda** and stated that within these lines was the territory that could reasonably be assigned to Britain. Ultimately the two parties agreed that the British should have occupation rights to the banks of the Gambia 10 kilometers (six miles) north and south of the river as far inland as Yarbutenda; there the eastern boundary of the Gambia was to be the arc of a 10-kilometer radius drawn from the center of the town.

Both the French and the British negotiators considered the agreements reached regarding the boundaries of the Gambia to be only temporary. The British believed that in the future they would be able to trade their exclusive rights to the downriver areas for concessions by the French elsewhere. The French believed that in time the British government would realize the nonviable character of their new **Protectorate** and would be more than willing to allow it to be absorbed by Senegal. Neither of these prognoses proved to be correct. The decade following the **Anglo-French Convention of 1904** saw both governments unwilling to test the new found entente by raising embarrassing questions about an area that neither party considered to be very important. Thus the boundary agreed upon in 1889 and demarcated on the ground in the 1890s became the permanent boundary between the Gambia and Senegal.

ANGLO-FRENCH CONVENTION (1904). This most important agreement cleared the way for the entente between France and Britain, which was to have such fateful consequences for European peace in the summer of 1914. The agreement finally settled the most outstanding differences between the two states regarding fishing rights off Newfoundland, spheres of influence in northern Africa, and border disputes in western and central Africa. Article five of the agreement ceded **Yarbutenda** to France with the stipulation that if the **Gambia River** was not navigable for seagoing vessels at that point, then the French would be given access to territory lower down on the Gambia River. While the Convention was quite explicit on this point, the British Foreign Office later resisted the claims made by the French for such mid-river enclaves. The excuse of the British for delaying action on the French demands for a river port was that such an enclave would allow the French to draw off the bulk of the **groundnut** exports and thus **Bathurst** and the British **Protectorate** would be even more poverty stricken than was then the case.

Although the French government in the period from 1906 to 1910 was very active in pressing for the mid-river port, and some of its officials in Senegal revived the plans for an exchange of territories, it was very careful not to allow this question to endanger the new found but shaky friendship between Britain and France. The thrust of French policy in the early 20th century was to gain support for what the government considered to be an inevitable confrontation with Germany in Europe. After 1910, the French government ceased to press Britain for territorial enclaves on the Gambia or exchanges of territory. World War I and the building of the railway and road system in Senegal, and the concentration of French capital in the ports of Kaolack and Ziguinchor, made possession of the Gambia less important to France. After 1918, virtually all diplomatic activity concerning an exchange of territory for the Gambia ceased. Thus the boundaries established in 1889, which had been considered temporary expedients, became permanent political realities.

ANTONIO, PRIOR OF CRATO (1531–1595). In 1580, one of the claimants to the Portuguese throne, Philip II of Spain, the champion of Catholicism and the enemy of England, amalgamated the thrones of Spain and Portugal. The Prior, claiming to be the true King of Portugal, rented certain trading concessions in Portuguese territory to English merchants. It was on the basis of these concessions that Queen Elizabeth I in 1588 granted exclusive trading rights for a period of 10 years to certain English merchants trading in West Africa. The company which was thus formed was the first organized effort on the part of the English to exploit the imagined wealth of western Africa.

ARCHER, FRANCIS BISSET. Government official and author, posted to the Gambia from Nigeria in January 1903, as Colonial Treasurer. He also served as acting Colonial Secretary in 1904 and 1905 and briefly in 1905 was Acting Governor of the Gambia. In 1905, he wrote the first book specifically devoted to the Gambia, entitled *The Gambia Colony and Protectorate: An Official Handbook.*

ARMED FORCES PROVISIONAL RULING COUNCIL (AFPRC). Name adopted by the group of four young army officers who overthrew **Dawda Jawara's** government on July 22, 1994. The members of the AFPRC were all lieutenants—**Yahya A. A. J. J. Jammeh** (Chairman), **Sana B. Sabally** (Vice Chairman), **Sadibou Hydara** (Minister of the Interior) and **Edward Singhateh** (Minister of Defence). A fifth junior officer, Lieutenant **Yankuba Touray,** subsequently joined the junta as Minister for Local Government. The AFPRC justified its seizure of power because of the alleged widespread corruption and undemocratic rule of the

People's Progressive Party (PPP). These "soldiers with a difference," as they described themselves, promised to restore "transparency and honesty" to government and reestablish full democracy. Several sympathetic civilians and civil servants were co-opted as ministers, in the junta's attempt to create a national consensus, but growing domestic and international pressure forced it to shorten its four-year program of transition to civilian rule to two years, but not before a serious split developed within the junta concerning the pace of change. Sabally and Hydara (the latter subsequently died in detention) were arrested following an alleged attempted coup on January 27, 1995.

Following a referendum on a new constitution, which was accompanied by the banning of the three major opposition parties, the AFPRC mutated into the **Alliance for Patriotic Re-orientation and Construction (APRC),** with Jammeh as its presidential candidate. He won the presidential election in September 1996, and several members of the junta remained as ministers (Secretaries of State) in the reconstituted civilian government.

ARMITAGE, CAPTAIN SIR CECIL HAMILTON (1869–1933). A medical doctor's son, Armitage was born on October 8, 1869. A soldier by profession, gaining his military commission in the South Wales Borderers in 1889, Armitage joined the colonial service as Assistant Inspector in the Gold Coast Constabulary in 1894. In 1895 he took part in the Ashanti Expedition, and he became Private Secretary to the Governor of the Gold Coast in 1899. He took part in the Ashanti Campaign of 1900, and the following year was made Acting Resident, Kumasi, and then Travelling Commissioner in the Gold Coast administration. In 1910, he became Chief Commissioner, Northern Territories, Gold Coast, from which post he was promoted to Governor of the Gambia, 1920–1927.

Armitage was in charge of administration during the recession following World War I and was partially responsible for the slowness in recalling from circulation the French **five-franc piece.** This demonetization crisis ultimately cost the Gambia over £200,000. Governor Armitage's main positive contributions to the Gambia were the establishment of the Agriculture Department in 1924 and the founding of a secondary school for the sons of chiefs at **Georgetown** in 1923. Armitage, DSO, CMG, KBE, died on March 10, 1933.

ARMITAGE SCHOOL. Established by Governor **Sir Cecil Armitage** at **Georgetown** in 1923 as a school for the sons of chiefs, to enable them to be educated locally, rather than in distant **Bathurst** with its unsettling possibilities, and to play a more informed role in local administration (it paralleled similar initiatives at Bo in Sierra Leone and Kaduna in Northern Nigeria). Initially it gave its students the rudiments of reading and writing. In the 1920s, there were only two main elementary schools for the **Protectorate.** One was a Catholic school at **Basse Santa Su,** and the other a **Wesleyan** school at Georgetown. There was, therefore, little demand for more secondary school facilities until after World War II. The expansion of all education in the postwar years dictated improvements to Armitage. It became a boarding postprimary school, the only one in the Protectorate. In 1961, its facilities were expanded to accommodate 200 pupils. Although created for the sons of chiefs, Armitage School subsequently became a nursery for many leading provincial political leaders.

ASSOCIATION FOR THE DISCOVERY OF THE INTERIOR RE-GIONS OF AFRICA. An organization created in 1788 by Sir Joseph Banks and other Englishmen with similar curiosity about the "unexplored" parts of the world. Of particular interest to the Association was the question of the existence of the Niger River. Whether it existed, where was its source, what direction did it flow in, was it connected with the **Gambia,** Senegal, and Nile Rivers, and what was its outlet? The Association first sponsored two expeditions, one to cross the Sahara from North Africa, and the other from Egypt. Both ended in failure. They next commissioned **Major Daniel Houghton,** who set out from the Gambia in November 1790, to penetrate the mysteries of the western Sudan. He was killed after accomplishing little. The most successful venture sponsored by the Association was that of the young Scottish physician, **Mungo Park,** who in December 1795 left the upper river station of Pisania on the Gambia. Park eventually reached Segu on the Niger before being forced to turn back. His two-and-a-half-year journey was the first successful European exploration of the interior of Africa and helped the Association convince the British government to support further exploration.

-B-

BADDIBU (or **RIP**). Today a district of The Gambia located on the north bank of the river, it stretches from the **Kerewan** creek to just below the town of Ballanghar in Lower Saloum. The bulk of the present-day population of Baddibu is **Mandinka,** although there is a significant concentration of **Wolof** in upper Baddibu. In the 19th century, Baddibu was one of the most important of the Gambian kingdoms. In the 1860s, **Ma Bah** used Baddibu as his base in attempting to create a large Islamic kingdom. At its greatest extent, the kingdom of Baddibu, or Rip, comprised not only the present-day riverine areas but also Saloum, parts of Cayor, and **Jolof.** "Baddibus" refers to the three Baddibu districts—Upper, Central, and Lower.

BADGE MESSENGERS. Created by a Protectorate Ordinance in 1909, which gave chiefs and certain headmen the right, with the permission of the British authorities, to appoint men to keep the peace in a given area. These men were called Badge Messengers because of the distinctive symbol of authority they were authorized to wear. They had the same rights, duties, and responsibilities as the regular police who operated in the **Colony** area. Although conditions in the **Protectorate** changed drastically in the 50 years after they were authorized, Badge Messengers remained the local constabulary that enforced the decisions of the district chiefs down to the very eve of independence.

BADOLO. **Wolof** term for a poor peasant. Normally it referred to someone who was neither a slave nor a caste member. Although free, a *badolo* had no wealth or power, nor any claim to a political title. He had the right to farm his land and pass it on to his sons. He owed a share of his harvest to the local chief (*lam*) and military service and other minor duties. The word *badolo,* although Wolof in origin, came to be applied by other ethnic groups in the Senegambia to persons of similar status.

BAH, HAMMAT NGAI KUMBAH. Hotelier and outspoken founder-leader of the **National Reconciliation Party (NRP),** one of the new political parties formed during the transition to civilian rule in 1996. His party came in third in the parliamentary elections of January 1997, winning just over 2 percent of the popular vote. Bah came in last in the presidential election in 1996, winning only 2.12 percent of the vote; but he defeated the **Alliance for Patriotic Re-orientation and Construction (APRC)** candidate in Upper Saloum in the general elections in January 1997, with 56.18 percent of the vote. Although the NRP put up only five candidates, two of them won. Bah is a leading critic of the APRC in the National Assembly.

BAH, MA (also known as AMAD BA or MABA) (?–1867). The son of N'Dougou Pende Bah, a Koranic teacher in a largely **Wolof** area of **Baddibu.** Ma Bah received Koranic education in Cayor and then later taught the Koran in **Jolof.** While in Jolof, Ma Bah married the niece of the **Burba** Jolof and thus forged ties with the premier Wolof state. After his father's death, he returned to Baddibu to assume his father's responsibilities. Probably in 1850, Ma Bah had his only meeting with **Al Hajj Umar Tall** at the village of Kabakoto, and at the conclusion of that meeting, Ma Bah was chosen as the **Tijaniyya** representative in Baddibu.

During the 1850s, Ma Bah continued teaching the Koran in Baddibu. There is some confusion as to why he turned away from such peaceful activities. The most likely conclusion is that he, an Islamic teacher with a considerable following among the people of Baddibu, was caught up in a clash between the **Mandinka** rulers and the British. In 1861, the British decided to punish the King of Baddibu for his harassment of **Bathurst** traders. Governor **G. A. K. D'Arcy** coordinated his offensive against Baddibu with the efforts of the French moving through Saloum, and the King of Baddibu was quickly defeated. Presumably Ma Bah had aided the British in the course of their invasion and had helped to arrange the peace terms.

After the war, the King of Baddibu decided to rid himself of this potential enemy with such a large Muslim following, and sent his son to kill Ma Bah. Instead, the son was killed by Ma Bah's followers, and the revolt in Baddibu began. Within a short period of time, the **Marabout** forces had overcome their Mandinka overlords, the king was killed, and large numbers of his followers were forced into exile.

The success of Ma Bah's revolt caused other Marabouts on the north bank to look to him for aid, and in May 1862, Ma Bah sent his army into **Niumi** to aid his fellow Muslims. An invasion of Baddibu by the *Bur* Saloum forced Ma Bah to retreat. Later, he recognized the independence of Niumi with the stipulation that it pay him a tribute through his lieutenant, **Amer Faal.** In the subsequent campaigning against Saloum, Ma Bah was generally successful, so that by the fall of 1863, the Marabout forces acknowledging Ma Bah controlled most of the territory between the **Gambia** and the Saloum rivers, except for part of Niumi.

Ma Bah's sphere of influence extended northward into eastern Saloum as far as Jolof. Unlike many of the other war chiefs or Marabouts of the Senegambia, Ma Bah was motivated primarily by the hope of creating a large, viable Islamic state. He was, like Usuman dan Fodio in northern Nigeria and, later, Muhammad Ahmed in the eastern Sudan, the director of a religio-political movement, rather than merely a warrior. Ma Bah's desires, however, ran counter to the plans of the French, who were concerned with dominating the trade of the **Serer** states of Sine and Saloum.

The anxiety of the French administrators and traders was increased by the conversion of Macadou and Lat Dior, both ex-*damels* of Cayor, who had been replaced by the French because of their opposition toward French policies. The French at first welcomed Ma Bah's activities since he was weakening the power of the Wolof and Serer *tyeddos*. In October 1865, the French by treaty recognized Ma Bah as the **Almamy** of Baddibu and of Saloum, and he agreed to respect the rights of French traders already in Saloum. In June 1865, Ma Bah sent his forces northward into Jolof, and within a few months he was in almost complete control of that Wolof state. A revolt in Saloum forced him to devote his total attention again to the south and doomed his plans for a union with the Trarza Moors to the north of the Senegal River. In November 1865, the French Governor, Pinet-Laprade, disturbed over Ma Bah's power and influence, led a large army, reported to be some 5,000 strong, overland to strike at Ma Bah's forces near Kaolack. The battle of Pathebadiane appears to have gone in favor of the Marabouts, and Pinet-Laprade withdrew his forces northward.

During 1866, Ma Bah's position in Jolof and the area around Kaolack declined as he was supporting Lat Dior in the invasion of southern Cayor and also his lieutenant, Amer Faal, in action against Niumi. Despite his weakened position, however, Ma Bah planned to rid himself of the kingdom of Sine, the last **Soninke** state standing between his kingdom and the French. After the rains began in 1867, Ma Bah accompanied his army in an invasion of Sine. The Serer *tyeddo* repulsed the invading forces in a major battle at Somb. Lat Dior fled the area, and after the battle, Ma Bah's body was discovered on his prayer mat. With Ma Bah's death, the most critical threat to European power in the Senegambia ended. He had come very close to restoring the old Jolof empire by utilizing the militant forces of **Islam** that he discovered in Baddibu, Saloum, and Jolof. None of his successors or any other Gambian leader came close to unifying the Senegambia. Ironically, the wars launched by Ma Bah had weakened the Senegambia states to the extent that the French and British found little resistance to their further penetration of the interior in the following two decades.

BAH, MAMADOU N'DARE. See MAMADOU N'DARE.

BAH, SAIT MATY. See SAIT MATY.

BAINUNK (BAINOUK). Possibly the earliest inhabitants of the coastal area of The Gambia between the **Gambia** and Casamance rivers. As a result of assimilation by later migrants to the area, the Bainunk are no longer a culturally distinct people.

BAJO, LAMIN (1940–   ). Secretary of State for Local Government and Lands since March 1998. Born in **Brikama,** Western Division, Bajo joined the Gambia National Gendarmerie (GNG) in April 1984, after completing his secondary education. He worked his way up to become Commander of the Presidential Guard in January 1994. He previously served as Commissioner for the Western Division, Minister of the Interior, and Secretary of State for Youth and Sports.

BALDE, ALFA MOLLOH EGUE. See ALFA MOLLOH.

BALDE, MUSA MOLLOH. See MUSA MOLLOH.

BALDEH, PAUL LOUIS (1937–1969). Schoolteacher and politician, born to a **Fulbe** family at Sare N'Gai in 1937 and educated at local Catholic mission schools and at the Catholic Secondary School at **Bathurst.** After completing a B.A. degree in Ireland, he returned to teach at the **Banjul** Catholic Secondary School. He early on aligned himself with the **People's Progressive Party (PPP)** and resigned his teaching position to campaign for the party in the upriver Fulbe areas. He was elected to Parliament in 1962 as MP for Lower Fuladu West and was appointed Minister of Education. Following disagreement with the party leadership, he was dismissed in 1963. However, just before independence, he was again appointed Minister of Education. He was reelected to parliament in 1966, but was passed over for further office. He was expelled from the PPP when he helped form the short-lived **People's Progressive Alliance (PPA).**

BANJUL. Capital city and chief port of The Gambia. The name initially given to the island ceded by the King of **Kombo** in 1816 to **Captain Alexander Grant,** who immediately constructed houses and barracks on the island to help control the entrance to the Gambia estuary. Grant renamed the island St. Mary's and called the new town Bathurst, in honor of the then Secretary of State for the Colonies, **Lord Henry Bathurst.** The streets were laid out in a modified grid pattern and named after the principal Allied generals of the war with Napoleon. Banjul Island thus became the center of British activity in the Gambia and the most populous part of the **Colony.** In 1973, in keeping with its status as the capital of an independent African country, its name reverted to Banjul. In mid-1993,

Banjul, including the adjacent Kanifing Administrative Area, had a population of 270,540. Because of overcrowding, there has been a steady migration of its population over several decades to the nearby mainland district of Kanifing (Bakau, **Serekunda,** and Fajara). Banjul's population fell by some 2,000 in the period 1983–1993, whereas Kanifing's doubled to 228,214. However, Banjul remains the administrative center of the country, the seat of government, and The Gambia's major port. It also remains the commercial and business center, although industrial activity is now concentrated in the Kanifing area, part of Greater Banjul.

BANTABA. A meeting place, usually a raised platform under a shade tree in each village, where the elders and the village head would come together to discuss matters of concern and to arrive at consensus decisions.

BANTA FARO. A **Mandinka** term for land areas above river levels that remain arid in the dry season although they are flooded during the rains. In The Gambia, these lands are higher than the mangrove swamps, but lie below the levels of the sandstone plateau that is an extension of the soil type found throughout southern Senegal and the **Casamance.** There are two types of *banta faros* in The Gambia—the estuarine and the upper river. The dividing line between the two is found roughly in the vicinity of **Kerewan** (Central River Division).

BARRA. Coastal settlement opposite **Banjul,** though the name (derived from the Portuguese for "narrows" or "strait"—a reference to the narrowing of the **Gambia River** at this point) was used more generally for the **Mandinka** kingdom of **Niumi.**

BARRA OR ANGLO-NIUMI WAR. In 1827, **Burungai Sonko,** the King of Barra, disturbed by Commodore **Charles Bullen**'s decision to build a fort at Barra Point, decided to abrogate the **Ceded Mile** treaty of the previous year. This decision resulted in a number of incidents culminating in the important Barra War, which did not end until January 1832. The hostilities forced Bullen to stop construction of the fort and, for a time, it appeared that the British would be driven out of Barra and the Ceded Mile. At one point the fledgling town of **Bathurst** was also threatened. The situation was reversed because the French at Goree dispatched a warship and troops to aid the British. This aid allowed the British to recommence construction of Fort Bullen in 1831, and this fort, with its three-gun battery, helped to give the British command of the entrance to the **Gambia River.**

BARRAKUNDA. A town in the **Wuli** district of the upper river area of The Gambia. It was the site of the furthest inland of the upper river factories (trading posts) established by English companies, because the falls at Barrakunda marked the limit of river travel in the dry season. A post was established there as early as 1651, but it was later destroyed by fire. An English factory was sited there again in 1678, and traders were posted there, intermittently, as late as 1810.

BASSE SANTA SU. Administrative capital and commercial center of Upper River Division. Conventionally known as Basse. It had a population of 15,930 in 1993.

BATHURST. See **BANJUL.**

BATHURST, HENRY, THIRD EARL (1762–1834). British Secretary of State for War and the Colonies, 1812–1828. **Captain Alexander Grant** in 1816 named his new town on St. Mary's Island in honor of Bathurst, who had authorized the project to restore British prestige on the **Gambia River.** Bathurst, a personal friend of William Pitt the Younger, held a number of senior government appointments and briefly served as MP for Cirencester in 1793. Born on May 22, 1762, he died on July 27, 1834.

BATHURST RATE PAYERS ASSOCIATION (BRPA). Founded in the early 1930s to act as a pressure group on the British administration to promote greater involvement of local people in municipal decision-making, particularly through direct African election to the urban authority. The influence of the Rate Payers Association was greatest between 1931 and 1935 when members of the newly created Urban District Council were normally chosen from its ranks. Although it continued to have a voice in Bathurst affairs, the BRPA gradually lost its unique position after the creation of the Bathurst Town Council in 1935. **Edward Francis Small** played a prominent role in the formation of the BRPA.

BATHURST TRADE UNION (BTU). A Bathurst-based general union organized by **Edward Francis Small** in 1929. Workers' combination in the Gambia dates back to a "Shipwrights' Society," which may have organized the country's first strike in 1856. A later body, the Carpenters' and Shipwrights' Society, negotiated a settlement of a general strike of artisans in 1921 and, after a period of obscurity, was revived in May 1929 to organize resistance to wage cuts imposed by private sector employers.

The Society was led by poorly educated Muslim **Wolof** artisans, who turned to Edward Small and other educated **Aku,** to turn their organization into the Bathurst Trade Union, with Small as Chairman. Other craft unions joined the BTU, so that by October 1929 it felt strong enough to confront employers over the wage cuts. Small and the BTU coordinated and extended strike action over a three-week period and succeeded in reversing the situation; the wage cuts were replaced by wage increases for private sector artisans and river craft workers, and the BTU was recognized by employers. The strike, which achieved international attention, is credited with having contributed to a change in official British thinking about the recognition of colonial trade unions. The "Passfield Memorandum" of 1930 (named for Lord Passfield [Sydney Webb] who was Secretary of State for the Colonies in the second Labour administration of 1929–31 and a leading socialist thinker, writer, and reformer, instrumental in setting up the London School of Economics) urged colonial governments to extend recognition to trade unions. As a result of this success, Small claimed a union membership of 1,000 in 1930.

The BTU was unable to capitalize on its victory, however, as it fell victim to a serious rift between Small and a rival faction headed by J. L. N'Jie, a shipwright, over union funds. The dispute spilled over into the community at large, with Small's political enemies in the "Gambia Representative Committee," headed by Legislative Councillor **Samuel John Forster, Jr.,** providing support for N'Jie. The latter's faction took advantage of the 1932 Trade Union Ordinance to register the BTU officially with government in 1933, under their leadership. The BTU was the first trade union to obtain such recognition in British colonial Africa. Suspicious of Small's leftist international links, the government also saw this as an opportunity to weaken his influence. Small was forced to form a new trade union, which he did in May 1935, calling it the Gambia Labour Union (GLU). Small remained its Chairman up to his death in 1958. After his death the GLU shifted to the far left ideologically, and though it still exists today, it has never attracted much of a following.

BATTIMANSA. Described by **Alvise da Cadamosto** in 1456 as the **Mandinka** ruler of part of the south bank approximately 60 miles from the mouth of the **Gambia River.** Battimansa received the Europeans in a very friendly fashion and treated them as honored guests during their 11-day stay, traded with them, and then signed a treaty of friendship.

BENSOUDA, MRS. FATOU (1961–   ). Minister of Justice and Attorney-General of The Gambia. Born in **Banjul** in 1961, she undertook legal studies at Ife University, Nigeria. Previously Solicitor-General, she assumed her present position in August 1998.

BINTANG. A village located approximately five miles up the **Bintang Bolon** from Bintang Point. It was the residence of the King of **Foni** and was one of the most important trade centers in the 18th century. Both the English and French maintained factories there in the hundred years after 1685. English independent traders continued to use Bintang as a trading base into the early 19th century.

BINTANG BOLON. This creek (*bolon*) is an important feature noted by early European visitors to the Gambia. It rises south of **Elephant Island,** north of the watershed of the **Casamance** River, and flows westward for approximately 80 miles before joining the **Gambia River** at Bintang Point some 30 miles from St. Mary's Island. It formed the dividing line between **Kiang** and **Foni.** From the earliest period of European activity there were always a number of temporary trading stations located along the Bolon. The **Royal African Company** maintained a major trade factory at **Bintang.** In some early literature, the waterway is referred to as the **Geregia** River.

BLACKBURNE, SIR KENNETH WILLIAM (1907–1980). Born on December 12, 1907, the son of a clergyman, Blackburne was educated at Marlborough and Clare College, Cambridge. He entered the Colonial Service in 1930 as an Assistant District Officer in Nigeria. He served in a similar capacity in Palestine, 1935–1938, and then took up an administrative post in the Colonial Office in London, where he remained until 1941. In that year he became Colonial Secretary of the Gambia and, during his two-year stay, headed a five-man development committee set up by the Governor, Sir Wilfrid Southorn. This committee was the Gambia's response to a Colonial Office directive that all colonies and territories prepare detailed analyses of their needs and make recommendations for the use of **Colonial Development and Welfare Act** funds at the conclusion of World War II. The Blackburne Report, published in 1943, was the first logical statement of the Gambia's needs encompassing all areas of the economy. The report, although many of its recommendations were ignored, served as the guide for Gambian development in the period 1945–1950. Blackburne left the Gambia in 1943 and spent the remainder of his career between the West Indies and the Colonial Office. He ended his official career as Governor of Jamaica. He retired in 1963 and died on April 4, 1980.

BLOOD, SIR HILARY RUDOLPH ROBERT, GBE, KCMG, CMG (1893–1967). Colonial administrator. The son of an Anglican clergyman and educated at Glasgow University, Blood was a captain in the Royal Scots Fusiliers during World War I. He served in the Ceylon civil service, 1920–1930, before becoming Colonial Secretary of Grenada from 1930–1934. In 1934, he was appointed Colonial Secretary of Sierra Leone. He was Governor of the Gambia from 1942 to 1947. After leaving the Gambia, Blood served as Governor of Barbados (1947–1949) and Mauritius (1949–1954). He was appointed Constitutional Commissioner in British Honduras (1959) and in Zanzibar (1960) and was also Chairman of the Constitutional Commission on Malta in 1960. In the Gambia, Blood's administration was responsible for drawing up proposals for improvements to the **Colony** area utilizing **Colonial Development and Welfare Act** funds. Although these funds fell short of expectations, the modernization of the water supply, the sewerage system, paved streets, and improvements to the port date to Blood's administration. Blood died on June 20, 1967.

BOJANG, DR. LAMIN. See **PEOPLE'S DEMOCRATIC PARTY.**

BOJANG, MOMODOU (MAJOR rtd.) (1957–   ). Secretary of State for the Interior. Bojang was born at Sanyang, Kombo South, Western Division, on October 23, 1957. Before joining the **Gambia National Army (GNA)** as an officer cadet in 1986, he worked in agriculture and banking, obtained a B.A. from Fourah Bay College, University of Sierra Leone, in 1985, and taught for a year at Gambia High School. He specialized in military intelligence in the GNA, becoming a company commander in 1994. After the army coup in July 1994 he was appointed Commissioner, Central River Division. He took up his present appointment in March 1997.

BOJANG, SANJALLY (?–1995). An untutored **Mandinka** of chiefly lineage from Kombo Central, Bojang was a successful dock labor contractor and played an important part in the setting up of the **People's Progressive Party (PPP).** Initially active in Mandinka charitable associations—Lilahi Warasuli and the Kombo and Niumi Burial Society—concerned with the welfare of **Protectorate** inhabitants living in the **Colony** area, he played a prominent role in the formation of the **Protectorate People's Party,** which became the People's Progressive Party (PPP). Previously, Bojang had alternated between the **Gambia Democratic Party (GDP)** and the **Gambia Muslim Congress (GMC),** but following attacks on him and on other Protectorate people by members of the **Bathurst** elite, he threw in his lot with the group of younger Protectorate Mandinka, a number of them graduates of **Armitage School,** who had formed the Protectorate People's Society early in 1957. He introduced David **(Dawda) Jawara** to the group and helped to finance and promote the newly formed PPP in the Protectorate, particularly among more conservative elders. Bojang, as National President of the PPP, led its enormously successful tour of the Protectorate, before the first national elections in May 1960.

During party leader Jawara's absence in Nigeria in late September 1960, Bojang sought to commit the PPP to a political union with the **Democratic Congress Alliance (DCA)** and the **United Party (UP)** in the short-lived Gambia Solidarity Party. Bojang was expelled from the PPP for his action, then he helped form the **Gambia National Union,** and on its demise he backed **Pierre Sarr N'Jie's** United Party (UP). Reconciled with Jawara in 1970, he rejoined the PPP as an ordinary member. He was appointed District Chief of Kombo Central in 1975, but was deposed after speaking against the government (allegedly under duress) on Radio Gambia during the abortive coup of 1981. He was *alkaaloo* of his home village, Kembuje, at the time of his death on October 23, 1995.

BOJANG, TOMANI. The last **Soninke** king of **Kombo.** After being hard pressed by the **Marabout** dissidents at **Gunjur** in 1863–1864, he agreed to the truce with **Fodi Kabba** and **Fodi Silla** arranged by Governor **G. A. K. D'Arcy.** For over half a decade there was relative peace between the two factions in Kombo, broken only by sporadic violence. In 1870, Tomani Bojang, upon learning of the proposed cession of British territories to the French, addressed a dignified note to Queen Victoria requesting that if she no longer wanted those areas ceded to her she could "return my territory back to me as an act of friendship." The British government informed him that it could not accede to his request. In the troubled years of the 1870s, neither could the British protect him completely from his Marabout enemies who had become even more powerful. Hostilities broke out in 1871, and within two years all of the Soninke towns in Kombo, with the exception of **Busumbala** and **Brikama,** were in Marabout hands. In the following year, Bojang lost Brikama, and a small remnant of his territory was saved only by a British-arranged truce in 1874. In the following year, Fodi Silla began the war again, and his forces took Busumbala, forcing the king to take refuge at Lamin, a few yards away from British territory.

The British Administrator, fearing that war would spread to British Kombo, warned Tomani Bojang not to expect any British aid. The king, therefore, was forced to accept Fodi Silla's humiliating terms. He shaved his head, became a Muslim, and tore down his stockade. His old enemy then allowed him enough land for himself and his people in the territory over which his dynasty had ruled for more than two centuries.

BOOKER, JOHN (?–1693). Chief agent of the **Royal African Company** in the Gambia from 1688 until his death in mid-1693. He was one of the most loyal and successful of the Company's servants in Africa. The outbreak of war with France in 1689 found him in charge of fewer than 200 men, and no ships of war were permanently stationed on the river. Nevertheless, he used visiting Company vessels to drive French shipping from the coast, to deal with privateers, and finally to transport an expeditionary force against St. Louis and Goree. Both French stations were captured in December 1692, their stores seized, and their defenses demolished. His death by fever removed the one man who might have resisted the French forces that recaptured St. Louis and Goree in 1693.

BRAVO, MAJOR ALEXANDER. Acting Administrator of the Gambia in 1870 who attempted to rebut the arguments of local and British merchants against the exchange of the Gambia for suitable French territory elsewhere.

BRIDGES, SIR PHILIP R. (1922–). Civil servant and solicitor. Born in England and educated at Aberdeen University, Bridges served with the Royal Artillery, and he was attached to the **Royal West African Frontier Force** in Burma during World War II. He first served in the Gambia as a Government Land Officer and was appointed Attorney General in 1964, a post he continued to hold after independence, being the only European in the Gambian cabinet. In 1968 he became Chief Justice, and he retired in 1983.

BRIKAMA. Administrative and commercial center of the Western Division and the second largest town in the country, located some 40 miles southeast of **Banjul.** Its population in 1993 was 41,761, more than doubling in a decade.

BRITISH WEST AFRICAN SETTLEMENTS. Until 1843, the administration of Sierra Leone and the Gambia was the primary responsibility of a Governor resident at Freetown. The Gambia was administered directly by an Administrator subordinate to Sierra Leone. In 1843, the Gambia was separated from Freetown under its own Governor. One of the major results of the parliamentary investigations of 1865 was a return to the older system, placing all the British territories—Sierra Leone, Gambia, the Gold Coast, and Lagos—under one Governor with overall responsibility, based once more in Freetown. Thus the administration of the Gambia became subordinate to decisions made in Freetown. In 1874, the British possessions on the Gold Coast and at Lagos were separated from Sierra Leone, but the Gambia remained under the control of the Governor of the British West African Settlements. It was not until November 1888 that the Gambia was released from this cumbersome and economically debilitating dependence and became a separate colony.

BROWN, THOMAS. British merchant whose firm was one of the largest in the Gambia in the late 1860s and early 1870s. Brown and Company had been trading in the hinterland since the early 1830s, and Brown had made enough money to retire to England in 1854. However, five years later he was back, and soon his agents were challenging French firms for supremacy on the lower **Gambia River.** He was a member of the **Legislative Council** during much of the early period of negotiations with France over exchanging the Gambia. He was one of the chief opponents of both attempts by Britain to be rid of the Gambia. He wrote long polemical letters, signed memorials, and personally lobbied the Colonial Office against the trade-off, since he was convinced that British and African firms would not receive adequate compensation and would be forced out of business by the French. Brown and Company continued in operation until 1880, and Brown was the last of the pioneer British merchants to continue to reside in **Bathurst.**

BRUE, ANDRE. Director-General of the French **Senegal Company** after 1697, with his headquarters at St. Louis. He was dedicated to driving English traders from the Senegambia and gaining French dominance of trade on the **Gambia River.** However, he was not able to accomplish this despite a quarter of a century of effort. Major reasons for his failure were his inability to control piracy, the losses sustained by the Senegal Company during the War of the Spanish Succession, and the growing economic weaknesses of the Company.

BULLEN, ADMIRAL SIR CHARLES (1769–1853). Bullen enlisted as a boy in the Royal Navy in 1779 and saw considerable action in the French wars, commanding HMS *Britannia* at Trafalgar in 1804. He first served on the West Africa station in 1801 and returned there in 1824–27 as a commodore on HMS *Maidstone,* sent to Gambian waters to support the Acting Governor of Sierra Leone, Kenneth MacAulay, in his negotiations with **Burungai Sonko,** the King of Barra. Subsequently a treaty was signed ceding to Britain the whole right bank of the river one mile inland from Jinnak Creek to Jokadu Creek. Immediately after the signing, Commodore Bullen transported two cannons to Barra Point. A military guard was placed over these guns and the site was named Fort Bullen in his honor. Bullen was appointed Superintendent of Pembroke Dock in 1830 and became an admiral in 1852. He died on July 2, 1853.

BUR. **Wolof** word for king or ruler (*bar* in **Serer**).

BURBA. The title given to the king in the earliest dominant **Wolof** state of **Jolof.**

BURTON, SIR RICHARD FRANCIS (1821–1890). Distinguished 19th-century explorer, translator, and author. As British Consul in Fernando Po, he visited the Gambia in 1863 and left his impressions of **Bathurst** and the British government in a book, *Wanderings in West Africa from Liverpool to Fernando Po,* which he published under the pseudonymous initials, F.R.G.S.

BUSUMBALA. A town midway between Sukuta and **Brikama** which was the main fortified base of the rulers of **Kombo.** By mid-1874, Busumbala was the only town loyal to the **Soninke** king, **Tomani Bojang.** Its capture in the following year forced him to capitulate and accept Islam in exchange for the right to continue to live in Kombo.

-C-

CADAMOSTO, ALVISE DA (1432–1488). A Venetian captain employed by Prince Henry of Portugal, commissioned in 1455 to investigate rumors of lands along the **Gambia River** where great quantities of gold could be obtained. Sailing in a 90-ton ship, he was joined off Cape Verde by **Antoniotto Usidimare** with two ships, and together they entered the estuary of the Gambia River. Armed resistance from Africans in canoes so unnerved the crews that they refused to proceed further. In the following year, Cadamosto returned with three ships to the Gambia and proceeded approximately 60 miles upriver. He was warmly received by the **Mandinka** ruler of **Baddibu, Battimansa,** concluded a treaty of friendship with him and acquired a few slaves and some gold in their trading. After staying in Baddibu for 11 days, he sailed downriver, explored the southern coastline as far as the Casamance River, and then returned to Portugal.

CADI (QADI, XADI). Arabic term for a judge. Sometimes reserved for the supreme judge or leader of an lslamic community.

CAMARA, ASSAN MUSA (formerly ANDREW DAVID CAMARA) (1913–). A Fula **(Fulbe),** born at Mansajang, **Basse,** Upper River Division (URD). Educated in **Bathurst,** he worked as a teacher/headteacher at the Anglican Kristikunda Mission School, URD, 1948–1960. He resigned to stand as an independent candidate in **Kantora** in the first national elections in 1960. Winning the election, he was pressed by his constituents to join the **United Party (UP)** in 1961. He defended Kantora successfully as a UP candidate in the 1962 elections. Disillusioned with the UP leader, **Pierre Sarr N'Jie,** he switched to the **People's Progressive Party (PPP)** in 1963. Camara served as Education Minister in the UP administration of 1961–62 and as Minister of Education, Labour and Social Welfare in 1963 on joining the PPP. In 1970, he moved to External Affairs and was appointed Vice President in 1972, following the postelection reshuffle. In 1974 he combined the Local Government ministry with the vice presidency. He returned to Education in 1977 and later was appointed to Finance and Trade. In 1981, he was appointed Vice President again and was the senior minister left in **Banjul** during the attempted coup in July.

Camara came under the President's suspicion in 1982 for allegedly backing independent candidates in URD at the general election, which saw the loss of Basse and other seats. In the May cabinet reshuffle he was demoted to Education Minister and resigned from the PPP in 1986 to form the **Gambia People's Party (GPP)** with two other former ministers, both of whom were disgruntled with the government. He lost Kantora, his parliamentary seat, in the 1987 elections as well as being defeated by **Jawara** in the presidential election. He met similar defeats in the 1992 elections. Following the military coup in 1994, the GPP was banned and Camara himself was barred from standing for Parliament. Camara changed his name when he reverted to Islam. See also **Gambia People's Party.**

CAMERON, SIR EDWARD JOHN, KCMG, CMG (1858–1947). Colonial administrator. An army doctor's son, born on May 14, 1858, Cameron was educated at Shrewsbury School and Clifton College, and at Merton College, Oxford. He joined the colonial service in 1882 as Private Secretary to the Governor of the Bahamas, moving to a similar position in the Leeward Islands in 1884. In 1885–1886 he served as Assistant Colonial Secretary and Treasurer, Sierra Leone, before returning to the Caribbean, first as President (Administrator) of the British Virgin Islands (1887–1893); then as Commissioner of the Turks and Caicos Islands (1893–1901); Administrator of St. Vincent (1901–1909); Administrator of St. Lucia (1909–1913); and Acting Governor of the Windward Islands. He served as Governor of the Gambia from 1913 to 1920. Cameron was responsible for putting into effect the provisions of the Comprehensive **Protectorate** Ordinance of 1913. In 1919, he issued another Protectorate Ordinance, which further defined the relative powers of the central government and the chiefs, and also introduced a new scale of Protectorate taxes. It was during Cameron's tenure of office that British firms gained supremacy in trade over their French competitors. The failure of Cameron and his successor, **Cecil Armitage,** to act quickly to equalize the exchange rate for the **five-franc piece** eventually cost the Gambia over £200,000. Cameron retired on leaving the Gambia and died on July 20, 1947.

CARROL, WILFRED DAVIDSON, M.A., B.C.L. (1900–1941). Gambian barrister-at-law and unofficial member of the **Legislative Council.** Carrol was born in **Bathurst** into a leading **Aku** merchant family, whose business dated back to 1883. Educated locally at the Methodist Boys High School, he proceeded to Britain in 1920 to study law at Oxford. After graduation he trained as a barrister and was called to the bar in 1924. He returned to the Gambia in 1925 and set up practice in Bathurst as a barrister and solicitor. In 1931–1934, he was an elected member of the Bathurst Urban District Council, representing **Jollof Town** North ward. He was appointed an unofficial member of the Legislative Council in 1932, as the nominee of the Bathurst Urban District Council. His advice was highly valued by that body. Carrol also served on several other public bodies and was associated with many sporting and social activities. Carrol was the only non-official lawyer in the **Colony** following the death of his uncle, **Sir Samuel J. Forster, Jr.,** in 1940. In poor health himself from about 1938, Carrol died on October 30, 1941.

CARTER, SIR GILBERT (1848–1927). Administrator of the Gambia from 1888 to 1890. Carter entered the Royal Navy in 1864 and first served in West Africa as Paymaster on the colonial steamer *Sherbro* in Sierra Leone. He took part in the Ashanti War in 1873 and then spent two years in the Leeward Islands, returning to West Africa as Collector of Customs on the Gold Coast in 1879. Carter's first appointment in the Gambia was as Treasurer in 1882. During his short term of office as Administrator, Britain reversed its decades-old policy against territorial expansion. In 1888, Carter was ordered to enter into definite treaties of cession with Gambian chiefs. His recommendation to his superiors that they claim a large segment of the hinterland of the **Gambia River** was largely ignored by the delegates to the Paris Conference in 1889. After the declaration of the **Protectorate,** Carter with his small force and few resources could do little but announce the change to the upper and middle river Gambian chiefs. On leaving the Gambia, Carter became Governor of Lagos, in which post he served from 1890 to 1897. Later he was appointed Governor of the Bahamas and of Barbados. He retired in 1910.

CASAMANCE. That part of the Republic of Senegal between The Gambia and Guinea Bissau, named after the river that flows through it. It presently comprises two of the administrative regions of the Republic of Senegal. The upper and middle parts of the territory belong to the sahel zone, while the lower Casamance marks the beginning of the West African rain forest zone. Inhabited by **Jola,** Papel, Balante, Tucolor, **Fulbe,** and **Mandinka,** the present-day Casamance was historically a part of the **Gambia River** complex and it was not until 1889 that it was arbitrarily separated from the Gambia. Ethnic ties between Jola in The Gambia and in Casamance and a guerilla struggle, dating back to 1982, against the Senegalese state by Jola, organized by the Movement of Democratic Forces of the Casamance (MFDC), led by Abbe Diamacoune Senghor, have contributed to the sensitivity of this region in Senegal-Gambia relations.

CEDED MILE. In June 1826, Kenneth MacAulay, Acting Governor of Sierra Leone, negotiated with **Burungai Sonko,** the King of **Barra,** the cession to the Crown of a coastal strip one mile in depth, beginning at Jinnak Creek in the west and stretching as far as **Jokadu** Creek in the east. In January 1832, following the **Barra War,** this cession was reconfirmed and the area controlled by the British was extended slightly. The Ceded Mile, though technically still part of the **Colony,** was administered by the

British as a part of the **Protectorate,** when the latter was declared over the hinterland areas in 1889.

CEESAY, EBRIMA (1959–). Secretary of State for Works, Communications and Information. Born of **Mandinka** parentage and educated at Fourah Bay College, University of Sierra Leone (Bachelor of Engineering, 1984), and Maastricht School of Management, the Netherlands (M.B.A., 1994), he spent his working career in mechanical engineering management in the Gambia Public Transport Corporation. He was appointed Minister (and subsequently Secretary of State) for Works, Communications and Information in September 1995.

CHAM, MOMODOU CADIJA (1938–). A former civil servant and politician, Cham was born at **Basse** on August 19, 1938, and educated at St. George's Primary School, Basse, and St. Augustine's Secondary School, **Bathurst.** He entered the civil service in 1958 and served four years until he was elected MP for Tumana, Upper River Division, in 1962, representing the **United Party (UP).** Although successfully defending the seat for the UP in the 1966 general election, Cham crossed over to the ruling **People's Progressive Party (PPP)** and held on to the seat until the 1992 general election, when he was defeated by the **Gambia People's Party (GPP)** candidate. Cham served as Minister of Education, Youth and Sports and later as Minister of Trade and Finance until the cabinet reshuffle of 1981, when he was dismissed, following press attacks on his ministerial performance. As a former minister, he was barred from standing for Parliament following the 1994 coup.

CHARLES ISLAND. See DOG ISLAND.

CHOWN, THOMAS, JR. British merchant who had taken control of the family business interests in the Gambia in 1870. He was one of the 10 members of the Gambia Committee which lobbied successfully in 1875 and 1876 against the revived plan of the Colonial Office to exchange the Gambia for French territory.

CHOWN, THOMAS, SR. British merchant who formed a family-owned trading company which operated in the Gambia from the early 1830s. He combined his efforts with those of other British merchants such as **Thomas Quin** and **Thomas Brown,** and Gambian traders such as J. D.

Cole and E. J. Nicol, to oppose the 1866–1870 plan to cede the Gambia to France.

CHRISTENSEN, ERIC HERBERT (1923–1990). A civil servant, born on October 29, 1923, in **Bathurst,** of mixed Gambian-Danish parentage. Educated at St. Augustine's Secondary School, he later taught there in 1941–1943. After military service in 1944–1945, he became a clerk in the Government Secretariat, 1946–1947, leaving to become Vice Consul at the French Consulate, 1947–1960, and Attaché at the Senegalese Consulate-General, 1961–1965. Returning to government service he was appointed Assistant Secretary, External Affairs, 1965–1966; then Assistant Secretary, Prime Minister's Office, 1966–1967. He was the first Gambian head (Secretary General) of the civil service in 1967, a post he combined with that of Secretary to the Cabinet. He was awarded the CMG in 1968. He died on July 30, 1990.

CISSE, BIRAM. Born into an important **Marabout** family at **Kaur,** he came under the influence of **Ma Bah** early in his life and proved himself one of the better military leaders of the kingdom of **Baddibu.** After Ma Bah's death, he precipitated a rebellion against **Mamadou N'Dare** by refusing to dismantle his fortifications at Kaur. He was aided in his struggle against Mamadou by **Musa Molloh** and by the Bur Saloum, Guedel M'Bodj. By the early 1880s, Cisse had managed to drive Mamadou from most of the vast territory he had once controlled. Complications arose, however, when **Sait Maty,** the son of Ma Bah, claimed the throne of Baddibu and Cisse found this new enemy more formidable than Mamadou. Despite considerable military success, particularly in the campaign of 1885, he was unable to completely defeat Sait Maty, and in 1886 he agreed to the proposal of British mediators to accept Sait Maty as his suzerain, provided he could keep his territory and receive a stipend from the British. When the stipend was not forthcoming, Cisse refused the agreement. In the civil war, both parties had encroached on the territory of Saloum, and the French, fearing a regrowth of Baddibu domination there, sent a military column against Sait Maty in 1887, defeated his armies, and forced him to flee. Cisse was not involved directly in this action, and he received guarantees of a part of the kingdom of Baddibu from the French. However, after rumors of an impending renewal of violence reached him, the French Commandant at Nioro arrested Cisse in June 1888. Cisse was exiled to Gabon.

COLONIAL/COMMONWEALTH DEVELOPMENT CORPORA-TION (CDC). Created by the British government in 1948 to devise development schemes that would secure the dual purpose of providing necessary income for the territories and also profits for the CDC. The management of the Corporation was the responsibility of a Board of Directors of eight members with Lord Trefgarne as Chairman. The Corporation was concerned with funding two major projects in the Gambia. The first was a large-scale mechanized project to clear, plant, and harvest rice mechanically on 4,700 acres of land near Wallikunda. The **Wallikunda rice scheme** was not successful, and after considerable expenditure, the facilities were taken over in 1953 by the Gambian government, which continued to operate the farm as an experimental station. The other CDC project in the Gambia was costlier and even more unsuccessful. From 1948 to early 1951, the Corporation expended nearly £1 million on the **Yundum Egg Project.** A combination of factors—poor management, over-optimistic estimates of profits, failure to confer with local officials, and chicken disease—combined to make the Yundum Project one of the Corporation's greatest African failures.

COLONIAL DEVELOPMENT AND WELFARE ACTS (CD&W). The first of these acts was passed by the British Parliament in early 1940 and represented a reversal of the previous doctrine for the dependent territories. Instead of demanding fiscal self-sufficiency of all territories, Parliament recognized a responsibility to assist the development of all of its territories even though an area might not itself have the available funds. Under these acts, Britain, although hard pressed in the years immediately after World War II, made massive grants of funds to its African territories. While falling far short of expectations, the Gambia in the decade after 1957 received over £1.5 million in Colonial Development and Welfare funds. These paid for the construction of a new bridge, a high school, The Royal Victoria Hospital (**Bathurst**), a better water supply, paved streets, and an adequate drainage system for the capital city. The bulk of the funds allocated for the **Protectorate** went for the improvement of **agriculture,** for the construction of an asphalt road from **Brikama** to **Mansakonko,** divisional capital of Lower River Division, and for the construction of a hospital at Bansang, MacCarthy Island Division.

COLONY. Correctly speaking, the Crown Colony of the Gambia was restricted to the capital city, **Bathurst,** and the surrounding area of British **Kombo,** the narrow strip of territory across the river estuary known as the

Ceded Mile, and **MacCarthy Island,** some 150 miles upriver. The remainder of the Gambian dependency, acquired at the close of the 19th century, constituted the **Protectorate.** The inhabitants of the Colony enjoyed a number of constitutional and legal privileges denied to the inhabitants of the Protectorate until the 1960s as well as greater access to medical, educational, and work opportunities.

COMPANY OF MERCHANTS TRADING TO AFRICA. Created by an act of the British Parliament in 1750, it was the successor to the bankrupt **Royal African Company** which, however, was not divested of all its powers until 1752. The Company of Merchants was prohibited from all trading in its corporate capacity. It was directed by an appointed executive committee, empowered to make rules regarding trading in West Africa, and thus could charge trading fees and customs duties. It received an annual subsidy from Parliament for the maintenance of trading forts and stations. The Crown exercised supervisory control over the activities of the Company. The fort on **James Island** was repaired and restaffed, and with the aid of ships of the Royal Navy, French attempts to dominate Gambian trade from **Albreda** were thwarted even before the outbreak of the Seven Years War.

During that war, the British beat off a French attack on James Island in 1757, and in the following year captured and garrisoned all the main French bases in Senegal. At the outbreak of the war, the Company had relinquished its rights of administration. Its territories were administered by the military until 1765 when the **Province of Senegambia** was created with its capital at St. Louis.

During the War of American Independence, a French force reoccupied St. Louis and razed James Fort in early 1779. The Treaty of Versailles of 1783 restored to the French all they had lost in the Senegambia, and in the same year the Crown returned control over the Gambia area to the Company of Merchants. The Company showed no great zeal in reestablishing trade relations. Parliament many times refused a grant that the Company directors felt necessary for the reconstruction of James Fort, and it was never rebuilt. British trade on the river was maintained by private merchants. Finally, in 1816, the Crown decided to send **Captain Alexander Grant** with a small party to build a fort near the river's mouth, a fort whose main function would be to prevent the **slave trade.** The Company of Merchants did not underwrite this venture, and there developed, in theory, a duality of control. Finally, in 1821, all the forts and territories were taken from the Company and placed under the direct jurisdiction of the Crown.

CONFERENCE OF PROTECTORATE CHIEFS. An annual meeting of the *seefoolu* of the Gambia was instituted in 1944 as a means of better communication with the Governor and the central agencies of the administration. The conferences, held in different places in the **Protectorate** each year, were occasions of great pomp and ceremony. The meetings all followed a similar format. The Governor would address the chiefs, outlining his proposals for action for the coming year. This would be followed by presentations by the heads of the central departments of their activities during the previous year and their plans for the coming year. Until 1958, the chiefs did not take an active role, asked few questions, and accepted the government's predetermined policy without demur. From 1958 onward, a number of chiefs, at times vehemently, began to comment on and question the performance of the government. However, political parties soon supplanted the chiefs as the dominant spokesmen for the Protectorate, and the conference never became more than a passive sounding board for the central administration.

CONTON, WILLIAM (1925–?). Bathurst-born educator and novelist. The son of a clergyman, Conton was educated in the Gambia and Sierra Leone, before leaving for university training at Durham in England. After receiving his B.A., he returned to West Africa where he became the principal of the Government Secondary School at Bo in Sierra Leone. He was author of *The African,* published in 1960, one of the first novels by an African to gain worldwide circulation and acclaim, and the first by a Gambian writer.

COURLAND, DUCHY OF. An independent Baltic duchy in the 17th century under the suzerainty of the kings of Poland. Jacobus (James), Duke of Courland, caught up in dreams of the wealth of Guinea, formed a trading company in 1650. In the following year his agents leased **Banjul** from the King of **Kombo,** a small plot of land at **Juffure** on the north bank, and most important, an island in the **Gambia River** from the King of **Barra.** The island was named St. Andrew's and later renamed **James Island** by the British. The company sent a group of settlers under Major Fock who built an excellent fort (Fort Jacobus) on the island from which the Courlanders hoped to dominate the river trade. The Duke's dream of a mercantile empire based on the Gambia and the West Indies was dashed by the corruption of his lieutenants, the open hostility of greater European powers, and events in the Baltic. The Duke was captured by Charles X of Sweden in 1658, and he assigned the rights to manage his Gambian holdings to the **Dutch West Indies Company.** In 1661, St. Andrew's Island was captured by the English under **Major Robert Holmes.** In 1664, Courland ceded its rights in the Gambia to England in return for a guarantee to respect the Duke's control over Tobago in the West Indies.

COURLANDERS. See **DUCHY OF COURLAND.**

-D-

DABO, BAKARY BUNJA (1946–). A **Mandinka** civil servant and politician, born at Dumbutto, Kiang West, in the Lower River Division. He was educated at Dumbutto and Kaiaf primary schools, Methodist Boys High School, **Banjul,** and the University of Ibadan, Nigeria, graduating in modern languages in 1967. Dabo received graduate training from the University of Abidjan, Ivory Coast, and specialized economic training from the Bank of America, National Westminster Bank, and Ghana Commercial Bank. He spent two tours in the Provincial Administration upriver at **Basse** and **Kerewan;** the first of these (1967–1968) was as Assistant Divisional Commissioner, and the second (1970–1971) as Divisional Commissioner. In the intervening years Dabo served as Assistant Secretary in the Ministry of External Affairs. In July 1971, he was appointed Director of Economic and Technical Affairs and three years later was made Manager of the commercial operations of the Gambia Commercial and Development Bank in Banjul.

In 1979, Dabo was appointed Gambian High Commissioner to the Republic of Senegal, a position he held until September 1981, when, following his key role at the time of the attempted coup d'etat in Banjul, he became a nominated Member of Parliament and was given the post of Minister of Information and Tourism. In 1982, Dabo replaced a former **People's Progressive Party (PPP)** minister, Howsoon Semega Janneh (who went on to form the **Gambia People's Party [GPP]**), as PPP MP for Kiang West, a seat he retained until the army coup in July 1994. He was also elevated to Vice President of the Gambia in May 1982, but was demoted to Finance Minister after the 1992 elections, as a result of President Jawara's suspicions of him, fueled by factional intrigue within the PPP. Dabo served briefly as Finance Minister under the **Armed Forces Provisional Ruling Council (AFPRC),** but fled to Britain in November 1994, from where he has continued to oppose the **Yahya Jammeh** government.

DABO, DARI BANA. The **Marabout** chief of Sankandi and a follower of **Fodi Kabba** in the late 1890s. When the longstanding quarrel over rice lands with the **Soninke** of Jataba became critical, **Travelling Commissioner Cyril Frederic Sitwell** investigated and awarded the lands to Jataba. Dari Bana Dabo refused to be bound by this decision and decided to fight when Sitwell, accompanied by Commissioner Silva and 11 African constables, appeared at Sankandi in early 1900 to enforce the award. In the ensuing skirmish, the two Travelling Commissioners, a neighboring chief, and six constables were killed. As soon as troops were available, the British, in conjunction with the French, moved to pacify those areas loyal to Fodi Kabba. French troops moved on Medina, Fodi Kabba's stronghold, in March 1901. The British, allied with **Musa Molloh,** had already taken Sankandi in January. Dari Bana Dabo fled to French territory where he was captured and turned over to the British for trial. He and two of his lieutenants were tried before the Supreme Court in **Bathurst** and found guilty of the deaths of Sitwell and his party. Dari Bana Dabo was sentenced to death and executed.

DARBOE, A. N. M. OUSAINU. A successful Muslim lawyer in **Banjul** and a leading civil rights campaigner in The Gambia. Darboe was instrumental in creating the **United Democratic Party (UDP)** in 1996. As Secretary General and leader of the UDP, he stood against **Yahya Jammeh,** former junta leader and candidate of the **Alliance for Patriotic Re-orientation and Construction (APRC)** in the presidential elections of September 1996, coming in second with a 39.2 percent share of the vote. Despite this setback, the UDP is the largest opposition party in the National Assembly, and Darboe remains a vocal critic of government policy.

D'ARCY, COLONEL G. A. K. Succeeded Lieutenant-Colonel **L. S. O'Connor** as Governor of the Gambia in 1859. He arrived in the midst of a yellow fever epidemic, which had reduced the European population of **Bathurst** to fewer than a dozen persons. His pleas to the Colonial Office for extra funds to be able to drain **Half Die** and improve the sanitation facilities of the **Colony** fell on deaf ears, and many of his recommendations were not put into effect until a half-century later.

D'Arcy's expedition against **Baddibu** in 1861 set in motion the series of events which brought **Ma Bah** to power. Throughout his tenure, D'Arcy was constrained from any policy toward Ma Bah and the middle and upper river areas which would have committed the British government to any more expense. The treaty of friendship D'Arcy signed with

Ma Bah in February 1863 concerning **Niumi** was a good example of the type of intervention D'Arcy was limited to. Although some of Ma Bah's lieutenants continued to cause trouble in Niumi, Ma Bah kept his word and did not again disturb the area. In **Kombo,** D'Arcy had the force to confront the **Marabouts** and **Fodi Kabba** and to maintain an uneasy status quo through 1864 and 1865. The chief disturber of the peace was **Amer Faal** who raided into the **Ceded Mile.** In July 1866, with naval support and a force of 500 warriors from Niumi, D'Arcy's West Indian troops stormed Tubab Kolon, Amer Faal's stronghold.

D'Arcy's ideas concerning British influence in the Senegambia were reflected in the report of **Colonel St. George Ord** in 1865, but aside from a few punitive forays such as that against Tubab Kolon, D'Arcy could do little to increase British control along the river.

DE JASPAS, MELCHIOR. An Armenian resident of Great Britain who was used by the **Royal African Company** to translate some of **Job ben Solomon's** Arabic letters. The Company decided to use his language skills and sent him to the Gambia in 1737. Because of maltreatment, he left the Company in the following year. However, in 1740 he was reemployed and accompanied Job ben Solomon to Bondu. In 1744, he journeyed overland to Cachau in what is today Guinea-Bissau. Little of concrete trading value was obtained for the Company by de Jaspas in his explorations, perhaps because the outbreak of war with France in 1743 focused the Company's attention elsewhere.

DEMA. **Wolof** term for witches, whom they fear greatly. A person becomes a *dema* through the mother. If the mother is a witch, then the children are also suspected of being able to do great harm. Witches are believed to be able to take animal or bird form and to eat people's souls and drink their blood.

DEMOCRATIC CONGRESS ALLIANCE (DCA). The DCA was formed in 1960 by a merger of the **Gambia Democratic Party (GDP)** and the **Gambia Muslim Congress (GMC),** because the leaders of the older parties, Reverend **John Colley Faye** and **Ibrahima Momodou Garba-Jahumpa,** wanted a stronger, **Protectorate**-wide party to contest the elections against the **United Party (UP)** and the **People's Progressive Party (PPP).** However, only three of their candidates were elected to the House of Representatives in 1960. In 1961 the DCA leaders reached an agreement with Jawara and the PPP and, although there was no merger, the DCA cooperated with the PPP in the elections of 1962. Despite the victory of the PPP, the DCA could win only one seat in the expanded House of Representatives. This failure, and political differences between Garba-Jahumpa and Faye, soon led to the breakup of the party. Garba-Jahumpa withdrew to form the **Gambia Congress Party (GCP),** while the rest of the DCA merged with the PPP in August 1965.

DEMONETIZATION CRISIS. See **FIVE-FRANC PIECE.**

DENHAM, SIR EDWARD BRANDIS, GCMG, KCMG, KBE (1876–1938). Educated at Malvern College and Merton College, Oxford, Denham joined the colonial service as a cadet in the Ceylon civil service. In 1920–1923, he was Colonial Secretary of Mauritius; he later held various positions in Kenya, including Acting Governor, in 1923–1928. From Kenya he moved to the Gambia, where he was Governor in 1928–1930. His final posting was Governor of British Guiana, 1930–1934. Denham died on June 2, 1938.

DENTON, SIR GEORGE CHARDIN, KCMG, GMC (1851–1928). A vicar's son from Dorset, Denton was born on June 22, 1851. After Rugby School, he pursued a military career, being commissioned in the 57th Regiment of Foot in 1869. He changed careers in 1880, joining the colonial service as Chief of Police, St. Vincent. Promoted to Administrator in 1885, Denton moved to West Africa in 1889, serving as Colonial Secretary and Acting Governor of Lagos (1889–1891 and 1893–1900) before assuming the Governorship of the Gambia from 1901 to 1911. Denton was the first chief executive of the Gambia in the modern era to be appointed Governor instead of Administrator. He completed the work begun by his successor, **Sir Robert B. Llewelyn,** in devising the framework of British rule in the **Protectorate.** This was done by a series of Protectorate Ordinances which refined and clarified the earlier system. The most important of these Ordinances were those of 1902 and 1909 (two modifying Ordinances being promulgated in that year). Denton's main contribution to the Gambia was his resistance to the requirements of the **Anglo-French Convention of 1904** which would have assigned a mid-river port on the **Gambia River** to the French.

His arguments that such a cession would destroy the British and Gambian merchants at **Bathurst** had considerable influence in determining the attitude of the British government in delaying the cession until after World War I, when subsequent events made the French abandon their designs on the middle river areas. Denton died on January 9, 1928.

DIBBA, SHERIFF, MUSTAPHA (1937–   ). Politician. The son of a **Mandinka** farmer from Salikeni, in the Central **Baddibu** district of the North Bank Division. His father later became district chief of Central Baddibu. Dibba was educated in government and mission schools and worked briefly as a clerk for the United Africa Company until he resigned in 1959 to work for the newly-formed **People's Progressive Party (PPP).**

Dibba was particularly active in organizing the youth wing of the party and stood successfully as PPP candidate for Baddibu (Central Baddibu from 1962) in the first national general elections in 1960 and subsequent elections, until he broke with the party. In 1964, he became Minister of Labour and in the following year Minister of Local Government. After the 1966 elections, he was appointed Minister of Works and Communications, and replaced **Sheriff Sisay** as Minister of Finance when the latter was expelled from the PPP.

When The Gambia became a Republic in 1970, Dibba was chosen to be Vice President while continuing as Finance Minister. He relinquished the latter portfolio in early 1973 and soon after was removed as Vice President and demoted to the less prestigious position of Gambian negotiator to the European Economic Community. His downfall was in part the result of the "butut scandal"; one of Dibba's brothers was arrested smuggling Gambian currency into Senegal and was found to have been working out of No. 1 Marina, Sheriff Dibba's official residence. On his return to The Gambia from Brussels, Dibba was made the first Minister of Economic Planning, but in 1975 he was expelled from the PPP following accusations of trying to take over the leadership of the party from **Sir Dawda Jawara** and soon after set up his own political organization, the **National Convention Party (NCP).**

In the 1977 elections, Dibba was unable to unseat the President, Sir Dawda Jawara, but the NCP captured five seats in the House and became the official opposition, with Dibba appointed Leader of the Opposition. He was detained for 14 months, on suspicion of complicity in the 1981 abortive coup in **Banjul,** before being exonerated by the courts. During the 1982 elections he campaigned for the presidency from his cell, managing to receive over 50,000 votes. But the accusations of NCP involvement in the abortive coup, though never proven, damaged its political reputation, and the party was fortunate to retain three seats in the House. Upon his release, Dibba continued as the major spokesman for the opposition against continued PPP rule and succeeded in regaining his parliamentary seat in Central Baddibu in the

1987 general elections, although he was yet again defeated in the presidential poll. The NCP was one of three parties banned by the military junta in July 1994 and, as a former government minister, Dibba was barred from standing for office.

DIEPPE MERCHANTS. They were the first French traders to trade openly with Cape Verde, the Gambia, and the Guinea coast, despite Portuguese claims to a monopoly of trade in all of western Africa. By 1560, they had established regular trade with Cape Verde, and in 1570, the first French ship entered the **Gambia River.**

DIOUF, ABDOU (1935–   ). President of Senegal since 1980 and of the **Senegambia Confederation** from 1982 to 1989. He had previously served as the Prime Minister of Senegal, one of President **Leopold Senghor's** most trusted lieutenants, from 1974 to 1980. A **Wolof** from Louga, Diouf was educated in Senegal and France and joined the civil service. Because of his abilities as an administrator, he was rapidly promoted to senior positions. When Senghor changed the name of Senegal's ruling party to Parti Socialiste (PS) and decided to reintroduce the office of Prime Minister, he chose the 38-year-old Diouf, ostensibly because he wanted a man little known in the country, who would be content to carry out Senghor's policies. Diouf replaced Senghor as President when the latter stood down in 1980.

He responded quickly to the Gambia government's pleas for assistance during the abortive attempt in 1981 to overthrow President **Dawda Jawara.** Senegalese troops drove the rebels out of **Banjul,** restored the legal government, and then maintained order in the damaged capital. Diouf shared Senghor's vision of a united Senegambia and persuaded Jawara to form the Senegambia Confederation in 1982. Diouf's irritation with the delaying tactics of the Gambian leadership led him to wind up the confederation in 1989.

DIOUF, COUMBA N'DOFFENE. *Bur* of Sine from 1853 to 1871, whose position in the 1860s was threatened by two external forces. The French, following a gradual process of extending their authority into the hinterland, had come to dominate the **Wolof** states of Baol, Walo, and Cayor to the north. At the same time, **Ma Bah's** armies had conquered large areas of the north bank kingdoms of the Gambia, Saloum, and **Jolof.** Sine was thus directly threatened by the raids of Ma Bah's lieutenants, although for six years Ma Bah avoided a direct confrontation with the *tyeddo* of Sine.

Coumba N'Doffene resisted French attempts to use him against Ma Bah. However, in 1867, Ma Bah decided to rid himself of the threat of the "pagans" and led a large army into Sine. In one of the most decisive battles in the western Sudan in the 19th century, Coumba N'Doffene's troops defeated the **Marabouts,** Ma Bah was killed, and within a short time the threat from a unified interior Islamic kingdom had disappeared. Coumba N'Doffene's later attempts to extend Sine's control over neighboring areas ended tragically with his death by gunshot at Joal in 1871.

DOG ISLAND. A small island located near the right bank of the **Gambia River** approximately midway between Barra Point and Lamin Point. In the 18th century it was called **Charles Island** by the British. Much of the stone used in the permanent buildings in early **Bathurst** was quarried on Dog Island, since the King of **Niumi** gave Captain **Alexander Grant** permission to transport stone from there.

DUMBUYA, FODI KABBA. See **FODI KABBA.**

DUTCH WEST INDIES COMPANY. See **WEST INDIES COMPANY (DUTCH).**

-E-

ECONOMY. The Gambian economy, since colonial days, has been largely a monocrop economy, based on the export of **groundnuts.** Despite attempts by postcolonial governments to diversify into other crops, such as rice and cotton, and to promote manufacturing, fisheries, and tourism, both personal incomes and national revenues still depend very heavily on groundnut production. Like other monocrop economies the country has been exposed to the vagaries of external shocks deriving from the uncertainties of crop output, world prices, and the knock-on effects of industrial recession and oil price hikes. These difficulties have been compounded by a very small national territory and population, a low educational and skills level, and a very heavy dependence on external markets and financial support. Gambian economic performance is also affected by relations with its only neighbor, Senegal, as it has been estimated that up to one-third of Gross Domestic Product (GDP) derives from the re-export trade across its borders to Senegal and the sub-region.

After initially confounding its critics, who in 1965 claimed the country was unviable, The Gambia enjoyed a measure of economic success until the mid-1970s, when a combination of adverse natural conditions and the impact of steep rises in the price of imported oil, led to mounting crisis, culminating in a political upheaval in 1981 and near-bankruptcy by 1985. National insolvency led the country to default on its loan repayments to the International Monetary Fund (IMF), which in turn forced The Gambia to accept an IMF-World Bank reform package. The Economic Recovery Programme (ERP), 1985–1990, compelled the government to take unpopular decisions in order to lay the foundations of economic recovery. In keeping with similar IMF-World Bank measures adopted elsewhere, The Gambia was required to cut back on public spending, through reducing the size of the public sector workforce and ministerial budgets, addressing the problems of corruption and inefficiency in public sector management, initiating the sale of state-owned enterprises, floating the currency and abolishing fixed exchange rates, and actively promoting agriculture and private enterprise as motors of economic recovery.

By 1990, sufficient progress had been made to proceed to the Programme for Sustainable Development (PSD), which permitted some easing back on social and economic cutbacks, while at the same time limiting government intervention in the economy to the facilitation of greater domestic and external private investment. GNP was calculated at U.S.$400 million in 1998 and GDP per head at U.S.$939. Foreign reserves stood at U.S.$102 million in 1996, and the country enjoyed a small trade surplus. However, this was only achieved through large transfers of foreign aid (some 80 percent of the development budget is met in this way) and remittances from Gambians working abroad. Agriculture contributed 40 percent of GDP in 1995–1996 and accounted for 75 percent of employment. Tourism and trade, and the public sector, formed the next two largest categories of employment.

Despite economic sanctions imposed by most of the country's external donors, in response to the army's seizure of power in July 1994, the military and post-military governments broadly kept to the earlier program of recovery, although some extravagance crept in before the 1996–1997 elections, in order to woo the electorate. In due course, external sanctions were lifted and there has been some recovery, if partial, in the state of the economy. The steady decline in groundnut exports has been partially offset by a recovery in tourism, now the second most important sector of the economy. In 1996, the government launched its **"Vision 2020"** policy statement, aimed at transforming The Gambia into the Singapore of West Africa by 2020, premised on the country becoming a regional center for high-technology service industries; though few, outside official circles, believe it likely.

ELEPHANT ISLAND. A large island located about 100 miles from the ocean at approximately longitude 15° 20', where the **Gambia River** begins a great bend to the north. It briefly divides the river into two channels. Above Elephant Island the water is normally not saline.

EROPINA (WUROPANA). One of the nine **Mandinka** kingdoms located along the south bank of the **Gambia River.** Eropina was one of the smaller polities located opposite Deer Island. During the **Soninke-Marabout Wars,** it was conquered by **Alfa Molloh** and incorporated into his kingdom of **Fuladu.** In the 20th century reorganization of the **Protectorate,** the area which was Eropina was joined to the old kingdom of **Niamina,** and this composite territory was divided into three districts, each under the direction of a chief.

EXECUTIVE COUNCIL. One of the two official councils established in British colonies to assist the Governor in making decisions. From 1843 to 1866, the Gambia had a small nominated Executive Council. There was no council from 1866 until the nominated Council was reinstituted in 1888. The official or government appointees constituted a majority. No provision was made for members of the Executive Council to be responsible to a legislative chamber, and it remained advisory until phased out by the new constitutional instruments just prior to independence.

-F-

FACTOR. An agent of a chartered company who was given the responsibility for disposing of trade goods for the company. A factor was in charge of a factory or trading post. The chief factors for most of the British companies in the Gambia also were held responsible for administering James Fort and the outlying trading stations and applying the common law to all Europeans in their jurisdiction. Although the position was primarily commercial, many factors, particularly during the century-long rivalry between France and Britain, were forced to assume military command as well.

FAIDHERBE, GENERAL LOUIS LEON CESAR (1818–1889). Governor of Senegal from 1854 to 1861 and from 1863 to 1865. He was one of the architects of the early French forward policy in West Africa. In his first term, he improved the economic structure of the small colony, constructed an efficient small African army, defeated the southern Mauritanian sheikhs, and sponsored the activities of French merchants in the **groundnut** producing areas of Cayor, Sine, and Saloum. It was Faidherbe's newfound strength which checked the westward movement of **Al Hajj Umar Tall** in the middle Senegal River region. By pressing for the building of a telegraph line to link St. Louis to Dakar, he committed France to a policy of interference in Cayor and Baol and, by constructing forts in the **Serer** states, he extended French influence almost to the banks of the **Gambia River.** Faidherbe and his successors in the 1860s followed a shifting policy of diplomacy and power in helping to check the expansionist activities of **Ma Bah.** The defeat of Ma Bah at Somb by the Sine *tyeddo* represented a vindication of French policy and laid the groundwork for eventual French expansion into the deep hinterland of the Senegambia.

FANAL. The Portuguese word for a lantern, today it refers to the lightweight wood and paper models of ships and other objects, constructed by competing local societies in **Banjul.** These highly detailed models are lighted by candles and are the focal point for a major celebration and parade through all the major streets of the capital on Christmas Eve. Fanal processions were banned in Senegal in 1954 because they became the focus of political clashes.

FARABANNA. The king's eldest son in the 19th-century state of **Wuli.** He had greater political influence than kings' sons in other **Mandinka** states and lived in a separate fortified compound in the chief town.

FARAFENNI. Fast-growing commercial center at the northern end of the Trans-Gambia Ferry; location of a **Gambia National Army (GNA)** engineers' base and of a new provincial hospital. It had a population of 10,168 in 1983.

FAYE, REVEREND JOHN COLLEY (1908–1985). Anglican priest, educator, and political leader. Of **Serer** stock, Faye was born in **Bathurst** and educated locally at St. Mary's Anglican School and the Methodist Boys High School. He received a first class teacher's certificate in 1927 and became a tutor at the Methodist Boys High School. In 1932–1934, he was headmaster of the Methodist Central School before transferring to St.

Mary's Anglican School where he became headmaster in 1938. He also organized the Gambia Teachers Union and was its first Liaison Officer, 1938–1942. Faye became headmaster of Kristikunda School in the Upper River Division of the **Protectorate** and held this position from 1942 until 1948. In 1947, he was ordained a deacon of the Anglican Church and received an MBE for his pioneering work in education upriver.

Faye was elected unopposed to the Bathurst Town Council on three occasions, representing **Jollof Town** and Portuguese Town wards in 1940–1942, before being posted to Kristikunda. From November 1947 to February 1951, at the request of the local chiefs, he represented the Upper River Division as a nominated member of the **Legislative Council,** in recognition of his pioneering educational activities in that area. In February 1951, he was instrumental in creating the **Gambia Democratic Party (GDP),** the first political party in the Gambia, and was elected to the **Legislative Council** at the head of the poll in the Bathurst constituency. In the elections of 1954, Faye was reelected to the Council and served until June 1960. From 1954 until 1960, he also served as ministerial head of Works and Communications. In 1960, Faye merged the GDP with the **Gambia Muslim Congress (GMC)** of **Ibrahima Momodou Garba-Jahumpa** to form the **Democratic Congress Alliance (DCA).** Despite this merger, Faye was defeated for election to the House of Assembly, managing only third place in Kombo West constituency. The other cofounder of the DCA, Garba-Jahumpa, also lost to a **United Party (UP)** candidate in the same election. Faye was leader of the DCA until 1963 when Garba-Jahumpa broke up the coalition. Soon after, he reconciled his differences with **Dawda Jawara** and the **People's Progressive Party (PPP)** and, in 1963, was appointed Gambia Commissioner to the United Kingdom. After returning to the Gambia in 1964, Faye retired from active politics and devoted his energies to the church. He died on December 10, 1985.

FERRIES. As no bridge links the north and south banks of the **Gambia River** the country is dependent on a number of ferry services to link its two halves and maintain surface contact with Dakar, the Senegalese capital. There are two principal ferry routes: **Banjul-Barra,** which provides the most direct route to Dakar; and the Trans-Gambia ferry at Yelitenda, in the middle reaches of the river, linking the commercial center of **Farafenni** on the north bank with **Mansakonko,** administrative center of Lower River Division, on the south shore. This latter ferry has been of considerable importance to Senegal, forming the shortest route between

Dakar and the troubled region of **Casamance.** During the period of the **Senegambia Confederation,** Senegalese troops controlled the Trans-Gambia ferry. Much commercial traffic from the Banjul docks to the hinterland also uses this ferry. Both these major ferries operate motorized craft, though breakdowns have been frequent in the past. A motorized ferry also operated on the **Kerewan** Creek in North Bank Division until the building of a bridge. Smaller and simpler ferries operate at Kuntaur, **Janjangbure,** Bansang, and **Basse.**

FINDEN, HARRY. Of Igbo (Nigerian) descent, Finden was a very successful trader and merchant in **Bathurst** during the third quarter of the 19th century and a leading Methodist. Barely literate, he was, nevertheless, elected leader of the Igbo Friendly Society in 1849 in succession to **Thomas Reffell.** He commanded a force of African troops during the **Baddibu** war in 1861, holding the rank of major, but at other times he clashed with the British administration and merchant group. He was one of the most important Gambians in the protest movement of the 1870s against Britain's proposed exchange of the Gambia for French territory. In concert with **Joseph Reffell, Thomas Brown** and **J. D. Richards,** he helped draw up and sign the many memorials to the British government officials in Bathurst and London stating the opposition of the Bathurst trading community to any such exchange.

FITZGERALD, CHARLES. Secretary of the Gambia Committee which opposed the cession of the Gambia to France in 1875–1876. He was a retired officer of the West India Regiment who, in 1875, authored a widely circulated pamphlet entitled, *The Gambia and Its Proposed Cession to France.* It is probable that he had written an earlier pamphlet, issued anonymously in 1870, entitled, *Has the Crown the Right to Cede the Gambia to France?*

FIVE-FRANC PIECE. A very handsome French coin which was accepted by an Order-in-Council as legal tender in the Gambia. The exchange rate was set at three shillings, ten and one-half pence. At the start of the 20th century, it made up over 80 percent of the total money in circulation in the Gambia. By the end of World War I, the franc had fallen in value, but nothing was done in the Gambia to make the official rate conform to the world rate. Issuance of the new West African alloyed coins in 1920 did not drive out the older currency. The Gambia was the only place in the world where the five-franc piece could be exchanged at a rate approximately 1.75 times its real value, and the area was thus flooded with the coins. They ceased to be valid for overseas transfers in March 1921, and in April their importation was prohibited. These actions did not halt the influx of the coins. Eventually, in 1922, the British decided to demonetize, and called in all the five-franc pieces at the legal rate. The cost of the failure of the British authorities to act promptly had to be borne by the Gambia. The demonetization cost the Gambia over £200,000 at a time when social and economic improvements were being denied, ostensibly because of a lack of funds.

FODI KABBA (?–1901). A **Mandinka** Muslim who as a young man was partly responsible for the beginnings of the **Soninke-Marabout** conflict in **Kombo.** With his power base at **Gunjur,** he collaborated with the inhabitants of Sabaji to attack the Soninke King of Kombo in 1855. The Governor, **Colonel Luke S. O'Connor,** responded with troops, and the British sustained extremely heavy losses in June of that year. Although convinced that Fodi Kabba was primarily responsible for the attack, O'-Connor could not retaliate against him because of the depletion of his force, and he arranged peace between the Marabouts and the Soninke in Kombo in April 1856.

In the next decade, Fodi Kabba and his fellow Marabouts drove out many of the older ruling classes in Kombo, **Foni, Kiang,** and **Jarra.** Fodi Kabba and his followers came into conflict with the British once again in 1864 with his attack upon the chief of **Yundum.** The British sent a relief column to support that ruler and the Marabouts were forced to sign another treaty of peace in 1864.

Some time after this, Fodi Kabba resettled his family in **Fuladu.** Whatever the reason for this action, it frightened **Alfa Molloh** and his son, **Musa Molloh,** who believed that Fodi Kabba was attempting to make inroads into their power in that **Fulbe**-dominated kingdom. Musa attacked the village and killed or kidnapped the entire family of Fodi Kabba. The survivors were released upon the personal intercession of Governor **G. A. K. D'Arcy.** However, Musa's action ushered in a new level of violence along the south bank, which until then had been relatively free of the marauding so prevalent in the north bank areas. Fodi Kabba came to rule over three districts that were isolated from one another. One was south of Bintang Creek, another was in western Jarra and eastern Kiang, and the third was in eastern Jarra.

In between these three territories the Soninkes managed to maintain a precarious independence. Fodi Kabba did not attempt to establish a centralized state such as the one that **Ma Bah** had attempted or the one that Musa Molloh would create. This failure meant that, in the 1870s, raids, looting, and burning were endemic throughout the frontier areas adjacent to Fodi Kabba's territories. Because of the ill-feeling between Fodi Kabba and Musa Molloh, the land between Jarra and Fuladu was particularly hard hit. The division of the Senegambia between France and Britain in 1889 brought considerable pressure to bear upon Fodi Kabba. He was viewed by the British as one of the primary disturbers of the peace and one of the reasons why the **slave trade** continued along the southern banks of the **Gambia River.** His followers and those of **Fodi Silla** threatened the members of the International Boundary Commission. After this, Fodi Kabba retired to the **Casamance,** but returned in the following year to raid the Foni district.

The British attacked him in January 1892, destroyed one of his main stockaded towns, and forced him to retire again into French territory. From his new base in the Casamance, he continued to support those Gambians who were discontented with the new British rule. His adherents would enter British territory, raid villages, take prisoners, and then recross the border into French territory before any effective pursuit could be organized. Such raids continued for almost 10 years until the murder of **Travelling Commissioners Sitwell** and Silva at Sankandi in 1900. This town was known to be allied to Fodi Kabba, and the British colonial authorities decided to destroy his power once and for all. Shortages of troops due to the South African War postponed the punitive expedition until 1901. The British were joined by the French and, in a two-pronged attack directed against Fodi Kabba, Sankandi was taken, and Fodi Kabba's territory on the British side was pacified very quickly.

The second phase of the campaign was carried out directly against the main Marabout force, and, in March 1901, Fodi Kabba's fortified town of Medina was taken and Fodi Kabba himself was killed. This action brought to an end a 50-year career, which spanned the entirety of the Soninke-Marabout Wars in the Senegambia.

FODI SILLA. He emerged in the early 1870s as the leader of the **Marabout** forces in **Kombo.** By 1874, the Marabouts had taken **Brikama** and most of the major towns in eastern Kombo. Many **Soninke** fled to safety in British Kombo and some, using this as a place of sanctuary, raided into Marabout territory. Because of the inherent danger in this to British Kombo, **Sir Cornelius Kortright,** the Administrator in 1874, concluded a treaty with Fodi Silla, creating a neutral zone between **Yundum** and

British territory. The arrangements were violated by both Soninke and Marabouts, and, in the following year, Fodi Silla's forces were everywhere victorious over those of the King of Kombo, **Tomani Bojang.** The king was forced to retreat to Lamin, a town within a few yards of the border of British Kombo. The rainy season prevented open warfare between Fodi Silla and the British. Tomani Bojang, receiving no direct assistance from the British, capitulated in September 1875, and agreed to become a Muslim. Fodi Silla, in return, allowed him and his people to continue to live in Kombo.

Fodi Silla then became the dominant factor in all of Kombo, having established good relations with his neighbor and fellow Marabout leader, **Fodi Kabba.** Except for his slave-raiding activities, he caused the British administrators little trouble until the joint Anglo-French Boundary Commission arrived in his territory in 1891. Understandably outraged at the implications of the **Anglo-French Convention of 1889,** both Fodi Silla and Fodi Kabba attempted to interfere with the work of the Commissioners. Subsequently three gunboats were stationed near the areas where the Commission was working. This show of force and the military actions taken against Fodi Kabba in **Foni, Kiang,** and **Jarra** caused Fodi Silla to remain relatively quiet in 1892. The British recognized him as chief of Western Kombo and paid him a stipend. Minor problems related to **Bathurst**-based traders in his territory, and his attitude toward the **slave trade** caused the British to mount a two-pronged offensive against him in February 1894. After initial failures, the British West Indian troops took **Gunjur** and forced Fodi Silla to flee to Foni. The **Jola** leaders there refused him sanctuary, and he and his followers retreated to the **Casamance.** There his followers were disarmed by the French. Fodi Silla was deported to St. Louis and later died in exile.

FONI (FOGNI). One of the nine **Mandinka** kingdoms along the south bank of the **Gambia River** in the early 19th century, lying south of **Bintang Bolon** and adjoining **Kombo** in the west. During the latter stages of the **Soninke-Marabout Wars,** the traditional rulers were overthrown and most of the territory was controlled by adherents of either **Fodi Kabba** or **Fodi Silla.** However, the large **Jola** population resident there resisted conversion and was never completely conquered. In 1887, most of the Jola chiefs placed themselves under British protection and seven years later, after Fodi Silla's defeat, they refused sanctuary to his forces, forcing him to flee to the **Casamance.** The non-Jola leaders also assumed a pro-British position in the 1890s, thus depriving Fodi Kabba of much-needed support.

In the 20th-century British reorganization of the **Protectorate,** Foni was divided into six districts—Foni Brefet, Foni Bintang, Foni Karenai (subsequently joined together as Foni Bintang-Karenai), Foni Kansala, Foni Bondali, and Foni Jarrol—each under the direction of a chief.

FOON, KEBBA WALLY (1902–   ). A **Bathurst Wolof** accountant and notary public, and political activist. He was educated at the Methodist Boys High School in Bathurst. He worked in government service in the Gambia and Britain before training as an accountant in London. In 1955, he started his own firm in Bathurst. In Britain he had formed the Gambia League and worked closely with nationalists from other British territories for African independence. Foon and a small group of other educated Gambians formed the **Gambia National Party (GNP)** in 1957, though this ceased to be a factor in politics by 1960. In the later 1950s, he and his wife, Marion, published a small, informative Bathurst newspaper. Foon, arguably, had the most unenviable political career in Gambian politics, failing to win a seat in every election from 1962 to 1987, standing successively for the **United Party (UP), UP/National Liberation Party (NLP),** UP again, and finally the **Gambia People's Party (GPP).**

FORDE, DR. ROBERT M. Surgeon and medical researcher who served in the Gold Coast from 1891 to 1895. He was appointed Colonial Surgeon in the Gambia in 1895 and became Senior Medical Officer in 1904. In April 1901, he discovered in the blood of a European patient a trypanosome, carried by the tsetse fly, that was the cause of "sleeping sickness." Forde's discovery of *Trypanosome gambiense* was the first major breakthrough in the treatment of this deadly disease whose cause had previously been a mystery.

FORO. The name given to a caste in **Mandinka** society. *Foro* are freeborn members of a lineage like the **Wolof** *badolo.*

FORSTER, SIR SAMUEL JOHN, JR., OBE, MBE (1873–1940). African barrister and political leader, son of **Samuel John Forster, Sr.,** and the first Gambian African to be knighted by the British. He was educated in **Bathurst** and the Anglican Church Missionary Society (CMS) Grammar School in Freetown before completing his studies in Britain. Forster read law at Merton College, Oxford, 1893–1896 and then qualified as a barrister at the Inner Temple. He returned to practice law in Bathurst in 1899. Official confidence in him was first seen in his appointment as Acting Colonial Registrar and Public Prosecutor in March 1901. Because the substantive post was regarded as too sensitive to be filled by an African at this time, Governor **Sir George Denton** nominated him to the **Legislative Council** instead, in March 1907, in succession to his late father. Forster was reappointed on successive occasions until his death in July 1940, a total of 33 years, such was his standing with the colonial administration. He was knighted in 1933 in recognition of his service to the colonial authorities. Yet, like his father he was prepared, on occasion, to criticize official policy, but he was widely regarded as the spokesman of the "moderate" section of the Bathurst African community. He was instrumental in founding the Gambia Representative Committee and the Bathurst Reform Club, which brought together politically like-minded elements in the capital. This reputation brought him into persistent conflict with **Edward Francis Small,** who emerged in the 1920s as the leader of the "radical" faction in Bathurst.

FORSTER, SAMUEL JOHN, SR., (?–1906). Wealthy African merchant and **Bathurst** political leader. One of three Igbo brothers who migrated voluntarily from southeast Nigeria to Freetown, Samuel Forster settled in Bathurst. He was the second African to be nominated to the **Legislative Council** in 1886, seemingly in order to replace the more outspoken **J. D. Richards.** Despite this, Forster was not an uncritical member of the **Legislative Council,** on which he served until his death in October 1906 at Las Palmas.

FORSTER, SMITH AND COMPANY. One of the oldest British trading firms in the Gambia, dating back to the early 1820s. After the death of Matthew Forster, the senior partner, the firm's business was drastically reduced and its assets transferred in 1870 to another British firm—Lintott, Spink and Company.

FOWLIS, ROSAMOND AROENKEH (1910–?). Teacher and union leader and one of the first Gambian women to take a prominent part in public life. Born in **Bathurst,** she was educated at Dobson St. Day School and the Methodist Girls High School in Bathurst. After completing her studies at Leicester Domestic Science College, in Britain, she returned home to a career as a teacher of domestic science, 1931–1965. Additionally, she organized nutrition and domestic science classes for women and girls in rural area; compiled a booklet on nutrition; and was elected President of the Gambia Teachers Union, 1941–1944. Her public activities also included membership of the Gambia Education Board, 1945, and of the Board of Governors of Gambia High School, 1967–1968. She was awarded an MBE in 1953.

FULADU. Late 19th-century state created by **Alfa Molloh** with the support of **Al Hajj Umar Tall** (leader of the **Tijaniyya** movement within West African Islam and head of the Tucolor Empire) and the rulers of **Futa Jallon** to whom Fuladu remained tributary until 1893. The Fuladu state was later extended by his son **Musa Molloh** Balde, but subsequently it was divided by the British into three chiefly districts — Niamina-Dankunku, Niamina East, and Niamina West, which are located in **MacCarthy Island** (now Central River) Division.

FULBE (FULA, FULANI, PEUL). A pastoral people whose homeland was in the vicinity of the upper Senegal River and who speak a language belonging to the Niger Kordofanian language family. They were the dominant group in the ancient Kingdom of Tekrur. After the overthrow of Tekrur, the Fulbe created a series of smaller states from the western segment of that state, where they continued in power until the Tucolor majority in those areas seized power and established a strict Muslim regime in **Futa Toro.** Between the 13th and the 18th centuries, in a series of long, complicated migrations, large numbers of Fulbe established themselves throughout the western and central Sudan as far east as the Cameroons. They were an important element in the population of Macina, were the base population for the theocracy of the **Futa Jallon,** and were present in large numbers in the Hausa states of northern Nigeria. Usuman dan Fodio, himself a Fulbe from Gobir, used them in the early 19th century as the nucleus of his **jihad,** which overran the Hausa states and created a reformist Muslim empire in northern Nigeria.

The Fulbe were present in large numbers in the upper Gambia region in the 19th century where, although living in **Mandinka** states, they maintained close ties both with Futa Toro and Futa Jallon. **Alfa Molloh** in his revolt of the 1860s used the Fulbe to create his kingdom of **Fuladu.** According to the 1993 population census, the Fulbe are the second largest ethnic group in The Gambia, numbering 168,284 or 16.21 percent of the total population.

FULBE BURURE. A dialect group of the **Fulbe,** who in the latter part of the 19th century migrated through **Fuladu** in great numbers and were the principal owners of cattle in the area in the 1870s. They participated in the Fulbe revolt against the **Mandinka,** but refused to serve **Alfa Molloh,** whose antecedents they held to be less pure than their own. Many of the Burure left Fuladu in the 1880s after their leaders quarrelled with Alfa Molloh.

FULBE FIRDU. A dialect group of the **Fulbe,** living in the upper **Gambia River** area. In the late 18th and early 19th centuries, they migrated in great numbers into the old **Mandinka** kingdoms of **Tomani** and **Jimara.** They were semi-sedentary, normally spending 15 or more years in one location, and they tended to intermarry with other peoples among whom they lived. The Fulbe Firdu composed the main support group for **Alfa Molloh**'s rebellion against his Mandinka overlords.

FULBE FUTO. A dialect group of the **Fulbe,** originally from the **Futa Jallon** region. In the second half of the 19th century they settled in the southern section of **Fuladu** in what is now the **Casamance.** Before the Fulbe uprising of the 1860s, groups of the Fulbe Futo continually raided into the riverine areas. Other members of this group had temporarily settled near the river to plant **groundnuts.** In the early years of his ascendency, **Alfa Molloh** paid tribute to the head of the Fulbe Futo in the Futa Jallon.

FUTA JALLON. A highland area in what is now Guinea, with elevations up to 5,000 feet. It is also the source of the **Gambia,** Senegal, and Niger Rivers. In the early 18th century, **Fulbe** reformers created a theocracy there, with the state controlled by elected *almamys.* The Futa Jallon experience acted as a model for Islamic reformers in the **Futa Toro,** northern Nigeria and the Gambia. Many Fulbe from the Futa Jallon regularly migrated to the area which would later become southern **Fuladu.** These **Fulbe Futo** became an important factor in the success of **Alfa Molloh,** and the Almamy of Futa Jallon loaned him fighting men to oppose the **Mandinka** traditional rulers. The state of Futa Jallon remained independent until the Almamy placed it under French protection in 1888.

FUTA TORO. An area adjacent to the middle Senegal River inhabited largely by Tucolor and **Fulbe** people. In 1776, a new theocratic state was created in the Futa Toro led by **Marabouts** of the **Qadiriyya** *tariq.* Later in the 19th century it became the center of the empire established by the **Tijaniyya** leader, **Al Hajj Umar Tall.** The Futa Toro area acted as a training ground for most of the Marabouts who wanted to convert the "pagan" peoples of the Senegambia region. In addition, the rulers of Futa Toro gave direct military assistance to some of the war chiefs of the Gambia during the **Soninke-Marabout Wars.**

FYE, SHEIKH OMAR (1889–?). Bathurst agent for a European trading firm and Muslim political leader in the period from the early 1920s to World War II, when he was engaged in a long rivalry with **Ousman Jeng** for the right to represent the Muslim community on the **Legislative Council.** For several years Fye enjoyed the support of the Muslim Juma Society, led by Momadu Jahumpa, and with its support, was able to gain nomination to the Legislative Council in 1932. By 1937, when Fye was up for renewal of his council membership, Jeng had made his peace with his Muslim opponents and their Christian allies, led by **Edward Francis Small,** and no support was forthcoming for Fye. The government was not prepared to reappoint Jeng, given his connections with the Small camp, so Fye's appointment was renewed for a further five-year term. In 1942, Fye was appointed for an additional two-year term by Governor **Sir Hilary Blood,** as no suitably qualified younger alternative could be found. "Sheikh" was a personal name, not a Muslim religious title.

-G-

GALWAY, LIEUTENANT-GENERAL SIR HENRY LIONEL (changed his name from Gallwey in 1911), KCMG, CMG, DSO (1859–1949). Born on September 25, 1859, Galway was the son of an army doctor. Educated at Sandhurst and commissioned in the 30th Regiment of Foot in 1878, Galway joined the colonial service in 1882 as ADC and Private Secretary to the Governor of Bermuda. In 1891, he was appointed Deputy Commissioner, Oil Rivers Protectorate, and took part in the Benin Expedition of 1897. Galway was appointed Divisional Commissioner in the Niger Coast Protectorate in 1899 and served as Acting Governor of Southern Nigeria in 1900. He was Chief Political Officer with the Aro Expedition of 1901. He was made Governor of St. Helena, 1902–1911, Governor of the Gambia, 1911–1914, and, finally, Governor of South Australia, 1914–1920. Galway died on June 17, 1949.

GAMBIA. The origins and meaning of the word "Gambia" are unclear. Even as late as the mid-18th century, "Gambra" was still an alternative spelling for the name of the river and the surrounding country. "Gamba" was another early variant of the name. One local account states that the word derives from

"Kambi-yaa," meaning Kambi's country, the response of a man called Kambi when asked the name of the country by early Portuguese visitors. The definite article has tended to be used casually, but the official name of the country is now "The Gambia." The article was insisted upon at independence, in 1965, to avoid confusion with Zambia. It was the convention during the colonial period to prefix the name with "the," rather than "The."

GAMBIA ADVENTURERS. A joint stock company which was allowed by the Royal Adventurers in 1668 to assume the monopoly of trade in the areas adjacent to the **Gambia River.** In 1684, after little profit and much litigation in London, the Gambia Adventurers and their parent company relinquished their trading monopoly to the **Royal African Company.**

GAMBIA AMALGAMATED TRADE UNION (GATU). A short-lived trade union formed by **Bathurst** politician **Ibrahima Momodou Garba-Jahumpa** in 1947–1948, to further his political career in opposition to his political mentor, **Edward Francis Small.** The government Labour Officer estimated its strength in 1947 as 250–1,000 members, compared with only 50 for Small's Gambia Labour Union (GLU). Hoping to recruit Muslim **Wolof** workers on an ethno-religious basis, against the **Aku** Christian Small in the 1947 **Legislative Council** election, Jahumpa was unsuccessful and disbanded the union soon afterwards.

GAMBIA DEMOCRATIC PARTY (GDP). The first political party in the Gambia. It was formed in June 1951, out of an earlier "Committee of Union and Progress," by supporters of **Reverend John Colley Faye** to support his candidature for one of the two elected **Bathurst** seats in the **Legislative Council** under the provisions of the Constitution of that year. Faye came in at the top of the polls. In the 1950s, this **Colony**-based party was the vehicle by which Reverend Faye successfully opposed his political rivals, **Ibrahima Momodou Garba-Jahumpa** and **Pierre Sarr N'Jie.** The GDP was able to ensure Faye's success in the second Legislative Council elections in 1954 and to win seats on the Bathurst Town Council, but the party went into decline subsequently, despite tactical alliances with the **United Party (UP)** in the mid-1950s and with the **Gambia Muslim Congress (GMC)** in 1959–60. Like other early parties in the capital city, the GDP was essentially a vehicle for the political advancement of its leader and, despite its attempt to present itself as a national champion of Gambian political advancement, it failed to overcome its Colony identity when elections were extended to the **Protectorate** in 1960. Prior to the elections of 1960, it was merged with the GMC to form the short-lived **Democratic Congress Alliance (DCA).** Many of Faye's adherents shifted their allegiance to the **People's Progressive Party (PPP)** or the UP, which had by then emerged as the only two viable parties.

GAMBIA FIELD FORCE. See **GAMBIA REGIMENT.**

GAMBIA MINERALS COMPANY. British company formed to explore and exploit the ilmenite deposits near Brufut in 1954. Ilmenite ore, the source of rutile and titanium oxide, was in short supply, and the major producers in India had raised the ore price. Gambian deposits were found to be marginal, but construction began, nevertheless, in 1956 on a railroad, electric dry mill, and other facilities. Although the company invested over £1 million, the entire operation was closed down in 1959, because the world price of rutile had fallen to the point where it was unprofitable to continue.

GAMBIA MOTOR DRIVERS AND MECHANICS UNION (GMDMU). A short-lived trade union formed by a Gambian politician, **Reverend John Colley Faye,** to advance his political career at the time of the 1951 **Legislative Council** election. The support of union members, claimed to number 600, may have contributed to Faye's narrow victory in 1951. Faye soon lost interest in the GMDMU, and it became inactive until revived in 1962. After a fitful existence it was wound up in 1970, most of its members joining a new union—the Gambia Motor Drivers and Allied Workers' Union.

GAMBIA MUSLIM CONGRESS (GMC). The second political party to be established in the Gambia. It was formed from the Bathurst Young Muslim Society and a number of smaller associations by **Ibrahim Momodou Garba-Jahumpa** in January 1952 and sought to combine religious affiliation with political activity. In this, the party was not successful, although individual members did gain some political standing. Garba-Jahumpa in the 1950s continued to work closely with the colonial government as a member of the Bathurst Town Council and as one of the elected members of the **Legislative Council.** In retrospect, this cooperation damaged the image of the GMC, and it became apparent before the elections of 1960 that the **United Party (UP)** was likely to sweep the elected seats in **Bathurst.** In order to obtain a broader support base, the leaders of the GMC agreed in 1960 to merge their party with the **Gambia**

Democratic Party (GDP) to form a new grouping called the **Democratic Congress Alliance (DCA).** After the failure of the DCA to become a major factor in Gambian politics, Garba-Jahumpa and his supporters broke away to form the Gambia Congress Party (GCP). By 1968, Garba-Jahumpa had settled his major differences with the ruling **People's Progressive Party (PPP),** and the GCP was disbanded.

GAMBIA NATIONAL ARMY (GNA). Formed in the wake of the dissolution of the paramilitary **Gambia Field Force** following the failed coup attempt of July 30, 1981. A separate Gambia National Gendarmerie (GNG) (subsequently renamed Tactical Support Unit) was merged with the army proper following the 1994 coup. Training was initially provided by Britain and later conducted by a Nigerian military mission, which was withdrawn after the 1994 coup. The current strength of the army is estimated at 800, divided into two infantry battalions and an engineers' squadron. There is also a 70-strong naval unit, which operates four inshore patrol boats. Elements of the GNA saw service with ECOMOG (the Economic Community of West African States Monitoring Group) in Liberia. Its main base is at **Yundum.**

GAMBIA NATIONAL PARTY (GNP). A **Colony**-oriented party formed in 1957 by a small number of educated **Bathurst** citizens, previously active in a "Committee of Gentlemen." Its leadership included E. J. Samba, a trader with a radical reputation; M. B. Jones, the outspoken anticolonial editor of *The Gambia Vanguard;* J. W. Bidwell-Bright, a leading businessman and owner of the *Vanguard;* and **Kebba Wally Foon,** an accountant and the party's President. Although the GNP never had much popular support, it took an active part in the public deliberations on the revision of the Constitution prior to the 1960 elections. However, its leaders were divided over the issue and went on to join other parties.

GAMBIA NATIONAL UNION (GNU). A small **Colony**-based political party formed at the time of the 1960 elections to present alternatives both to the **United Party (UP)** and to the **People's Progressive Party (PPP).** Its founders included **Sanjally Bojang, Kebba Wally Foon,** E. J. Samba, and M. B. Jones. However, in the elections of 1962 and for some time afterward, it cooperated with the UP. The GNU was never large, and, by 1965, most of its members had either joined the UP or had ceased to be active. Following the retirement of some of its key leaders, the party had ceased to function by 1967.

GAMBIA NATIVE ASSOCIATION. See J. D. RICHARDS.

GAMBIA PEOPLE'S PARTY (1). A short-lived political organization set up in 1954 by George St.Clair Joof, a barrister and former elected member of the **Bathurst** Town Council. It ceased to exist after Joof's crushing defeat in the 1954 **Legislative Council** elections.

GAMBIA PEOPLE'S PARTY (GPP) (2). Formed in early 1986 to contest the general elections of May 1987. Its leaders were **Assan Musa Camara, Lamin Muhammad Saho,** and Howsoon Semega-Janneh, all former ministers in the **People's Progressive Party (PPP)** government. Camara, who had been a member of the PPP Central Committee and Vice President of The Gambia for seven years, was chosen to head the new party. Although it contested general elections in 1987 and 1992, it lacked the resources and distinctive political program necessary to achieve much success. It was also too dependent on Camara, as the other two leaders had no political standing by this time. Indeed, Saho was serving a jail sentence in Britain and sought to rejoin the PPP. The GPP also suffered from a government campaign to discredit it for seeking to raise funds from a Nigerian businessman in return for post-election business concessions and for its perceived pro-Senegalese stance. In 1987, the GPP managed to field candidates in all but two of the 34 constituencies, but failed to win a single seat, though winning 12 percent of the vote. Two-thirds of its candidates lost their deposits. Hopes of a major breakthrough in the **MacCarthy Island** (MID) and Upper River (URD) Divisions, with their large **Serahuli** and Fula communities, thought to be sympathetic to Camara, failed to materialize, and even the party leader failed to hold on to his seat at **Kantora.** Only in six constituencies could it manage to obtain more than a quarter of the vote. In 1992, it could field only 17 candidates; though, on this occasion, it did win two seats—Tumana and Upper Fuladu West, in the URD and MID, respectively. Once again, Camara failed to win back his old seat. Camara also trailed behind **Sir Dawda Jawara** and **Sheriff Mustapha Dibba** of the **National Convention Party (NCP)** in both presidential elections, his share of the vote slipping from 13.5 percent to just over 8 percent. The party and Camara were barred from contesting the 1997 elections, and, by then, both Semega-Janneh and Saho had died.

GAMBIA PRODUCE MARKETING BOARD (GPMB). Previously called the Gambia Oilseeds Marketing Board, it was created by the

British colonial government in 1949 to act as the chief purchasing agent for the **groundnut** crop. The appointive board established a fixed payment per unit of decorticated and undecorticated nuts and all groundnut byproducts, based upon the previous year's experience. The GPMB followed the practice of paying the bulk of the purchase price immediately to the farmers. Senegal, by contrast, for many years paid higher prices, but on a three-payment system. A large portion of the Sine and Saloum crop was brought to the Gambia to obtain the immediate payment. The name of the board was changed in 1971 when it became necessary for the government to fund and purchase the ever-increasing Gambian rice crop as well as the groundnut crop. As part of the government's economic reform program the GPMB has now lost its monopoly to purchase groundnuts.

GAMBIA REGIMENT. In 1901, the British recruited and trained a unit of company strength which formed part of the Sierra Leone Battalion of the Royal West African Frontier Force. During World War I, the Gambia Company saw active service in Cameroon and East Africa. In 1939, the Company was stationed in Sierra Leone, but in the following year was posted to **Bathurst** where it became the nucleus of the First Battalion of the Gambia Regiment. In 1941, the Second Battalion was formed. The First Battalion in 1943 was attached to the Sixth Brigade of the 81st (West Africa) Division in Nigeria. From there, the Division was moved to the Far East, and the Battalion took part in the eight-day defense of Frontier Hill in Burma. The Second Battalion was also sent to the Far East and attached to the 81st Division. It took part in the Allied victory at Myohaung and in the liberation of Rangoon.

Both units returned to the Gambia in 1945, and after demobilization, selected elements were combined to form once again the Gambia Company of the Sierra Leone Battalion. In 1950, "A" Company became a separate entity and was presented with its colors in April 1951, the only unit of company strength to have them. The Company was disbanded for financial reasons on the recommendation of Governor **Sir Percy Wyn-Harris,** but some of the soldiers were regrouped in 1958 as the **Gambia Field Force,** a paramilitary unit of some 140 men initially, eventually increased to about 700. The Field Force had a separate command structure from the police force and was deployed principally to deal with civil unrest in the capital and to maintain order in the provinces at election time. It was disbanded following the abortive coup attempt of July 1981, in which a number of its personnel had supported the insurrection.

GAMBIA RIVER. The river which gives its name to the country rises in the **Futa Jallon** uplands of Guinea, some 12 miles (19 kilometers) northwest of Labe and heads north into eastern Senegal before turning in a westerly direction into Gambian territory at Koina. From here it meanders across the length of The Gambia before reaching the Atlantic a few miles west of the capital, **Banjul.** The river is 680 miles long overall, with about half its length in The Gambia. It is tidal to the Senegalese border and saline as far as **Elephant Island.** Salinity and water level vary according to season, though even during the dry season small seagoing vessels could reach the **Barrakunda** Falls, and the river is some 200 yards wide at the eastern extremity of The Gambia. At its estuary, bordered by Cape Point to the south and Jinnak Creek to the north, it is 12 miles wide. For most of its length in The Gambia the river is bordered by dense growths of mangrove and swamps; where salinity is low. Some of the swamps sustain rice cultivation. Ironstone scarps are a feature of the river in its upper Gambian reaches; where the rock traverses the river shallow rapids are found. Silt deposited on rock outcrops over time has formed a series of islands, the most important historically being **MacCarthy Island** and **James Island.** Numerous creeks (*bolons*) feed into the river, the most important of which is the **Bintang Bolon,** which rises some 80 miles away in the **Casamance** region of Senegal. A deep bar at the estuary of the Gambia and sufficient draught as far as Barrakunda enabled European sailing ships to trade into the African interior from the 16th century onwards. Until the advent of modern roads, the river was the principal means of transport; during the colonial period both government and trading companies constructed a string of wharftowns (*tendas*) along its length to load **groundnuts** and sell imported goods to the local farming communities. The width of the river has prevented bridge construction, and **ferries** are the only means of crossing.

More recently the use of the river has declined. Despite plans going back to the early 1960s to harness the river's resources for transportation, irrigation, and hydroelectric power generation, nothing has come of these to date. The collapse of the **Senegambia Confederation** in 1989, the enormous costs of constructing a bridge-barrage across the middle reaches of the river, and the concerns about environmental damage caused by a river barrier, following a major environmental impact study conducted by researchers from the University of Michigan, have led riparian states and potential donors alike to shelve any plans for the present. The most recent Gambian government development plan — **Vision 2020 (The Gambia Incorporated)** — no longer gives central place to exploitation of the river. Instead, there is a policy of seeking to develop the waterway for ecotourism, so as to distribute the benefits of tourism away from the coastal resorts to upriver communities. Although the numbers of larger animals such as crocodiles and hippopotami have been greatly reduced as a result of overhunting, the river attracts a wide range of bird life, which in turn has made The Gambia popular with ornithologists. See also **Organization for the Development of the Gambia River Basin/Organisation pour la Mise en Valeur du Fleuve Gambie**

GAMBIA SOCIALIST REVOLUTIONARY PARTY (GSRP). Obscure self-styled marxist opposition movement formed circa 1980 by "Dr." Gibril ("Pengu") George, a disaffected small-scale businessman. Banned, together with the **Movement for Justice in Africa-Gambia (MOJA-G),** following the discovery of a plot against the government in October 1980, it went underground. It was during this time that **Kukoi Samba Sanyang** returned to The Gambia and joined the movement. On July 30, 1981, members of the party, together with disaffected members of the **Gambia Field Force,** launched an unsuccessful coup against the government. George was killed during the fighting and Sanyang fled abroad. Although he continued the struggle in exile, the party itself ceased to exist.

GAMBIA WORKERS UNION (GWU). The most important trade union in the history of The Gambia, the GWU was founded in 1956 as a general workers' union, rather than a craft union, by **Momodou Ebrima Jallow,** Henry Joof and others. It organized a successful one-day strike of unskilled laborers in **Bathurst** in February 1960, on the eve of the country's first nationwide elections. Rather than seek confrontation, the government set up a wages enquiry and agreed to a 25 percent increase in the minimum wage. This greatly increased the popularity of the GWU, and in the mid-1960s it claimed over 1,100 paying members. Spurred on by his earlier victory, Jallow called a second two-day strike in January 1961, in pursuit of a much larger pay claim. A large public demonstration organized by the GWU in support of the striking workers was dispersed by the police, and Jallow was charged with incitement to riot. This merely inflamed public opinion, which readily identified the GWU action with the wider independence struggle; Jallow escaped with a nominal fine and the employers, with the tacit support of the administration, negotiated an acceptable pay rise.

The GWU was now at the height of its popularity, but, like the **Bathurst Trade Union (BTU)** three decades earlier, it failed to build on its initial success, and, by 1967, it had gone into decline. The GWU's difficulties lay in part with Jallow's decision to affiliate it with the anticommunist International Confederation of Free Trade Unions (ICFTU) in 1963; this divided its membership, promoted misuse of external funding by union officials, and drew Jallow away to Lagos as Secretary of the ICFTU's African Regional Organisation (1964–1965). Equally damaging was the decision to join the **United Party (UP)** in denouncing the **People's Progressive Party (PPP)** government's attempt to introduce a republic in late 1965. This further split the membership and caused a serious rift with the new PPP government. Jallow even stood as an independent candidate in the 1966 elections against the UP leader, **Pierre Sarr N'Jie,** as well as against the PPP. Finally, Jallow's attempt to regain popular support by organizing another general strike in February 1967 was a dismal failure. Worker support was divided, and Jallow and the GWU were no longer feted as heroes; on the contrary they were seen as undermining the efforts of the new Gambian government. The GWU had to abandon the strike on its second day and accept terms it had earlier rejected. Another unsuccessful general strike was called in January 1970, which forced the GWU onto the defensive in subsequent years.

Union rank-and-file militancy pushed the GWU to call another general strike in July 1975. The PPP government, faced with an internal crisis during the strike — the expulsion of **Sheriff Dibba** — decided to settle on this occasion, but it left the PPP deeply suspicious of the GWU. Further industrial unrest in 1976 led to tougher legislation on strike action. GWU militants forced the union into supporting an illegal strike at the Gambia Utilities Corporation (power and water) in the **Banjul** area. This was too much for the government, and it used legislation from colonial days to deregister the GWU in January 1977 for repeatedly failing to send in annual financial returns to the Registrar-General's office. It was only in 1982, after the failed coup attempt of the previous year, that the government decided to grant temporary recognition to the GWU, following Jallow's constructive role during and after the uprising. Recognition was subsequently withheld when younger and more radical GWU leaders supported workers in an industrial dispute at the Jahali-Pachaar rice project in **MacCarthy Island** Division. Jallow was forced to adopt a new name, the Gambia Workers Confederation (GWC), for his revived union. Leadership of the GWC passed to Pa Modou N'Jie after Jallow's death in 1984.

GARBA-JAHUMPA, IBRAHIMA MOMODOU (1912–1994). Teacher, labor leader, and one of the first Gambian politicians. Born in **Bathurst,**

son of a **Wolof** shipwright and senior figure in the local Mohammedan Society, whose family had emigrated to the Gambia from Senegal in 1816. He attended Koranic school and primary and secondary schools in Bathurst and qualified as a teacher in 1936, teaching at the Mohammedan School in Bathurst and in **Georgetown,** except for a brief period during World War II when he worked for the British Overseas Airways Corporation (BOAC). Initially enjoying the political patronage of **Edward Francis Small,** Jahumpa served as Assistant Secretary of the **Bathurst Rate Payers Association (BRPA)** in 1935 and as Secretary of the Gambia Labour Union (GLU) from 1942 to 1945. He was also nominated by Governor **Sir Wilfrid Southorn** to serve on the Bathurst Advisory Town Council in 1941, to which he would be elected after World War II. He became the first Chairman of Bathurst Town Council in 1959.

After 1945, Jahumpa broke with Small and sought to establish an independent power base to promote his political career. He created a short-lived **Gambia Amalgamated Trade Union (GATU)** in 1947–48, but his main means to political office was through organizing the Muslim community in Bathurst. Already active in the Bathurst Young Muslim Society (BYMS), a spin-off from the Mohammedan Society in which his father had been prominent, Jahumpa sought to play on the grievances of Bathurst Muslims, particularly with respect to the dominance of the smaller Christian community in public life and modern employment. Unsuccessful against Small in the 1947 **Legislative Council** election, Jahumpa went off to teach in Georgetown until he returned to contest the Legislative Council elections of 1951. With BYMS support he came in second in the polls, which gave him a seat in the Legislative Council and, together with **Rev. John Colley Faye,** the new status of "Member of Government," a proto-ministerial appointment created by Governor **Sir Percy Wyn-Harris.**

In January 1952 Jahumpa sought to strengthen his position politically by forming the **Gambia Muslim Congress (GMC)** out of some 40 Muslim societies, including the BYMS. He was returned to the Legislative Council in the 1954 elections and was given the Agriculture and Natural Resources portfolio by Wyn-Harris, who was widely seen as favoring Jahumpa over Faye and **Pierre Sarr N'Jie,** the **United Party (UP)** leader and the third elected member for Bathurst. The GMC entered into a loose alliance with the UP against the **Gambia Democratic Party (GDP)** in the mid-1950s, but the personal animosity between the two leaders and the growing strength of the UP led Jahumpa to abandon N'Jie in order to merge the GMC with his earlier rival, Faye's GDP, to form the **Democratic Congress**

Alliance (DCA), before the 1960 elections to the new House of Representatives. Notwithstanding the new alliance, Jahumpa lost his seat and the DCA won only one seat.

In 1961, the DCA formed a tactical alliance with the new force in Gambian politics, the rural-based **People's Progressive Party (PPP),** which was anxious to win a foothold in the capital. Neither Garba-Jahumpa nor the DCA fared any better in the 1962 general elections, doing no more than hanging on to their one seat. Breaking with other elements in the DCA over his opposition to a republican constitution, Garba-Jahumpa created his own Gambia Congress Party (GCP), allied with the UP. He succeeded in winning a seat in the House in the 1966 elections, only to disband the Congress Party two years later in order to join the PPP. He was rewarded with ministerial office at Health and Social Welfare. He held on to **Half Die** (Banjul South) constituency in the 1972 general elections and was subsequently promoted to the prestigious Finance Ministry, which he held until his electoral defeat in the 1977 general elections. He never stood for Parliament again and faded from public life.

Garba-Jahumpa was the ultimate political chameleon, changing his political color as the pursuit of his political career dictated. At various times he posed as a radical pan-Africanist, cultivating links with Ghana's Kwame Nkrumah, and yet he was a cooperative member of the Wyn-Harris administration; he sought early on to exploit the religious ticket and yet he was prepared to enter into tactical alliances with both his Christian rivals in Bathurst; and, finally, though spokesman for the **Colony,** he readily came to terms with the rural-based PPP in the 1960s and so ensured himself a political future. He died in **Banjul** on September 4, 1994.

GARRISON SCHOOL. The school created by the British for the education and training of African soldiers stationed in the Gambia. The school at **Bathurst** was particularly important during Governor **G. A. K. D'Arcy's** tenure in producing a small number of competent African noncommissioned officers.

GEORGETOWN (JANJANGBURE). Administrative center of Central River Division (previously MacCarthy Island Division). See also **MacCarthy Island.**

GEREGIA (JEREJA). The site of a Portuguese settlement on the south bank of the **Bintang Bolon** approximately 20 miles from the village of **Bintang.** The name is a corruption of the Portuguese word for a church—

igreja. It is conjectured that the site of Geregia is near the present-day village of Kansala. In the 1650s, the area near Geregia was a favorite trading location for the English. They established a factory there as early as 1689 and continued to maintain trading posts there throughout the early 18th century.

GEWEL (cf. *jali* in **Mandinka**). Praise-singers, musicians, and oral historians among the **Wolof,** constituting one of the inferior and intermediate social castes (*nenyo*) between freeborn and slaves. *Gewel* were attached to the courts of royalty and nobility, earning their living as bards, musicians, and keepers of oral genealogies. Despite this close association with nobility, until the colonial period they were required to live in a particular part of a village, could not marry outside their caste, and were denied the usual forms of burial after death. *Gewel* were known as *griots* by the French. With the decline of traditional aristocracy, *griots* found a new career with the introduction of modern party politics, praising or insulting rival political leaders, according to who paid for their services.

GOMES, DIEGO. A one-time page to Prince Henry of Portugal, he led an expedition which entered the Gambia estuary in 1457. Gomes met with chiefs who the year before had received **Alvise da Cadamosto,** traveled upriver to **Kantora,** and traded for considerable amounts of gold. His reports of the rich goldfields of the interior, combined with the gold he brought back, helped convince Europe of the wealth to be had from interior trade. Gomes's reports also led to the first two Portuguese missionaries being sent to the Gambia in an abortive attempt to convert the riverine Africans.

GOULDSBURY, SURGEON-MAJOR VALESIUS S., CMG. Administrator of the Gambia from 1877 until 1884. In 1880, the Governor-in-Chief, **Sir Samuel Rowe,** proposed that part of the £19,000 surplus in the Gambian Treasury be used to finance an expedition into the hinterland as far as the **Futa Jallon,** with the purpose of investigating trading possibilities and entering into friendly relations with African rulers. When this was approved, Administrator Gouldsbury was chosen to lead the exploration. In 1881, Gouldsbury, following his instructions, proceeded as far as the Futa Jallon. He made a number of treaties with the rulers of the upper river and the Futa Jallon. The expedition was valuable only because it gave the government up-to-date information on the events then transpiring in the interior and because it confirmed what Governor **Richard**

Graves MacDonnell had said in 1849 about the paucity of trading opportunities there. Gouldsbury believed that any profits to be made there would be more than offset by the expenses involved. His negative report helped support the general British attitude that the interior lands were worthless, and it predisposed the Colonial Office to adopt a quiescent attitude toward French expansion into the interior during the 1880s.

GOVERNMENT HOUSE. Residence of colonial Governors and Administrators, situated on the foreshore in central **Bathurst.** After independence in 1965, it was renamed State House and is now the official residence of the President. A smaller Government House was located at Cape St. Mary, some eight miles from the capital, where the **Gambia River** joins the Atlantic. Owing to its cooler climate, it was used as a weekend retreat to escape the heat and humidity of Bathurst.

GRANT, CAPTAIN (later LIEUTENANT-COLONEL) ALEXANDER. Captain Grant was sent from Goree in March 1816 with two officers, 50 men of the African Corps, and 24 artisans with orders to reoccupy James Fort, in order to protect British trade rights to the Gambia and to check the trade in slaves. Grant arranged with the ruler of **Barra** for the reoccupation by agreeing to pay him approximately £75 per year. He soon discovered that the fort was almost beyond repair and suggested to his superiors that **Banjul** be occupied instead. Colonel Brereton with 30 more men joined Grant in April, and together they negotiated with the King of **Kombo** the cession of the island for a payment of approximately £25 per year.

On April 23, 1816, Grant took formal possession of the island and began work on barracks and gun emplacements. The King of Barra allowed the British to take stone from **Dog Island** for their construction work. The British at Goree advertised special privileges for merchants who established themselves at the new settlement called **Bathurst.** By early 1819, there were 700 civilians in the town and within a decade, over 1,800. Grant was responsible for laying out the basic pattern of the city of Bathurst with its streets named after generals who fought at Waterloo. He built the earliest section of **Government House,** and parts of the barracks he constructed are still used as government offices. Grant took the lead role in urging merchants towards legitimate trade and, from the beginning, used all the forces at his command to stop the riverine **slave trade.** He also encouraged the missionary activities of the Society of Friends and the **Wesleyans.** In 1823, he negotiated the occupation of Lemain Island (renamed **MacCarthy Island**) and ordered the construction of a mud fort, called Fort George, which was then manned by a dozen soldiers. Grant also served as Acting Governor of Sierra Leone in 1820 and again in 1821. He was promoted to major in the Second West India Regiment just before he turned over command of the Gambia garrison to Captain Findley in 1823.

GRAY, SIR JOHN MILNER (1889–1970). Gray was born in Cambridge on July 7, 1889, the son of the Master of Jesus College. He was educated at the Perse School, Cambridge, and King's College, Cambridge. He took articles as a solicitor in 1911–1914, and enlisted with the Sherwood Foresters for the duration of World War I, ending as a captain. He qualified for the bar (Gray's Inn) in 1932, while working as a District Magistrate in Uganda, having joined the Colonial Service there in 1920 as an Assistant District Commissioner. After serving as an Acting Judge in Uganda, Gray was promoted Judge of the Supreme Court of the Gambia in 1935. He ended his career as Chief Justice of Zanzibar, 1943–1952. Gray was a scholar of some repute. In The Gambia he is best remembered for his long, detailed, scholarly work, *A History of the Gambia,* covering the period up to the end of the 19th century, published in 1940, which has remained the standard work on Gambian history. Gray also wrote scholarly works on East African history. He died on January 15, 1970.

GRIOT. See ***GEWEL.***

GRIS-GRIS. Charms which the wearer believes have the power either to ward off a specific evil or to enable the wearer to perform certain tasks. The name could be a corruption of "[blessed] Gregory," an amulet popular with Europeans at the time of their early contacts with the Gambia. In traditional society these charms were prepared by someone who was believed to have unique powers in communicating with the spirit world. **Mandinka** warriors customarily went to war wearing great numbers of charms about their bodies. Muslim **Marabouts** also acquired a reputation for making such amulets, and it is common for many Muslims today to wear small leather-bound verses of the Koran which they have received from a Marabout.

GROUNDNUTS. A spreading, hairy, annual leguminous herb (*Archis hypogasa*), which provides the main cash crop of Gambian farmers and the main source of export earnings for the government. The plant is native to

Brazil. In the 16th century it was brought to Europe, from where it was taken to all parts of the world. The groundnut, or peanut, was introduced to the Gambia by the Portuguese and was noted by such early English visitors as **Richard Jobson** and **Francis Moore.** However, its cultivation as a cash crop did not begin until the great increase in demand for fats and oils which occurred in Europe in the course of the 19th century. The first shipment of groundnuts from the Gambia was in 1830, and was worth only slightly more than £10. In 1890, over 18,000 tons, worth £130,000, were exported. Groundnut production peaked in the 1970s when over 140,000 metric tonnes were grown.

Groundnuts are planted in April or May, just before the rainy season. The **Mandinka** and **Jola** plant the groundnuts in ridges, while the **Wolof** plant them on the flat. Weeding is a continuous process during the growing season. Harvesting is normally done by digging the plants by hand, generally during October. The plants are then stacked to dry, and threshing is done after the trading season opens in December. The nuts are then bagged and transported to the buying stations.

GUELOWAR. The name of the matrilineage from which the rulers of Sine and Saloum were chosen. This matrilineage was historically that which had led a northward-moving **Mandinka** migration which in the 13th or 14th centuries encountered the southward-migrating **Serer.** It is from this meeting that the complex political institutions of the Serer states can be dated.

GUINEA COMPANY. This was formed in 1651 by the Commonwealth (the English republic under the Lord Protector, Oliver Cromwell, 1649–1660) in expectation of riches to be gained from West African trade. Two trading expeditions were sent to the Gambia, a factory established on **Bintang Bolon** and traders sent as far into the interior as **Barrakunda.** A series of accidents destroyed much of the trade goods, large numbers of the Europeans were incapacitated by illness and many died, and, finally, in early 1652, **Prince Rupert** and a small royalist fleet entered the **Gambia River** and seized the Company ships. Following this disaster, the Commonwealth abandoned all attempts to trade in the Gambia.

GUM TRADE. Established in the 16th century, the trade in gum arabic (derived from the *Acacia arabica* tree) had by the 18th century become very important for some West African traders. The **Royal African Company** began to trade for this item at **Portendic** in Mauritania. Both French and

British gum merchants suffered because of the European wars of the 18th century. One of Governor **Louis Faidherbe's** first goals in the 1850s was to end the exclusive power of the Mauritanian sheikhs over this trade. Soon afterwards, in 1857, Britain relinquished its rights to the trade at Portendic in return for French abandonment of their trading post at **Albreda** on the **Gambia River.**

GUNJUR. A town in southern **Kombo** which was the main base of operations of the young **Marabout Fodi Kabba** in the 1850s who, in collaboration with **Omar of Sabaji** (now called Sukuta), almost defeated the British forces in **Bathurst.** It continued to be a Marabout stronghold during the 1860s and was a particularly important base during the final conquest of the **Soninke** in Kombo during the 1870s. **Fodi Silla** had by this time come to control Gunjur, and his activities against the Boundary Commission finally brought a British punitive expedition into Kombo. Gunjur and Fodi Silla's other main towns were taken in 1894, and he was forced to flee to the **Casamance** where he was captured by the French.

-H-

HALF DIE. A swampy and unhealthy area at the southern extremity of St. Mary's Island. This area, also called Wildman Town or Moka Town, was inhabited by the poorer residents of **Bathurst.** Until protective measures were taken in the 20th century, Half Die was nothing but a sandbank in the dry season and a swamp during the rains. Reputedly, it acquired its name because of the high mortality rate there in the 19th century.

HANNO. Carthaginian soldier and mariner who in about 500 B.C. was commissioned to investigate the western coastline of Africa. According to writing on a stone column at the Temple of Baal in Carthage, Hanno's ships reached the Chertes (Senegal) River and then the Bambotus, "a large and broad river" full of crocodiles and hippopotami. This latter has been identified by some scholars as the **Gambia River. Sir Henry Richmond Palmer,** a former Governor of the Gambia, in *The Carthaginian Voyage to West Africa,* comments that Hanno probably reached the vicinity of Sierra Leone before turning back.

HAY, SIR JAMES SHAW, CMG KCMG (1859–1924). Hay was born on October 25, 1859, and was an army officer before entering the colonial service. Commissioned in the 89th Foot in 1857, he served during the Sepoy Mutiny the following year. His colonial service was divided mainly between West Africa and the West Indies. He served as District Officer (1875–1877), Inspector-General, Gold Coast Constabulary (1877) and Assistant Colonial Secretary (1878–1880) in the Gold Coast, before being appointed Inspector-General of Police, Mauritius (1880–1885). Hay served as Administrator of the Gambia in 1886–1888. He then became Governor of Sierra Leone (1888–1892) and of Barbados (1892–1900). He died on June 20, 1924.

HELM, HENRY (HEINRICH). A Prussian-born naturalized British citizen and resident of **Bathurst** who was responsible after 1870 for managing the Gambian affairs of **Thomas Chown** and Sons. He became a member of the **Legislative Council** in 1878 and continued the Chowns' opposition to any cession of the Gambia to France.

HOLMES, MAJOR ROBERT. Appointed in 1661 as commander of a small fleet of ships outfitted by the **Royal Adventurers of England Trading into Africa** to establish their dominance on the **Gambia River.** He occupied **Dog Island,** cultivated the friendship of the ruler of **Kombo,** and finally forced the surrender of the **Courlanders** on St. Andrew's Island. Holmes renamed the island after James, Duke of York. Although Holmes's action against the Courlanders was unauthorized, English possession of the Courlanders' fort and trading stations was used to force the cession to the English of the Courlander rights in 1664. In 1663, Holmes was again sent with two ships to the Gambia to unload stores and ascertain the situation of the garrison he had left. Upon being informed of the presence of a hostile Dutch ship in Gambian waters, Holmes took his three ships northward and captured the Dutch trading entrepôt of Goree. His actions precipitated the second Anglo-Dutch war, for the Dutch States-General dispatched Admiral de Ruyter and 13 ships to recapture Goree. Although de Ruyter bypassed **James Island,** he achieved one of the first victories in the second trade war between the two great maritime powers.

HORTON, DR. JAMES AFRICANUS BEALE (1835–1883). Army physician, scholar, and businessman. He was born in Gloucester, Sierra Leone, of Igbo (Nigerian) parentage. Horton attended village schools and then the Church Missionary Grammar School (CMS) and Fourah Bay College in Freetown. He was one of three Africans selected by the British in 1855 for medical training in Britain. On qualifying he entered the army as a staff assistant-surgeon and was posted to the Gold Coast. He took part in the Ashanti War of 1864 and was sent to the Gambia the following year. He accompanied the British troops sent to **MacCarthy Island** to counter the threats to the British presence there. After the soldiers were withdrawn, Horton stayed behind as commandant, entered into friendly relations with neighboring chiefs, and helped organize a provisional government for the island.

When the regular British magistrate arrived in June 1866, Horton left, and he arrived in **Bathurst** in time to give his professional aid during the yellow fever epidemic. In 1867 he returned to the Gold Coast, where he died in 1883. Though a loyal servant of the British Crown, Horton was also a notable champion of African rights and author of a widely admired book, *A Vindication of the Negro Race*. He also wrote several other books relating to the economy, geography, and ethnography of West Africa.

HOUGHTON, MAJOR DANIEL (1740?–1791). A British army officer and explorer. He was stationed at Goree in 1780 when ordered to **Bintang** with 80 men and four small ships to cut timber. While there he was forced by a French man-of-war to sink his ships and take refuge with the **Jola.** Aided by them, Houghton managed to drive off the French landing parties and was later rescued by a British warship. In 1790, Houghton was chosen by the **Association for Promoting the Discovery of the Interior Parts of Africa** to try to open communications between the Gambia and Timbuktu and to search for the River Niger. He traveled to Medina near **Barrakunda** Falls and from there proceeded to Bambuk. He was last heard from in July 1791, trying to make his way to Timbuktu. He is believed to have died of disease or to have been murdered. **Mungo Park** would later take up Houghton's quest for the Niger.

HUNGRY SEASON. Concentration on **groundnuts,** the one cash crop of the Gambia, poor roads, and a faulty system of distribution of local surpluses of foods led to chronic food shortages by the early 1930s for the period just before harvest time. In some of the upper river areas, near-famine conditions prevailed during this "hungry season." To offset this, the colonial government had to import large quantities of rice, usually of an inferior quality, which was distributed to the people. Beginning in the 1950s, more farmers were induced to plant rice, fertilizers were used, ox-ploughing schools were started, and foreign rice experts were brought to the **Protectorate.** This concentration on rice production, coupled with more improved market facilities and all-weather roads, has ended the hungry season which was once such an accepted part of the lives of so many Gambians.

HUNTLEY, SIR HENRY VERE (1795–1864). Naval captain, colonial Governor and author. Son of an Anglican clergyman, Huntley joined the Royal Navy in 1809 and served, initially, on the West Indian and North American stations. In 1818, he was posted to the Mediterranean and, after a spell in Britain, was transferred to anti-slavery duties on the west coast of Africa. Following his successes and promotion to captain, he was appointed Lieutenant-Governor of the Gambia in 1839, succeeding William Mackie who had governed for only six months.

Huntley found the **Colony** in debt, the problems of the **liberated Africans** still unsolved, and British prestige in the upper river at a very low level. Huntley provided space for the resettlement of liberated Africans by convincing **Suling Jatta,** the ruler of **Kombo,** to cede to the Crown the district now known as Kombo St. Mary. In the **MacCarthy Island** area there was a brief period of violence between various factions during which the chief of Nyanibantang was killed. After Huntley ordered the British there to maintain strict neutrality between feuding factions and denied the island as a place of sanctuary, British prestige was soon restored. Huntley reinforced the garrison at MacCarthy Island, gained the cession of land for a small fort at Kataba, and entered into a treaty of protection with the chief. This treaty of protection, however, was disavowed by the Colonial Office. In 1841, Huntley was made Lieutenant-Governor of Prince Edward Island and afterwards served in the consular service in Luanda and in Santos, Brazil.

HUTTON, WILLIAM. Administrator temporarily in charge of the British administration at **Bathurst** in 1829. Without consulting the Colonial Office, he had induced Bathurst merchants to subscribe some £7,000-worth of goods for interior trade, contingent upon satisfactory treaties with hinterland chiefs. In April and May 1829, he entered into agreements which would allow the British to build factories at Kantalikunda, and the King of **Wuli** ceded Fattatenda outright. Hutton's agreements were repudiated by the British government, and he was later dismissed from the service because of questions over his handling of public finance.

HYDARA, LIEUTENANT SADIBOU (1964–1995). One of the four organizers of the army coup of July 22, 1994. Born at Dippakunda, near

Banjul, in April 1964, he spent most of his childhood in Sierra Leone. Hydara joined the Gambia National Gendarmerie (GNG) in 1984 and transferred to the army in 1993. He was a founding member of the **Armed Forces Provisional Ruling Council (AFPRC)** and Minister of the Interior until his arrest with **Lieutenant Sana Sabally** on January 27, 1995, for allegedly seeking the overthrow of junta leader **Yahya Jammeh.** He died in Mile Two prison, outside Banjul, of natural causes (his family denied he had a record of ill-health) on June 3, 1995, before coming to trial.

-I-

IBRAHIMA, ALFA. One of the powerful **Fulbe** rulers of the **Futa Jallon** in the late 19th century, who played an important role in the success of **Alfa Molloh** in his wars against the traditional **Mandinka** rulers of **Jimara, Tomani,** and **Eropina.** In the late 1860s, he sent his son with Fulbe reinforcements to aid Alfa Molloh's armies and continued to support the Fulbe throughout the 1870s. In 1879, large numbers of Ibrahima's troops took part in the campaign against **Simotto Moro** at Tubakuta. Although Alfa Molloh did not consider himself subject to Ibrahima, there was a mutually advantageous relationship between **Fuladu** and the Futa Jallon.

ILER. The name of a tool with a short handle and an inverted, heart-shaped blade used in cultivation by **Wolof** and **Mandinka groundnut** farmers in Saloum and The Gambia. The *iler* is the main tool used to clear weeds and also to loosen the soil around the plants at harvest time.

INDIRECT RULE. The term which describes the general administrative policy followed by Great Britain in governing most of its African territories. First introduced by Sir Frederick (later Lord) Lugard in Uganda, and, more systematically, in Northern Nigeria at the start of the 20th century, the system was subsequently extended across the African dependencies and beyond. In theory, African traditional rulers, under the supervision of European District Officers, would be authorized to continue to make the basic administrative and legal decisions for their people. In the Gambia this was complicated because the **Soninke-Marabout Wars** had disturbed and in some cases destroyed the older kingdoms and their ruling classes. The first attempt at indirect rule came with the appointment of **Travelling Commissioners** in 1893 and the Protectorate Ordinance of

1894. By 1945, subsequent Ordinances had created a system whereby most of the Gambia was governed by 35 appointed chiefs.

Legislation sponsored by Governors **Sir Henry Richmond Palmer** and **Sir Arthur Richards** from 1933 to 1935 brought the theory and practice of government in line with the concepts of Lord Lugard and Sir Donald Cameron. A Senior Commissioner was appointed in 1944 to provide continuity of policy and centralization of planning. In the same year the government established the annual Conference of Protectorate Chiefs.

ISLAM. See **AHMADIYYA; JIHAD;** *KHALIFA;* **MARABOUTS; MOURIDE; QADIRIYYA; RELIGION; SONINKE-MARABOUT WARS; TIJANIYYA.**

ISMAIL, AL HAJJ. A Mauritanian teacher who, in the early 1850s, traveled through the western Sudan preaching against the infidel. He probably never visited the Gambia, but one of his agents, **Omar [of Sabaji],** took up residence in Sabaji where he, in conjunction with the **Marabouts** of **Gunjur,** planned an attack in 1855 upon the **Soninke** of **Kombo,** which almost succeeded in taking **Bathurst.** Shortly afterwards, Ismail was captured by the French and sent into exile to Cayenne.

-J-

JACK, SIR ALIEU SULAYMAN (1922–). Sometime civil servant, **groundnut** mill manager, and politician. Born at **Bathurst** into a Muslim **Wolof** family, he was educated at the Roman Catholic mission school and joined the civil service during World War II. In 1950, Jack began his political career when he was elected to the Bathurst Town Council. At an early date, he associated himself with the **Democratic Congress Alliance (DCA),** but became Speaker of the House of Representatives after the elections of 1962 with the assistance of the **People's Progressive Party (PPP)** government. Jack served briefly as Acting Governor General during **Sir Farimang Singhateh's** absence on leave. He resigned the Speakership to become Minister of Works and Communications after the 1977 general elections. Subsequently dropped from the government, he was Speaker of the Senegambia Confederal Assembly, 1982–1989.

JALLOW, MOMADOU EBRIMA (1927–1987). The Gambia's most distinguished labor leader. Born in **Georgetown** in June 1928, he received secondary education at St. Augustine's School, **Bathurst.** He joined the civil service as a clerk in the Education Department and later served in the Income Tax Division. Jallow also worked in the mid-1950s as a secretary-accountant for private firms in Bathurst. At the urging of friends, he formed the Gambia Construction Employees Society, which led to the creation in late 1956 of the **Gambia Workers Union (GWU).** Although possessing little experience of unionism, Jallow was able in 1958 to negotiate a number of favorable contracts with employers. In late 1958, he attended a four-month course in trade unionism at Kampala in Uganda and began to make contacts outside the Gambia. Throughout 1959, he concentrated on building union strength among the dock workers and daily paid employees. In 1961, at the height of the **groundnut** season, his union conducted the first successful large-scale strike in the Gambia. This strike achieved a substantial increase in the wages of daily workers and eventually led to the formation of Joint Industrial Councils for the arbitration of labor disputes. The British government decision to indict him for taking part in a riot merely increased his popularity among Gambians.

Jallow's decision not to enter politics at this period in Gambian history was crucial, since his popularity might have created a political vehicle that could have challenged the older parties. Even so, he was considered important enough to attend, as a non-party representative, the constitutional discussions in Bathurst and London, which preceded the transfer of power. In 1964, Jallow became the full-time Secretary General of the African Regional Office of the International Confederation of Free Trade Unions (ICFTU) with headquarters at Lagos. On his return to The Gambia Jallow continued to lead the GWU, but both personal problems and clashes with government adversely affected his career. He failed twice, in 1966 and 1972, as an independent parliamentary candidate in **Banjul** North. His relations with government improved after the abortive coup of July 1981, and, just before his death on May 23, 1987, he was selected as a nominated MP to represent the interests of labor in the House of Representatives (a post subsequently taken by his lieutenant, Araba Ba), even though, at this time, the GWU had failed to be formally reregistered. Jallow was widely regarded as the ablest trade union leader of his time in The Gambia.

JAM. A **Wolof** word for non-free persons. Slaves in Wolof society belonged to one of two groups—those born in captivity and those captured in war. Although some slaves held high positions and most were treated well, they were always considered to be the property of their masters who could do with them what they wished.

JAMBUR. The **Wolof** name for freeborn persons. The freeborn were divided into three categories—those belonging to royal lineages, nobles not of such lineages, and *badolo* (peasants), who made up the bulk of the population in a Wolof state.

JAMES ISLAND. See **COURLAND, DUCHY OF.**

JAMMEH, HIS EXCELLENCY ALHAJI YAHYA ABDUL AZIZ JEMUS JUNKUNG (COLONEL Retd.) (1965–   ). President of the Republic of The Gambia and leader of the ruling **Alliance for Patriotic Re-Orientation and Construction (APRC).** Born at Kanilai in the **Foni** Kansala District, Lower River Division, of a Muslim **Jola** farming family, he completed primary education locally and then moved to Gambia High School, **Banjul,** where he completed his education in 1983. Jammeh joined the Gambia National Gendarmerie (GNG) in April 1984, progressing to sergeant in 1986 and officer cadet in December 1987.

Commissioned in September 1989, he was promoted to lieutenant in February 1992. His promotion to captain took place after the July 1994 army coup and his promotion to colonel shortly before he left the army to head the civilian government. Jammeh was assigned to various duties as a junior officer: Gendarmerie Training School as an Escort Training Instructor (1987–1989); Presidential Escort in the Presidential Guards (1989–1990); Commander of Mobile Gendarmerie (January-June 1991); Commander of the Military Police, GNG (June-August 1991); and, finally, head of the army Military Police at **Yundum** Barracks. Jammeh attended a Military Police Officers Basic Course in the United States, September 1993 to January 1994. He was also in charge of presidential and VIP security on a number of occasions (1990–1992). Jammeh was one of four junior officers who organized the army coup of July 22, 1994, and he was Chairman of the military junta, the **Armed Forces Provisional Ruling Council (AFPRC),** from July 1994 to September 1996. He retired from the army following his election as President of the Republic, in the elections of September 9, 1996.

JANJANGBURE. See **MacCARTHY ISLAND.**

JARRA. One of the nine **Mandinka** kingdoms located along the south bank of the **Gambia River** in the early 19th century. It adjoined **Kiang** on the west and extended eastward to Sofaniama Bolon. During the latter stages of the **Soninke-Marabout Wars** much of Jarra was controlled by the powerful **Marabout** leader, **Fodi Kabba.** Because of the antipathy between Fodi Kabba and **Musa Molloh,** eastern Jarra became a particular arena of conflict. In the 20th-century reorganization of the **Protectorate,** Jarra became a part of the Central Division (later Lower River Division) and was divided into three districts, each under the direction of a chief.

JATTA, FAMARA L. (1958–   ). Secretary of State for Finance and Economic Affairs since March 1998. He undertook university training in the United States at Cheney State College, Pennsylvania (M.A. Regional Planning and Economics, 1983) and Harvard University (M.A. Public Enterprise Policy and Management, 1992). After a career as a senior economist and planner, rising to Permanent Secretary, Jatta was appointed Minister (and subsequently Secretary of State) for Trade, Industry and Development in 1994.

JATTA, SIDIA. Former educationalist, radical politician, and community activist, elected Leader of the **People's Democratic Organisation for Independence and Socialism (PDOIS),** more commonly known as DOI, in December 1987. He stood as DOI presidential candidate in the 1992 and 1996 elections, losing on both occasions. In 1996, his share of the vote was 2.7 percent, compared with 5.2 percent in 1992. Jatta was more successful in parliamentary elections, in which he finally won **Wuli,** his natal district, on his third attempt, with 48.93 percent of the vote. Since his election to the National Assembly, Jatta has been one of the most trenchant critics of the **Alliance for Patriotic Re-orientation and Construction (APRC)** government.

JATTA, SULING (?–1855). The King of **Kombo** who in 1840 was pressured by Lieutenant-Governor **Sir Henry Vere Huntley** to cede to Britain a part of his kingdom, which afterward became known as British Kombo or Kombo St. Mary. This area was enlarged by a later cession in 1853 and gave the British approximately 25 square miles of land adjoining St. Mary's Island. Suling Jatta renounced his right to collect customs duties and rents in the ceded territory in 1850, in return for a small annual payment.

His kingdom was one of the first Gambian areas to be invaded by Islamic proselytizers. These **Marabouts** were particularly strong in **Gunjur** and Sabaji (Sukuta). By the end of 1851, it was apparent that Suling

Jatta was losing much of his support to the preaching and raiding of the Muslims. Governor **Sir Richard Graves MacDonnell** tried to persuade the Colonial Office to take much of Kombo under British protection and thus bring an end to the internecine struggle. He was only authorized, however, to seek the cession of a small strip of land from the king to add to British Kombo. This included the town of Sabaji, most of whose elders were **Soninke,** but the bulk of whose population was loyal to the Marabouts. After much consideration, Suling Jatta agreed to the cession in May 1853. The townspeople of Sabaji refused to accept the agreement, and British forces took the town by storm in 1853.

This was not the end of the affair, since the Marabout leaders, Omar and **Fodi Kabba,** launched an attack in June 1855 against both Suling Jatta and British Kombo. The Marabouts almost succeeded in taking **Bathurst.** Marabouts from Gunjur tried to take **Busumbala,** the king's town. The attack was beaten off, but Suling Jatta was killed. The ensuing struggle for power between the Soninke families of **Yundum** and Busumbala over the succession greatly helped the Kombo Marabouts in their bid for power.

JAWARA. The title given to a general appointed to command the armies in a **Mandinka** state.

JAWARA, SIR DAWDA KAIRABA (1924–   ). Prime Minister of the Gambia from 1962 to 1970 and President of the Republic from its inception in 1970 to July 22, 1994, when he was deposed and forced to go into exile. He was born at Barajally in the **MacCarthy Island** Division, and his father, a prosperous **Mandinka** farmer, chose him from among his six sons to be educated at **Bathurst,** first at the Muslim primary school, then at the Methodist Boys High School. After graduation in 1945, he worked at the Royal Victoria Hospital and won a scholarship to Achimota College, in the Gold Coast (Ghana). He later graduated as a veterinary surgeon at Glasgow University and gained a further diploma in tropical veterinary medicine. In 1954, he returned to the Gambia and became a veterinary officer in the **Protectorate.** The following year, he was converted to Christianity and married Augusta, a daughter of **Sir John Andrew Mahoney,** one of the leaders of the **Aku** community in Bathurst. In 1965, Jawara reverted to **Islam,** changing his name back to Dawda and divorcing his Christian wife in a controversial incident in 1967. He then proceeded to marry Chilel, daughter of a leading Bathurst **Wolof** trader, Modou Musa N'Jie, previously the principal financial backer of the opposition **United Party (UP)**. Jawara subsequently took a second wife, Lady Ngaime, according to Islamic practice.

One of the founders of the **People's Progressive Party (PPP)** in 1959, whose constitution he helped draft, Jawara was elected as its leader. At the time Jawara was one of only two Mandinka university graduates in the country and, despite his humble social status as a member of the leatherworker caste, was widely respected throughout the Protectorate on account of his work as Government Senior Veterinary Officer. Following the elections of 1960, in which the PPP won nine parliamentary seats to the UP's seven, Jawara was appointed Minister of Education. However, he and other PPP ministers resigned in 1961 when the Governor passed him over for **Pierre Sarr N'Jie** of the UP as the territory's first Chief Minister. In the elections of 1962, the PPP won an overwhelming victory and Jawara became Prime Minister. His government cooperated fully with the Governor and the Colonial Office in negotiating the transfer of power in The Gambia. When The Gambia became independent on February 18, 1965, Jawara continued as the head of government. He was knighted by the British in 1965. Jawara became Executive President when The Gambia voted for a republic on April 24, 1970.

When national presidential elections were held in 1982, Jawara defeated **National Convention Party (NCP)** leader **Sheriff Dibba** soundly, winning over 72 percent of the vote. In subsequent multi-candidate presidential elections in 1987 and 1992, Jawara's share of the vote slipped to about 60 percent, but even the 58.4 percent he achieved in 1992 was over 2 percent more than **Yahya Jammeh** obtained in the 1996 election. The PPP, likewise, obtained overwhelming majorities in the general elections of these years.

Both in his domestic and his foreign policy, Jawara was characterized as a political moderate. At home he sought successfully to create a national political coalition to replace the old **Colony**-Protectorate hostility through the judicious use of state patronage and ministerial office. He headed off several internal challenges within the PPP during his period in office, as well as two splits in the party. Within the constraints imposed on him, he sought to pursue democratic leadership and rejected the more authoritarian style of leadership frequently found among Africa's new rulers. In his economic policy he sought a middle-of-the-road approach, encouraging domestic and overseas private enterprise as well as direct state involvement through parastatals. Priority was given to shifting government spending to the former Protectorate, in recognition of the decades of neglect of that part of the country, an area which generated whatever wealth The Gambia possessed. While important results were obtained in terms of the redirection of public investment, Jawara came under increasing criticism by the late 1970s for failing to cope with growing economic difficulties, the solving of which, in several instances, lay beyond his capacity. The oil price crises and adverse climatic conditions in the course of the 1970s, the domestic hardships that resulted from these, and Jawara's inability (or unwillingness) to deal firmly with the frequent cases of corruption eroded his standing among the urban populace, although he continued to enjoy considerable support in the countryside. Surviving the abortive coup of 1981, he faced severe economic difficulties in the mid-1980s, which nearly bankrupted his country and forced him to accept painful and unpopular recovery measures imposed by the International Monetary Fund (IMF) and World Bank. By the early 1990s measurable recovery had been achieved, but Jawara and the PPP continued to be accused of tolerating corruption in senior governmental circles. Jawara himself would be found guilty of misappropriating public funds, by commissions of enquiry set up by the military government.

In foreign policy Jawara was seen as a pragmatist and a moderate, emerging as an honest broker in African and inter-Islamic relations. He was rare among his African peers in denouncing despotic government, and he was instrumental in getting the Organization of African Unity (OAU) to accept a Charter of African Human Rights and to set up monitoring institutions in The Gambia. His environmental concerns were seen in the **Banjul** Declaration on the management of his country's environment. Jawara's pro-Western stance on most international issues, while earning him the condemnation of local radicals, did not stop him from speaking out on such issues as South Africa and Israel. His frequent overseas visits, though winning The Gambia useful diplomatic and financial assistance, became another object of local criticism. Jawara was a strong supporter of inter-African cooperation and he played a full part in the affairs of the OAU and the Economic Community of West African States (ECOWAS). His pragmatic approach to pan-Africanism was seen in his handling of the delicate relations with Senegal, particularly after the 1981 coup attempt. From a position of weakness, he was able to maintain Senegalese support while not yielding his country's sovereignty. It is likely that with the passing of time Jawara's political reputation will undergo further revision.

JENG, OUSMAN (1881–1960). Educated **Wolof Bathurst** trader and Muslim political leader in the interwar period. He initially supported the

Gambia Section of the **National Congress of British West Africa** in 1920, but broke his links with it when Governor Sir **Cecil Armitage** intimated that he intended to appoint a Western-educated member of the Bathurst Muslim community to represent the wider Islamic society on the **Legislative Council** when a vacancy occurred in November 1921. Armitage's choice of Jeng enjoyed the support or consent of the **Protectorate** chiefs and of **Samuel John Forster, Jr.,** the Aku spokesman, but split the Bathurst Muslim community, although, when consulted by the Governor, they did not put forward any alternative name.

Jeng's rival as political spokesman for Bathurst Muslims was a younger educated Wolof trader, **Sheikh Omar Fye,** but his *griot* (low caste) origins counted against him on this occasion. Jeng was subsequently accused of high-handedness by the Juma Society, a group of influential Muslim elders led by Momadu Jahumpa (father of **Ibrahima Momodou Garba-Jahumpa,** the postwar Bathurst politician), who unsuccessfully sought to have him replaced by Fye when his membership came up for renewal in 1927. Unable to stop the reappointment, they accused Jeng of adultery, and therefore of being unworthy to represent the community. This further split the Muslim community between the Jeng and Fye-Jahumpa factions and spilled over into a drawn-out struggle for control of the Mohammedan school in Bathurst. **Edward Francis Small,** though a Christian, supported the anti-Jeng faction, due to Jeng's close political ties to S. J. Forster. Jeng was not reappointed in 1932; instead his rival, Sheikh Omar Fye, was appointed for five years. In a political about-face, Jeng went on to win a seat on the newly-created Bathurst Advisory Town Council as a **Bathurst Rate Payers Association** (BRPA) candidate. Edward Small, the *éminence grise* of the BRPA, brokered a settlement between Jeng and the Jahumpa faction, which led to Sheik Omar Fye, now out of favor, being politically isolated.

JIHAD. According to Muslim theology, taking up the sword either to defend or to expand the true faith was the obligation of every believer. He should resort to violence only after persuasion and argumentation have failed. The term, "jihad," originally Arabic, is found in all the Senegambian languages. The first major jihads in West Africa were those of the Almoravids of the llth century. From that time forward there were many jihads, aimed at spreading the influence of Islam. Any war undertaken against non-Muslims was likely to be pursued as if it were a jihad, although technically most were not. The most notable of the 19th-century jihads in Senegambia were those led by **Al Hajj Umar Tall** and the

Soninke-Marabout Wars, which ravaged the areas adjacent to the **Gambia River** for over half a century.

JIMARA. One of the nine **Mandinka** kingdoms located along the south bank of the **Gambia River** in the early 19th century. It was one of the larger and more prosperous of the upriver polities and had a long history of trade with Europeans, since **MacCarthy Island** was adjacent to its middle areas. **Alfa Molloh** was a resident of Jimara and it was there that he made his first conquest, overthrowing the traditional Mandinka dynasty. Jimara became the nucleus of his new kingdom of **Fuladu.** In the 20th-century reorganization of the chiefdoms, the area which was Jimara became the Districts of Fuladu West and Fuladu Central.

JOAR. A village on the north bank of the mid-**Gambia River** which was the site of a number of trade factories established by the Portuguese and later by English trading companies. The English had factories there in 1704 and between 1723 and 1727. The **Royal African Company** post there in the 1730s was their principal out-factory on the river. The settlement is now known as Ballanghar.

JOB BEN SOLOMON (JOB JALLOW). Son of a **Fulbe** ruler in Bondu. In the early 18th century he was captured in the Gambia and sold into slavery. Job was transported to Maryland where he labored for over a year. Fortunately, one of his letters, written to his father in Arabic, fell into the hands of General Oglethorpe, who was so impressed that he ransomed ben Solomon. General James Edward Oglethorpe (1696–1785) was a soldier, philanthropist, and social reformer. He was the leading light in the creation of the colony of Georgia in 1732, where slavery was barred. Job then began a 14-month stay in Britain where he assisted Sir Hans Sloane with Arabic translations and was presented at the court of George II. Sir Hans Sloane (1660–1753) was a leading physician and natural scientist with direct knowledge of the West Indies. He was elected president of the Royal Society in succession to Sir Isaac Newton. Agents of the **Royal African Company** were ordered to treat him with great respect when he returned to the Gambia in 1734. He and **Francis Moore** became good friends and Job accompanied Moore on a number of journeys to trading stations before returning to Bondu in 1736 with a Company servant, Thomas Hull. Job was responsible for interceding with one of his patrons, the Duke of Montagu, to free a friend, **Lahamin Jay,** from slavery in Maryland. Jay, after returning to Gambia, joined Job in Bondu. The last record of Job dates to 1740 when he came to **James Island** and led a Company agent, **Melchior de Jaspas,** back to Bondu.

JOBE, MOMODOU LAMIN SEDAT (1944–   ). Secretary of State for External Affairs. Born at Bansang, Central River Division, on July 24, 1944. He undertook his higher education in France, finishing with a doctorate from the University of Grenoble in 1976. When he was not working as a Gambian career diplomat, Jobe taught at the University of Dakar (1974–1978) and Howard University, Washington, D.C. (1978–1980), and worked for UNESCO (1981–1996 and 1996–1997). He returned to the Gambian diplomatic service as an Ambassador at Large (1996–1998) and was appointed to his present post in January 1998.

JOBSON, RICHARD (fl. 1620–1623). A supercargo for the English **Guinea Company** who arrived with two ships and much trade goods in the Gambia in 1620. After seizing property from local Portuguese inhabitants in reprisal for their looting and massacre of the crew of an English ship, Jobson's ships proceeded to Tendaba. Jobson took one of the ships to Mangegar, where a house was purchased from the chief, to be used as a trading factory. It was decided that Jobson, with seven men, should continue the exploration of the river. He reached **Barrakunda** Falls in January 1621, and Tenda the following month. He made friends with the local rulers, discovered the nature and type of trade to be had in the upper river, and found that the Portuguese were no longer a force on the river. By the time that Jobson returned to his ships, disease had reduced the crews to such an extent that Jobson left the Gambia in May.

Jobson was convinced of the wealth that could be obtained by trading in the Gambia and labored to convince the English royal family to subsidize further ventures. One of the propaganda weapons he used was his book on the expedition, entitled *The Golden Trade.* In 1624, he was entrusted with command of another expedition to the Gambia, but the venture was a failure. A later book, *The Discovery of the Country of King Solomon,* did not change the minds of English sponsors, but played an important role in spurring French interest in the Senegambia. The French formed a company in 1626 to exploit the river trade. Jobson, however, never returned to the Gambia.

JOINER, THOMAS (?–1842). A **Mandinka** merchant who, in the early 19th century, became one of the most affluent **Bathurst** traders. He had been a *griot* as a young man, but was captured and sold into slavery in one of the southern states of the United States of America. There he learned the craft of carpentry (which probably gave him his name). He was fortunate to be able to purchase his freedom, and, in about 1805, he returned to the Gambia. Beginning with only a small amount of money, he had, by trading with the upper river areas, become wealthy even before the town of Bathurst was founded. Joiner owned a number of ships and boats engaged in the river trade, among them the largest craft operating from the port of Bathurst. His ships made regular journeys with passengers and cargo to Sierra Leone, the Cape Verdes, the Isles de Los, and the Madeiras. At one time he employed over 100 persons to help carry on his trading activities. Joiner considered himself, and was considered, a prominent member of the largely European trading community of Senegambia. He had become by the time of his death the most respected Gambian trader in Bathurst.

JOKADU. One of the five **Mandinka**-controlled kingdoms on the north bank of the **Gambia River** in the early 19th century, bounded on the west by Jurunku Bolon and on the east by Kutang Bolon. In 1862, the area was captured by **Amer Faal,** one of **Ma Bah's** lieutenants, and the people were forced to accept **Islam.** It was then incorporated into Ma Bah's kingdom of **Baddibu** (Rip), and its history in the later years of the century was bound to the struggles for control of this larger state by the successors of Ma Bah. The chieftaincy was restored by the British reorganization of the **Protectorate** in the 20th century when it became a district in the Lower River Division (subsequently North Bank Division).

JOLA. This ethnic group comprises approximately 8.5 percent of the population of the Gambia (1993 census) with the majority residing in the **Foni** areas south of **Bintang Bolon.** Some Jola traditions suggest a common origin for themselves and the **Serer** in the upper Gambia region. They still maintain a joking relationship with the Serer. It is probable that the Jola are the people longest-resident in the Gambia region and that they were overcome by a series of **Mandinka** invasions. Some of the earliest European visitors mention the Jola, whom they called Feloops, living in the same places as they do now. Their political and social organization was village-oriented and not as sophisticated as that of the Mandinka or **Wolof. Francis Moore** and **Mungo Park** both reported in the 18th century that, although the Jola paid tribute to their Mandinka overlords, they had not been completely subjugated and continued to exercise great freedom.

The Jola were noted for their competence in war. A number of times in the 18th century, the Jola came to the assistance of British traders and soldiers during conflicts with the French. In the latter part of the 19th century many Jola served as mercenaries in the **Soninke-Marabout Wars.** Disdaining the religious positions of both Muslims and Mandinka, they served both sides. However, they strongly resisted the attempts by **Fodi Kabba** to convert them to **Islam.** In 1887, the chiefs of 16 Jola towns signed a treaty with **Sir Samuel Rowe** at Kansala, whereby they placed themselves under British protection. In the age of modern politics, the Jolas tended to be eclipsed by other ethnic communities until the emergence of **Yahya Jammeh** as junta leader and elected President. **Kukoi Samba Sanyang,** leader of the abortive coup of July 1981, is also a Jola.

JOLLOF TOWN. A section of **Bathurst** between **Soldier Town** and **Half Die,** fronting on Wellington Street; it was also known as Melville Town. It is today the site of most of the major trading and business establishments. In the early 19th century this section of the city was largely inhabited by **Wolof** artisans.

JOLOF. The original **Wolof** state, it was formed before the 14th century. Its rise was probably occasioned by the breakup of the kingdom of Tekrur and the demise of Malian power in the Senegambia region. The Wolof probably migrated from Tekrur into most parts of what is now Senegal. Eventually, by the 16th century, five major states—Walo, Cayor, Baol, Sine, and Saloum—owed allegiance to the ruler (*burba*) of Jolof. In the course of the following century all these revolted against Jolof domination, and the state became relatively isolated from the lucrative trade with Europeans. Because of its location, it was open to attacks from Mauritania and from the more prosperous coastal states of Cayor, Walo, and Baol. Much of the population was at an early date converted to **Islam.** In the **Soninke-Marabout Wars,** Jolof was conquered by **Ma Bah's** forces and briefly became a part of the kingdom of **Baddibu.** The Burba Jolof in the 1880s allied himself with the faction supporting **Sait Maty** in Baddibu. The use of Jolof territory for raids into French-protected areas led to a French expedition in 1890 and the subsequent absorption of this state into the French empire.

JONGO. The name for a slave in **Mandinka** society, comparable to the **Wolof** *jam.*

JOW, MRS. SATANG (1943–   ). Secretary of State for Education. Born in **Banjul** on August 31, 1943. She received her education at Fourah Bay College, University of Sierra Leone (B.A., 1966), and the Institute of Education, London University (Postgraduate Certificate in Education, 1969). Satang taught at Gambia High School, Banjul, 1966–1994, and was principal for the last five years. She was appointed Minister (and subsequently Secretary of State) for Education in July 1994.

JUFFURE. A **Mandinka** village on the north bank of the **Gambia River** opposite **James Island.** In the early 18th century a large number of mixed-blood Portuguese also resided there. The English maintained factories there for a century after 1680. At first these were sponsored by the large chartered companies, but later they were maintained by independent traders. In the early 18th century, Juffure provided the garrison at James Fort with a large part of their vegetable requirements. Juffure gained considerable prominence in the 1970s because the African-American author Alex Haley claimed that this was the village of his ancestor Kunta Kinte in the very popular semi-fictional book, *Roots*. Because of this work Juffure has become a tourist attraction.

JULA (DIOLA). **Mandinka** word for a trader. It has also come to denote a number of related groups of Mandinka of merchant origin who settled along the major trading routes in the Western Sudan, Sierra Leone, Guinea, and the Gambia.

JULY 22 MOVEMENT. Mass organization set up by the **Armed Forces Provisional Ruling Council (AFPRC)** in 1996 as part of its national program of civic education and national development. Its Secretary General is Lamin Kongira. The organization was also seen as a propaganda organ of the AFPRC in its process of transition to civilian rule. The national network of the movement is credited with having played a major role in ensuring the victory of **Yahya Jammeh** and the **Alliance for Patriotic Reorientation and Construction (APRC)** in the presidential and general elections of 1996–1997.

JUSTOBAQUE, PETER. The **factor** of the **(Dutch) West Indies Company** at Goree who in mid-1661 attempted to oust the British from their newly won superiority in trade on the **Gambia River.** Sailing up the Gambia River, he partly neutralized the small British garrison at Charles Fort on **Dog Island.** However, he was thwarted by the firm action of the British factor at Fort James who refused all Justobaque's arguments, promises of reward, and threats. Finally, Justobaque withdrew from the river and the directors of the Dutch Company and the States-General took no further immediate action to drive the English from the Gambia.

-K-

KABILO-TIYO. In **Mandinka** kingdoms, the *kabilo-tiyo* was in charge of a *kabilo* or a collection of yards (extended family households). He was normally the senior man of a particular lineage.

KAH, KEBBA A. H. (1923–?). Teacher and politician born to a Muslim **Wolof** family at Medina Mas Kah in the **Protectorate.** He was educated in Koranic schools, at the Catholic mission school, and at the Teachers Training College. Kah taught at a number of Protectorate schools until he resigned to enter politics in 1959. He stood as an independent candidate in the first national elections in 1960 but joined the **United Party (UP)** on his election. When **Pierre Sarr N'Jie** became Chief Minister, Kah was appointed to head the Ministry of Health. After the 1962 election, he joined the **People's Progressive Party (PPP)** and was appointed Minister of Finance and later of Works and Communication, before becoming Minister of Health in 1965. Forced to resign to make way for **Ibrahima Momodou Garba-Jahumpa,** when the latter merged his Gambia Congress Party with the PPP in 1968, Kah helped establish the short-lived **People's Progressive Alliance (PPA).** Though he returned to the PPP, he was one of three PPP MPs involved in a scandal concerning passport irregularities and was expelled from his parliamentary seat and from the PPP in 1971. He subsequently disappeared from political life.

KANTORA. The uppermost of the **Mandinka**-controlled kingdoms on the south bank of the **Gambia River.** The rulers and traders of Kantora are mentioned in 15th century Portuguese accounts because of their alleged possession of great quantities of gold. Kantora was one of the Mandinka states which the **Alfa and Musa Molloh** attempted to absorb into **Fuladu** during the **Soninke-Marabout** conflicts in the 1870s. Although they were never completely successful, the older traditional rule in Kantora was broken. In the British reorganization of the chiefdoms of the Gambia in the 20th century, the area of the ancient kingdom and its name were revived as a district in the Upper River Division.

KAUR. A trading post on the middle Gambia, which later became an important **groundnut** exporting port accessible to smaller ocean-going vessels.

KELEPHA-SAMBA, I. B. A. (1915–1995). Banjul-born civil servant and politician. He was the National President of the **People's Progressive Party (PPP)** and its elected representative for Banjul North from 1977 until the army coup of 1994. Kelepha-Samba spent most of his working life as a civil servant, first with the Gambia Post Office, then as a purser and senior accounting officer in the Marine department. On his retirement in 1972 he took a prominent part in political life. He failed to unseat **United Party (UP)** leader, **Pierre Sarr N'Jie,** in the 1972 parliamentary election in **Bathurst** North, but won the seat in 1977 (after N'Jie had been barred from office) and in all subsequent elections up to 1992. Kelepha-Samba held several public positions—Parliamentary Secretary, Ministry of Health, 1977–1979, Minister of Works and Communications, 1979–1982, and Mayor of Bathurst, 1968–1969. He died on 18 July 1995.

KEMINTANG (?–1843). A **Soninke** chief who in the 1820s was contesting with Kolli, the chief of Kataba, for the overlordship of **Niani.** The power relationship between these two was partially upset by Kolli's ceding Lemain Island (**MacCarthy Island**) to the British in 1823. But the British could not maintain a large enough force on the island to bring peace to the adjoining areas, and the endemic warfare continued. In 1834, a dispute arose between Kemintang and a **Bathurst** merchant at Tendaba, and Kemintang seized a vessel belonging to another merchant and held it for ransom, asking the British to redress the wrongs he had suffered. Instead, Lieutenant-Governor **George Rendall** declared an embargo on upper river trade and in August dispatched a 120-man force against the chief. Kemintang retired to Dungaseen, a fortified town near the headwaters of Sami Creek. The invaders dragged their cannon and ammunition through 20 miles of sand and mud, only to find the walls of the town impervious to artillery. Abandoning the guns, two of which could still be used, they retreated to the **Gambia River.** Kemintang mounted these guns on the walls of his town, and his victory gave him added prestige in Niani. Despite a number of British efforts, he refused to surrender the artillery and continued to make sporadic war against Kataba until his death.

KENNEDY, SIR ARTHUR EDWARD (1810–1883). An Irishman, born on April 9, 1810, and educated at Trinity College, Dublin. Kennedy initially served as a soldier, enlisting in the British army as an ensign in the 27th Foot. He retired from the army in 1848 and joined the colonial service as Governor of the Gambia in 1851, but was transferred to Sierra Leone as Governor before he could visit the Gambia. He left West Africa in 1854, to become Governor of Western Australia. After leaving Western Australia in 1862, Kennedy was put in command of Vancouver Island, before returning to Africa as Governor of the West African Settlements in 1867. He remained in this post for five years and then moved to Hong Kong, where he served as Governor until 1877. His final posting was to Queensland. Kennedy died at sea on June 13, 1883, while returning home on leave.

During his time as Governor of the **British West African Settlements** he was one of the key figures in the negotiations for the exchange of British possessions in the Gambia for French territory elsewhere. The Colonial Office, responding to French offers, ordered Kennedy to investigate and report on the situation in the Gambia. In 1869, he visited **Bathurst** for the first time and spent 10 days in the Gambia. Thus the detailed reports on conditions in the territory that he submitted to the Colonial Office during the following six years were not based on personal observation or detailed knowledge, but on reports from subordinates and merchants who did have experience of Gambian conditions. Despite this obvious lack of firsthand knowledge, the Colonial Office viewed Kennedy as their expert.

Even before his visit to Bathurst, Kennedy was in favor of some exchange that would consolidate the West African territories claimed by both nations. Kennedy further argued that the Gambia was a useless appendage that cost Britain in military expenditures more than the territory was worth. What trade there was, was in the hands of French merchants, and the "peculiar population" was resistant to all attempts to extend civilization to the areas outside the **Colony.** Kennedy's first long reports, along with similar ones from the administrator, **Rear Admiral C. G. Patey,** convinced the British government to propose to France a sweeping exchange of territory. By March 1870, all the details of the exchange had been worked out except the rights of English and French subjects in the ceded territories. However, the Franco-Prussian War interrupted the negotiations for exchange, and discussions were not resumed until 1875.

KËR. Wolof word for a compound or yard, a cluster of dwellings inhabited by members of an extended family. By extension, *kër* could mean an extended family, a lineage, or the village of an important person.

KEREWAN. Administrative center of North Bank Division. It had a population of 33,102 in 1993, having nearly doubled its size in 10 years.

KESSELLIKUNDA. A town in **Fuladu** which was the residence of **Musa Molloh** after his movement in 1903 from the **Casamance** into British territory. The British recognized Musa Molloh's position as head of British Fuladu and paid him a handsome stipend until they could no longer ignore his practice of slavery and rumored atrocities. In 1919, they destroyed Musa's compound at Kessellikunda and exiled him to Sierra Leone for a number of years.

KHALIFA. **Wolof** and **Fulbe** title for the leader of a community of believers. The term was originally Arabic and was among the many borrowed from that language by West Africans. In Wolof the term is normally applied to the head of an Islamic religious brotherhood or one of its branches.

KIANG. One of the nine **Mandinka** kingdoms located along the south bank of the **Gambia River** in the early 19th century. It stretched from the confluence of **Bintang Bolon** and the Gambia River eastward to a spot opposite Devil's Point. Bintang Bolon separated Kiang from **Foni** to the south. The major port towns of Tankular and Tendaba are in Kiang. Because of its location and wealth, Kiang was a major prize in the **Soninke-Marabout** conflicts. **Ma Bah's** attempt to gain a firm foothold on the south bank was thwarted at **Kwinella** in Kiang. Eastern Kiang by the 1870s was firmly controlled by **Fodi Kabba,** while the central and western parts of Kiang were still in the hands of the **Soninke** or owed allegiance to **Fodi Silla.** Kiang continued to be an area of disorder until after the killing of **Travelling Commissioners Sitwell** and Silva and a large part of their force at Sankandi in 1900. After the British reorganization of the **Protectorate** in the 20th century, Kiang was placed in the Central Division (subsequently Lower River Division) and divided into three districts, each under the direction of a chief.

KILHAM, HANNAH (1774–1832). A member of the Society of Friends who in 1823 arrived in the Gambia as the leader of a party of four Europeans and two Gambian men, Mamadi and Sandani, educated in Europe, to set up one of the first industrial missionary schemes in Africa. The two European men and one of the Gambians started an agricultural school at Cape St. Mary, while Mrs. Kilham and another woman, Anne Thompson, opened a school for girls in **Bathurst.** The other Gambian took charge of the school for **liberated Africans.** Later, a **Wesleyan** missionary arrived in the Gambia, and Mrs. Kilham turned her school over to him and took up residence in Bakau where she opened another girls' school. Within a few months all the members of the Friends' mission were stricken with fever and were forced to return to England, thus ending the Quaker experiment in Western technical education. Hannah Kilham died at sea while en route to Freetown to undertake further educational work.

KING'S BOYS. Recaptive slaves who had served with the **Royal African Corps** and the **West India Regiments** and had been pensioned or discharged. They were the first of the **liberated Africans** to be sent to the

Gambia. Beginning in the early 1820s, a number of these ex-soldiers settled along Oyster Creek with grants of land and free farming implements. Some of the King's Boys became government ferrymen, others burned lime from the oyster shells for the **Bathurst** market, and still others found employment in the construction of the first public buildings in Bathurst.

KOMBO. One of the traditional south bank **Mandinka** kingdoms. The rulers of Kombo controlled the lands adjacent to the mouth of the **Gambia River.** The peoples of Kombo had long been in contact with Europeans because of the kingdom's location. **Captain Alexander Grant** purchased St. Mary's Island, on which to build the town of **Bathurst,** from the King of Kombo. The price was an annual payment of 103 iron bars (approximately £25). In 1853, the British negotiated a further cession of land from **Suling Jatta,** another ruler of Kombo. This new area became British Kombo, and the transaction helped to precipitate the **Soninke-Marabout** conflict in the lower river territories. The wars began in Kombo with the activities of **Omar of Sabaji** and **Fodi Kabba.** The greatest threat to the continued British presence on the river came from the warfare between the contending factions in Kombo in the mid-1850s. The problem was not resolved until 1855, when Suling Jatta was killed and the **Marabouts** loyal to Fodi Kabba controlled western Kombo.

KONKO. A short handled mattock-shaped tool that is used for planting **groundnuts.** The sower uses the *konko* in one hand to make holes in the ground, while with the other hand he drills the seeds into the holes. The tool is featured in the coat of arms of the Republic of The Gambia and as an emblem by the **People's Protectorate Party (PPP).**

KOORAA (KORA). **Mandinka** 21-string harp-lute played by a caste of professional musician-singers known as *jalis* (cf. **Wolof** *griot*).

KORDA-TIYO. The **Protectorate** Ordinance of 1902 and all those which followed until 1933 accepted the *korda* (yard) as the basic political institution throughout the Gambia. A yard was defined as a collection of several huts held by a kindred grouping. The head of a yard was normally referred to by the **Mandinka** term *korda-tiyo.* These household leaders were under the supervision of a village head, called the *satee-tiyo.*

KORTRIGHT, SIR CORNELIUS HENDRICHSON, KCMG (1817–1897). Administrator of the Gambia from 1873 to 1875. Kortright began and ended his career in the colonial service in the West Indies. He was President (Administrator) of the British Virgin Islands, 1854–1856, and then Lieutenant-Governor of Grenada (1856–1864) and Tobago (1864–1872), before transferring to West Africa. On leaving the Gambia Kortright was appointed Governor of the **British West African Settlements,** and he ended his career as Governor of British Guiana. He was deeply involved in the 1874–1876 Colonial Office plans to cede the Gambia to France and acted as the chief source of information for the Colonial Office planners. His report that **Bathurst** mercantile opinion would not be hostile if proper compensation was paid proved to be wrong, since opposition from this section became very organized and vocal. Kortright died on December 23, 1897.

KOTO, MANSA. The chief of Battelling whose town was selected by **Travelling Commissioner Cyril Frederic Sitwell** in 1900 as the neutral ground on which to adjudicate the quarrel between the **Marabouts** and the **Soninke** in **Kiang.** When **Dari Bana Dabo,** the Marabout leader of Sankandi, refused to parley, Mansa Koto and some of his retainers accompanied Sitwell and his party to Sankandi. When the people of Sankandi opened fire, Mansa Koto was killed, along with the Travelling Commissioner and the majority of the armed escort.

KWINELLA (QUINELLA). A village in **Kiang.** In 1863, a son of the former **Soninke** ruler of **Baddibu** attempted to overthrow **Ma Bah's** regime, and having failed, recrossed the **Gambia River** where he and his followers regrouped themselves near Kwinella. Ma Bah's forces pursued them across the river, and there ensued one of the major pitched battles of the **Soninke-Marabout Wars.** Ma Bah was defeated, his army retreated, and he was forced briefly to seek sanctuary among the **Fulbe** at Sumbundu. Although this defeat was not as important a factor in the downfall of Ma Bah as the British believed, it did deny him a major foothold on the south bank and forced him to concentrate his expansionist activity northward into Saloum and **Jolof.**

-L-

LAHAMIN JAY. A **Mandinka**-speaking **Fulbe** who had been captured, sold into slavery, and sent to Maryland with **Job ben Solomon.** Job, after his release, petitioned the Duke of Montagu to secure the release of

Lahamin Jay who was returned to the Gambia by the **Royal African Company** in 1738. He became a part of the mission headed by **Melchior de Jaspas** in 1740, which sought to improve trade between the Company and the kingdom of Bondu.

LAIDLEY, DR. JOHN. A surgeon who in 1791 joined Robert Aynsley, a trader, at his station at Pisania (Karantaba). He acted as the banker for **Major Daniel Houghton** and later **Mungo Park** in their expeditions into the western Sudan. Park spent the latter six months of 1795 at Laidley's house while studying **Mandinka,** and it was there that he returned after his successful exploration.

LAM (pl. *LAMAN*). **Wolof** and **Fulbe** title for a chief. In some cases it refers to the original chief of a lineage.

LAMINE, MOMADU. A Muslim leader from Bondu who had contested French domination and was driven to take refuge at Toubacouta where he was welcomed by the son of **Simotto Moro.** A French expedition followed Lamine to the Gambia, and **Musa Molloh,** then an ally of the French, crossed the **Gambia River** with a large army. The combined forces took Toubacouta in 1886 and Momadu Lamine, according to legend, was killed by Musa.

LEBANESE. An extremely successful minority business community, originating in Lebanon and Syria, who are to be found in most West African countries from Senegal to Cameroon and even beyond. The first immigrants began arriving in Senegal at the turn of the 20th century, and their numbers increased until independence, when African governments sought, often half-heartedly, to restrict the numbers and activities of the Lebanese, owing to popular resentment at their economic success. Their ascendency in middle-level business was originally due to the preferences given to them, rather than to their African competitors, by the large European commercial firms. Although their numbers and influence have decreased, they are still the dominant mid-level merchants in The Gambia and are also active in transport and the service sector. With rare exceptions—such as the **Madi** family—the Lebanese have avoided direct participation in politics, although they are known to offer financial support discreetly to politicians as part of their efforts to protect their economic interests.

LEGISLATIVE COUNCIL. One of two councils found in British Crown Colonies to assist the Governor in making decisions. The small nominated

Gambian Legislative Council was first created in 1843. When the Gambia was made dependent on Sierra Leone in 1866, its Council was abolished only to be reestablished after the Gambia was made a separate colony in 1888. In 1893, the authority of the Council to make rules and orders was extended to the **Protectorate.** In 1915, the Council was enlarged to include four official and three nominated unofficial members. In 1932, its size was increased by an additional African member nominated by the Urban District Council and by one of the Commissioners from the Protectorate. The Council was reorganized in 1947 to contain three ex-officio members, three nominated government officials, six unofficial nominated members, and one elected member from **Bathurst.** In 1951, the number of elected members was increased to three (two for Bathurst and one for **Kombo** St. Mary). The constitutional revision of 1954 provided for five ex-officio official members, two nominated officials, seven directly elected members from the **Colony,** and seven indirectly elected members from the Protectorate. After 1954, certain elected members were appointed to the **Executive Council** and allowed a share in directing the affairs of the government departments. Although they were not yet really responsible, this was the necessary first step toward ministerial government. According to the Constitution of 1960, the legislative instrument for the Gambia was renamed the House of Representatives.

LEMAIN ISLAND. See MacCARTHY ISLAND.

LIBERATED AFRICANS. Africans in transit as slaves to the New World who were liberated, normally by warships of the British West African Patrol. Because they were taken twice, the term **"recaptive"** came to be used to describe these Africans. Most of the recaptives were taken to Freetown, although they came from various parts of West Africa and represented many different ethnic and cultural groups. They presented a considerable problem to the British government in Freetown, which had only limited funds available for resettlement. Many of the recaptives in the 1820s and 1830s found their way to the Gambia where they became the nucleus of a Westernized population in **Bathurst.** By 1836, they numbered 2,386 and a manager had to be appointed to look after them. Attempts to persuade them to accept free passages to the West Indies in 1841 and 1845 were largely unsuccessful, though a group did emigrate to St. Vincent. The **Aku** (Yoruba) became particularly important in trade and commerce, and their descendants were among the first Africans to occupy important posts in the civil service and government of 20th-century Gambia.

LLEWELYN, SIR ROBERT BAXTER, KCMG (1845–1919). Administrator of the Gambia, 1891–1900. Llewelyn started his career as a clerk in
the Colonial Office, London, in 1868. Apart from his Gambia service, he
spent all his career in the West Indies. After serving in junior posts in Jamaica he headed, in turn, the administrations of the Turks Islands, Tobago, St. Vincent, and St. Lucia. Llewelyn was the man most responsible
for establishing the early forms of **indirect rule** in the Gambia **Protectorate.** British control over most of the **Gambia River** areas after the **Anglo-French Convention of 1889** had been exercised in an ad hoc, intermittent manner until 1893 when Llewelyn appointed the first **Travelling
Commissioner.** After months of study of other British colonial dependencies, particularly India, the Governor and his staff issued the Protectorate Ordinance of 1894. Later Governors modified this legislation, but
the basic form and mechanics of Protectorate government as stated in the
1894 Ordinance remained in effect until the eve of Gambian independence. Llewelyn was also primarily responsible for modifying the more
extreme demands of the French representatives on the various boundary
commissions of the 1890s. He and his advisors drew up and instituted the
plans for the joint operation with the French in 1901 that finally destroyed
the influence of **Fodi Kabba.** On leaving the Gambia, Llewelyn ended his
career as Governor of the Windward Islands, 1900–1906. He died on February 19, 1919.

-M-

**MacCARTHY, SIR CHARLES (1768–1824) (also written as M'-
CARTHY).** Governor-in-Chief of the **British West African Settlements,** 1814–1824. An Irishman, MacCarthy joined the British army in
1794 as an officer in the 5th Regiment of the Irish Brigade. He served in
the West Indies and New Brunswick before being appointed Lieutenant-
Colonel in the **Royal African Corps** in 1811 and sent the following year
to Sierra Leone as Governor. He took over command at Cape Coast on
the Gold Coast as well and was killed in action against the Ashanti on
January 21, 1824, at Bonsaso. His head was taken as a trophy by the
Ashanti.

It was MacCarthy who made the recommendation to the Colonial Office in 1815 that Britain should reoccupy **James Island.** He supported
Captain Alexander Grant in his decision not to attempt the rebuilding
of the fort on the island, but rather to purchase **Banjul** (St. Mary's) Island

from the King of **Kombo** and build the British base there. Although until 1821 the government of the Gambia was military and seemingly temporary, MacCarthy had enlisted the support of the newly arrived **Bathurst** merchants for the government, and he had established a courts system. After 1821, the Gambia was officially made a part of the British West African Settlements, which he controlled from his headquarters in Freetown. **MacCarthy Island** was subsequently named after him.

MacCARTHY (McCARTHY) ISLAND. Called Lemain Island by Europeans in the 18th century, its original local name was Janjangbure. It reverted to this name in the 1970s. MacCarthy Island was an important trading site for trans-Gambian trade from areas in Senegal to the north as well as from the upper **Casamance.** Europeans had maintained temporary trading stations on the island since **Richard Jobson's** time. In 1823, the island was ceded to the British by Kolli, **Soninke** ruler of Kataba, and renamed MacCarthy Island, in honor of the Governor-in-Chief of the **British West African Settlements.** Despite much pressure from the **Soninke-Marabout Wars** and a penurious treasury, it remained throughout the century the chief British enclave in the interior. Georgetown, its major settlement, was once one of the larger settlements of the interior, and became administrative center of MacCarthy Island Division (now Central River Division). It was also the location for a **Wesleyan** missionary settlement.

MacDONNELL, SIR RICHARD GRAVES. Governor of the Gambia from 1847 until early 1852. In 1844, while serving as first Chief Justice of the **Colony,** he made one of the longest journeys into the hinterland seeking information on the people, their customs, and potential trade. He traveled by water to Fattatenda where he met three Frenchmen who had just visited Bondu. From Fattatenda he traveled on foot to the capital of Bondu where he induced the ruler to repudiate the exclusive trade treaty he had just made with the Frenchmen and extracted a promise that the route from Bondu to the **Gambia River** would be kept open. After being appointed Governor, MacDonnell in 1849 and 1850 undertook yet more explorations. In 1849, he traveled by boat over 100 miles beyond **Barrakunda** Falls. In the following year, he reached Jallakotta on the Neriko River. He was disappointed by both expeditions since he found the river above the falls difficult to navigate, the country sparsely settled, and little sign of major cultivation of any exportable crop. On the return journey in 1850, Governor MacDonnell's party narrowly escaped death when he visited Kunnong near **Kwinella.** The inhabitants of Kunnong, after driving off MacDonnell, then pillaged a trading post nearby. On his return to **Bathurst,** MacDonnell organized a punitive expedition, which eventually forced the chief of Kunnong to submit to the British Governor. Earlier in 1849, MacDonnell had helped organize a joint French-British expedition against the Papels on Bissago Island who had made a practice of capturing shipwrecked vessels and their crews.

MacNAMARA, MATTHIAS. An ensign in O'Hara's Corps in the Senegambia who was selected over senior officers to be Lieutenant-Governor at **James Island** in 1774. He disobeyed orders, seized French trading ships, and traded privately with the Africans. Despite such actions, he became the Governor of Senegambia in late 1775. Almost immediately he began a quarrel with **Captain Joseph Wall,** who had taken his place at James Island. MacNamara ordered Wall's arrest and kept him in confinement for 10 months at the fort before bringing him to trial. Wall was subsequently cleared of the charges and in two civil suits won damages from MacNamara, who was removed as Governor of Senegambia by the Council of Trade in August 1778.

MADI, HENRY (1913–1965). The most prominent member of the leading **Lebanese** commercial family in the Gambia. Unusually for a Lebanese, Henry Madi and, to a lesser extent his brothers, Joseph and Robert, took an active part in the political life of the community. Henry Madi won the **Kombo** St. Mary seat in the 1951 and 1954 elections to the **Legislative Council** on a nonparty platform, but was widely believed to have discreetly provided financial support to all the fledgling political parties in the 1950s. As testimony to his public standing, he was appointed as an independent delegate to the constitutional conferences in **Bathurst** and London in 1961 and in London again in July 1964. His brothers, Joseph and Robert, were appointed nominated MPs in the House of Representatives, in succession, in the mid-1960s and early 1970s. Henry Madi died unexpectedly, at the age of 52, in London, in September 1965, from where he had directed the British end of the family's extensive business activities.

MAHONEY, SIR JOHN ANDREW (1883–1966). Chief Clerk with the French trading company, Morel Prom, Mahoney emerged as one of the leaders of the **Bathurst** African community in the second quarter of the 20th century. He was the recognized head of the Mahoney family, perhaps the most prominent **Aku** family, which counted some of the most educated and influential people in Bathurst. These included Augusta, the first wife of Prime Minister **Sir Dawda Jawara.** Sir John was a longtime friend of **Edward Francis Small** and other early nationalists, and he was active in the Gambia Section of the **National Congress of British West Africa (NCBWA)** and the **Bathurst Rate Payers Association.** Despite his earlier reputation as a radical, he was a nominated member of the **Legislative Council,** from January 1942 to 1947, and Vice President of the Council in 1951. He was the first and only Speaker of the Legislative Council, 1954–1960, and Speaker of the new House of Representatives until his retirement in 1962. He was knighted in 1959 and died in January 1966.

MALI EMPIRE. After the Almoravids overthrew the kingdom of Ghana in the 11th century, there ensued a century and a half of military and commercial rivalry between a number of powerful city states in the western Sudan. Eventually, in the 13th century, the **Mandinka** ruler, Sundiata, defeated his Soso rivals. On the basis of Sundiata's conquest, later rulers built the Mali empire, the most powerful and richest empire ever developed in the Sudan. It reached its apex under Mansa Musa in the 14th century, its fame being underscored by Mansa Musa's legendary trip to Mecca. Before its downfall, the empire included eastern Senegal, and many Gambian riverine rulers paid homage and tribute to the great King of Mali.

MALTA PLAN. In the late 1950s, this was one solution suggested for small British dependencies that were considered to be incapable of achieving complete independence due to weakness or economic nonviability. It was at first proposed as a solution of the problem of the island of Malta, and was also proposed for the Gambia. The chief feature of the plan was some type of federal association between the dependent territories and Great Britain. With the political leaders of most of the smaller areas opting for independence, the plan was abandoned even before details of association were seriously discussed.

MAMADOU N'DARE (?–1889). Chosen by the chiefs of **Baddibu** to succeed his brother, **Ma Bah,** in 1867. Before the wars on the north bank, he had studied the Koran in Mauritania and helped Ma Bah run a religious school in **Jolof.** Like his brother, he was an austere and orthodox Muslim. He continued the wars begun by Ma Bah along the **Gambia River** and reached the apex of his power when he loosely controlled much of the north bank from the Atlantic to **Wuli.** The British signed a treaty with him, recognizing his hegemony in all these areas except **Niumi.** However, his **Marabout** forces were not able to conquer Sine and the inland **Wolof** territories where the French had become dominant. Mamadou was not successful in establishing permanent institutions of government that could keep his war chiefs in check, and, in 1877, one of them, **Biram Cisse,** decided to build his own fortified base and refused Mamadou's order to tear down the walls of his town.

This began a devastating civil war which was to last until the French invasion of 1887, when those territories farthest from Nioro were freed from Mamadou's control. **Musa Molloh** and the *Bur* Saloum allied themselves with Cisse, and by the early 1880s, Mamadou had lost most of the territory over which he had ruled. His problems were further complicated by the actions of **Sait Maty,** Ma Bah's son, who claimed the kingship created by his father. In 1886, the British withdrew the stipend paid to Mamadou as ruler of Baddibu. In the same year, Cisse and Maty had almost reached an agreement whereby Cisse recognized the younger man as suzerain, but each wanted the stipend, which Governor **Sir Gilbert Carter** decided to pay to neither. The conflict continued into the next year when French forces defeated the Marabouts, forced Sait Maty to flee, and divided what was left of Ma Bah's patrimony between Cisse and the aged Mamadou. Once again king, if only over a small area and by the grace of the French, Mamadou enjoyed this shadow power until his death in 1889.

MANDINKA (also written as **MANDINGO,** cf. **MENDE; MALINKE**). One of the most important ethnic groups in the Gambia, presently constituting 34 percent of the Gambian population. The Mandinka are spread fairly evenly throughout the length of the country. The Gambian Mandinka are the most westerly extension of the Manding group of people who speak kindred languages belonging to the northern subgroup of the Niger-Congo family and have similar political and social organizations. Some of the other West African Manding speakers are the Bambara, Malinke, Mende, **Jula,** and Kuranko. The Mandinka have long been resident in the Gambia, probably moving into the area during the period of disorder in the western Sudan following the breakup of the empire of Ghana in the 11th century. **Richard Jobson** noted in the 17th century that Mandinka rulers in the Gambia still showed deference to the ruler of **Mali** long after the breakdown of Mali's hegemony over the western Sudan.

Mandinka society was divided into three endogamous castes—the freeborn *(foro),* slaves *(jongo)* and artisans or praise singers *(nyamalo).* Age groups (*kaafoo*) were important in Mandinka society in contrast to the socio-political organizations of neighboring **Wolof** people. The basis of life for the Mandinka was and is **agriculture,** although they were also the dominant traders on the river. In the second half of the 19th century, cultivation of **groundnuts** became the major activity for most Mandinka farmers.

In the 19th century almost all the riverine territories of the Gambia were controlled by a number of Mandinka rulers (*mansolu*), organized in separate and competing kingdoms. These were **Niumi, Jokadu, Baddibu,** Upper and Lower **Niani,** and **Wuli** on the north bank; and **Kombo, Foni, Kiang, Jarra, Niamina, Eropina, Jimara, Tomani,** and **Kantora** along the south bank. Rule in each of these states was based upon kinship, and each king surrounded himself with a complex bureaucracy. The kingdoms were subdivided into the territorial units of the village, ward, and family compound. Village administration was carried out by the *satee-tiyo (alkaaloo)* in council. Each village was further divided into *kabilos,* or wards, which were administered by a *kabilo-tiyo.* Each of these officials was chosen on the basis of his lineage as well as his abilities. The kings each maintained an armed force to defend the state and impose their will on their subjects. Since they were not themselves permitted to lead troops, the rulers chose a general (*jawara*) for this function. The Mandinka systems of rule were challenged in the later 19th century by proselytizing teachers who wished to convert the Mandinka to **Islam.** The ensuing conflicts led to the half-century series of wars called the **Soninke-Marabout Wars,** which resulted in the conversion of most of the people to Islam and a breakdown of traditional Mandinka authority structures in the Gambia.

MANE, KOLLIMANKE. King of **Barra** at the time when **Captain Alexander Grant** began the construction of the first buildings in **Bathurst.** The king allowed the British to quarry stone on **Dog Island** free of charge. Instead, the king was paid a proportion of the duty levied on merchant ships entering the river. This was greatly reduced in 1820, and, after Kollimanke Mane's death in 1823, this incident was remembered by the new king and his advisors and was one of the reasons for the **Barra War** of 1831.

MANJAGO (MANJACK). A small ethnic community found in the **Kombos,** tracing its origins to the Manjago people of Guinea-Bissau. Although no longer Portuguese-speaking, they often retain Portuguese names such as Mendy and Gomez. They numbered some 7,500 in 1993.

MANSA (pl. *MANSOLU*). **Mandinka** title for the ruler of one of their traditional states.

MANSAKONKO. Administrative center of Lower River Division, situated on the south bank of the **Gambia River** some 110 miles from **Banjul.** It had a population of 10,206 in 1993.

MARABOUTS. Initially Muslim religious teachers who later came to exercise considerable political and economic influence. At the court of every Senegambian ruler who had accepted **Islam,** there would be at least one Marabout whose responsibilities in normal times were to pray for the ruler, give advice, and handle correspondence. In the disturbed conditions after 1850, some of the Marabouts came to wield great political influence, and some, such as **Ma Bah,** themselves became the rulers of large kingdoms. This was the case in many areas adjacent to the **Gambia River** where traditional rulers and their entourages refused to accept Islam. The series of civil wars called the **Soninke-Marabout Wars** were initially based on the desires of reforming Marabouts to overthrow the "pagan" Soninke rulers and convert the people to Islam. Whereas Marabouts came to play a vital role in the administrative and economic life of the French colony of **Senegal,** a role continued after independence, there were no Grand Marabouts in the Gambia and the British tended to ignore them in favor of local chiefs in the administration of the territory.

Gambian Marabouts are to be found throughout the country, but enjoy a more local following than in Senegal. While many seek to avoid open association with political parties, some have come out in support of the UP or PPP. A number of prominent Gambian politicians have visited Marabouts, usually the more prestigious ones living in Mauritania and Senegal, before elections, to seek spiritual guidance and intercession or to obtain the support of their followers in The Gambia.

M'BAKI, OMAR. Politician and former district chief *(seefoo)* of Sami District, **MacCarthy Island** Division. One of the few educated chiefs in the Gambia in the late 1950s. He served for 14 years as a member of the **Executive Council** during British rule. After the election of 1960, he was a minister in the government of **Pierre Sarr N'Jie** and was the spokesman for the indirectly elected **Protectorate** chiefs. At this time he was considered by some as a political alternative to the leaders of the two major parties. When the **People's Progressive Party (PPP)** came to power, he fell out of favor and, in 1965, he and six other chiefs were dismissed by the central government for antigovernment attitudes. After this M'Baki withdrew from political life to take up a business career.

MBENGA, MUSA SAIHOU (1961–). Secretary of State for Agriculture and Natural Resources. Mbenga was educated in the United States of America at Texas Technical University (B.Sc. Plant and Soil Science, 1983) and Cornell University (M.Sc. Plant Breeding and Biometry, 1989). He worked with the Gambian Department of Agriculture as a research scientist until appointed Minister (and subsequently Secretary of State) of Agriculture and Natural Resources in July 1994.

MEDICAL RESEARCH COUNCIL (MRC). One of the major African tropical medicine research units was established at Fajara soon after World War II and maintained by the Medical Research Council of Great Britain and by **Colonial Development and Welfare Acts** funds. Later a field station was established at Keneba in **Kiang** in the Lower River Division. A 40-bed research ward was maintained at Fajara. The MRC has been engaged in the study of tropical diseases, particularly malaria, sickle-cell anemia, and filariasis.

MENDY, DOMINIC (1959–). Secretary of State for Trade, Industry and Employment since March 1998. He was born at Sibanor, Lower River Division, on October 13, 1959, of **Manjago** parentage. Mendy graduated from Fourah Bay College, University of Sierra Leone (Economics and Social Studies, 1987) and the University of Malaya, Kuala Lumpur (M.B.A., 1995). He worked as government auditor at the Social Security and Housing Finance Corporation, 1982–1983, and with Standard Chartered Bank, **Banjul,** 1993–95. Mendy was appointed Minister of Trade, Industry and Finance in August 1995 and Secretary of State for Finance and Economic Affairs in March 1997. He was dismissed without explanation in January 1999.

MIDDLETON, SIR JOHN, KCMG, CMG, KBE (1870–1954). Educated at Edinburgh University, he joined the colonial service in Nigeria in 1901 and by 1907 was Senior Assistant Colonial Secretary. Middleton served as Assistant Colonial Secretary and Colonial Secretary in Mauritius, 1908–1920, and was Governor of the Falkland Islands, 1920–1927. He served briefly as Governor of the Gambia, 1927–1928, and ended his career as Governor of Newfoundland, 1928–1932.

MOLONEY, SIR CORNELIUS ALFRED, KCMG (1848–1913). Administrator of the Gambia from 1884 to 1885. Moloney was educated at the Royal Military College, Sandhurst, where he was commissioned in 1867. He began his career in the colonial service in the Bahamas in 1871. He served in the Gold Coast administration, 1873–1879, taking part in the Ashanti War of 1873, and as Colonial Secretary in the Gold Coast. In 1880 he was appointed Acting Administrator of Lagos Colony, and he moved to the Gambia in 1884. Moloney returned to Lagos as Administrator in 1886 and was upgraded to Governor in 1887. Leaving West Africa in 1890, he spent the rest of his career as Governor, successively, of British Honduras, the Windward Isles, and Trinidad and Tobago. He retired in 1904 and died on August 13, 1913. His major contribution during his brief tenure in the Gambia was the completion of the 300-yard-long bridge over Oyster Creek.

MOORE, FRANCIS. Representative of the **Royal African Company** and writer. He was sent to **James Island** in 1730. During his nearly five-year stay in the Gambia, Moore traveled throughout much of the area. He was a trade **factor** in many places, most notably at **Joar** and **Yamyamakunda.** Much of our knowledge of Gambian social, economic, and political institutions in the 18th century is due to Moore's keen interest in the riverine Africans and their customs. His observations were published in 1735 in what became one of the classic books detailing West African life, *Travels in the Inland Parts of Africa*.

MOURIDE. A syncretic sufi Islamic brotherhood established in Senegal by Amadou Bamba M'Backé (1851–1927) in the late 19th century. Initially treated with suspicion and hostility by the French authorities, Bamba was twice exiled, to Gabon and Mauritania, yet he and his followers came to terms with colonial rule and became its economic mainstay through their dominance in **groundnut** cultivation. The Mourides, a highly disciplined religious organization owing political as well as spiritual allegiance to Bamba and his lineal descendants, also proved an invaluable ally to African rulers of the postcolonial state. Both **Leopold Sedar Senghor** and **Abdou Diouf** cultivated the leaders of the M'Backé family. Although the center of the Mouride brotherhood is Touba in Senegal, and most of its devotees are Senegalese, the brotherhood also enjoys a following among Gambians, mainly in the **Baddibus** and **Jarra.**

MOVEMENT FOR JUSTICE IN AFRICA-GAMBIA (MOJA-G). Radical political movement formed in late 1970s, influenced by marxist and pan-Africanist ideology and by a Liberian movement of the same name, to challenge the **Dawda Jawara** government. Principally engaged in consciousness-raising activities, MOJA-G was also accused of acts of political vandalism. It was banned following a failed plot by elements of the security forces in October 1980. Its leaders fled to Europe, principally Sweden, where they continued to denounce the **People's Progressive Party (PPP)**. Although restored to legality before the army coup of 1994, MOJA has not sought to contest elections. Elements of MOJA supported the coup and helped form the **July 22 Movement** and the **Alliance for Patriotic Re-orientation and Construction (APRC)**. While MOJA-G does not appear to have a clear political hierarchy, Ousman "Koro" Sallah and Ousman Manjang have served as prominent spokespersons.

MUMBO JUMBO. Described by **Francis Moore** in the 18th century as a figure of considerable importance in **Mandinka** society. He was said to be a man dressed in leaves who was called upon to judge the virtue of individuals in a particular village. He spoke a particular secret cant language not understandable to women or outsiders. This is the origin of the English usage of the term.

MUSA MOLLOH (?–1931). The son of **Alfa Molloh,** founder of the **Fulbe** kingdom of **Fuladu.** During the 1870s, Musa was content to act as the commander of his father's military forces, and it was he more than any other person who expanded the areas under the control of the Alfa, at the expense of the traditional **Mandinka** rulers as well as those of such other **Marabouts** as **Fodi Kabba** and **Simotto Moro.** The death of Alfa Molloh in 1881 fractured the recently created state of Fuladu, since Musa had no intention of meekly surrendering his power to his uncle who had inherited the throne. Musa took his faction southward, established a fortified base at Hamdallai, and in 1883 placed himself under the protection of the French. With their aid he soon reestablished his authority through much of Fuladu, and eventually killed his uncle and other members of the family who stood in the way of his maintaining control of the state. Finally, in 1892, he proclaimed himself king. The state Musa Molloh created was a reflection of his need for a stable kingdom that would respond quickly to his desires. He exercised complete military authority and controlled the political life of the state by a close watch over the 40 district leaders he appointed to act in his name throughout the territory. Musa also used a central bureaucracy to check on the activities of the district heads.

Unfortunately for Musa's centralized state, the partition of the Senegambia after 1889 brought fundamental changes to Fuladu. It was clear to Musa that in order to maintain the unity of his kingdom, he would have to choose peace rather than war with the Europeans, and he therefore promised to live quietly in the newly established French territory. In 1901, he participated in the joint expedition against his old enemy, Fodi Kabba. However, with the greater presence of the French and British in the interior, his days of freedom of action were almost at an end. The French interfered more and more with his rule, particularly as rumors of his tyranny against his subjects reached the centers of authority. In 1903, the French decided to build a military post at Hamdallai.

In response, Musa burned his town, cut the telegraph lines, and retreated to British territory where he established himself at **Kessellikunda.** The British recognized his control over what was then only a small part of his once large kingdom. They paid him an annual stipend and in general left him alone to rule. Without an army and cut off from the bulk of his previous territory in the south, he was, in effect, a British prisoner. The British could depose him whenever they wished, but it was to their advantage to have a strong ruler acting as a unifying force in the upriver areas. In 1919, finally reacting to reports of atrocities, the British deposed Musa, destroyed his royal compound, and exiled him to Sierra Leone. He was allowed to return in 1923, shorn almost entirely of his power. Until his death, he remained nothing but a shadowy reminder of the time when he was the most powerful of the kings of southern Senegambia.

-N-

NATIONAL CONGRESS OF BRITISH WEST AFRICA, GAMBIA SECTION (NCBWA). The first modern political organization in the Gambia. It developed out of the Gambia Native Defensive Union, which its organizer, **Edward Francis Small,** converted into a local Congress committee in 1919. Interest in holding an intercolonial conference among the British West African elite dated back to 1914, but it was only after World War I that it could be held. Initially, there was broad support in **Bathurst** for Gambian participation, and sufficient funds were collected to enable Small to attend the founding meeting of the NCBWA in Accra in March 1920, a meeting held under the leadership of Gold Coast barrister and nationalist, J. E. Casely Hayford. The NCBWA put forward 83 resolutions, covering a wide spectrum of issues of concern to the Westernized elite, the most important being a call for half the seats in colonial legislatures to be filled, through direct election, by Africans.

On his return from Accra in May, Small converted the committee into a Gambia Section of the NCBWA. Most members were Bathurst Christian **Aku,** with some urban Muslim **Wolof** involvement, but few links with the **Protectorate** populace. The Gambia Section, from its inception, was divided into a radical group led by Small and a conservative faction headed by **Samuel John Forster, Jr.** The latter and other wealthier conservative members left the organization and thereafter opposed it. Governor Sir **Cecil Armitage,** like his counterparts in the other British West African dependencies, denounced the NCBWA as an unrepresentative clique of educated coastal Africans, with no mandate to speak for the vast majority of rural Africans, and he refused to make more than minor constitutional changes at this time.

Support had begun to slip by 1922 when Small decided to travel abroad, leaving his brother-in-law, **John Andrew Mahoney,** in charge. By the time Small returned in 1926 the local Congress section was in serious difficulties, and it ceased to exist after 1928. The death of Casely Hayford and the rise of new anticolonial protest organizations elsewhere in West Africa, as well as official hostility or indifference, led to the collapse of the NCBWA everywhere save Freetown by the early 1930s.

Elsewhere along the West African coast, the pan-African form of colonial protest gave way to more inward-looking successor organizations, distracted by limited opportunities to directly elect Africans to local legislatures. In the Gambia, political activity focused instead on municipal representation through the formation of the **Bathurst Rate Payers Association.**

NATIONAL CONVENTION PARTY (NCP). Formed on September 7, 1975, by former **People's Progressive Party (PPP)** founder and Vice President of The Gambia, **Sheriff Mustapha Dibba,** on his expulsion from the PPP. Not to be confused with an earlier, but defunct, party of the same name founded by Noah Sanyang in 1965, the NCP replaced the moribund **United Party (UP)** as the major political opposition to the PPP. Although claiming a national following and an alternative political program, called the "**Farafenni** Declaration," the NCP differed little in substance from the PPP and its manifesto was little more than a rewriting of the original PPP one. Consequently, it failed to make more than limited inroads into the governing party's popular support. Dibba was denounced, to some effect, by the PPP as a disaffected and ambitious renegade and his party as a **Mandinka** tribalist movement. The NCP also lacked the financial resources to present an effective challenge to the PPP, given the latter party's control of the government apparatus, and had to rely too heavily on Dibba.

It contested every election between 1977 and 1992 (despite the detention of Dibba and other party leaders following the failed coup attempt of July 1981), but never won more than six seats, even though it won up to 30 percent of the vote. Neither was Dibba able to win more than 27 percent of the vote in any presidential election. The NCP's strength was greatest in Dibba's home area of the **Baddibus** in North Bank Division and in the Greater **Banjul** area, where Baddibu Mandinkas had settled. Attempts to forge an alliance with the **Gambia People's Party (GPP)** at the time of the 1987 and 1992 elections foundered due to differences between the two leaders. Together with the PPP and GPP, the party was banned by the **Armed Forces Provisional Ruling Council (AFPRC)**, and Dibba was barred from contesting further elections.

NATIONAL LIBERATION PARTY (NLP). Small and short-lived radical political party set up by **Banjul** lawyer Pap Cheyassin Ousman Secka in October 1975 to contest the 1977 general elections. It failed to forge a political alliance with the main opposition party, the **National Convention Party (NCP),** but did put up joint candidates in six constituencies with the ailing **United Party (UP).** Despite this, all its candidates lost their deposits and party organizer Alassan Touray was killed in a road accident while on campaign in **Jokadu.** Secka, already defeated in Sabach-Sanjal, was decisively beaten a second time, soon afterwards, in a by-election in Banjul Central, following the death of its UP MP. After this double defeat, Secka dissolved the NLP and established links with the **Gambia Socialist Revolutionary Party (GSRP)** in 1980. He was sentenced to death (later commuted) for his part in planning the unsuccessful coup attempt of July 30, 1981. Following his early release from prison Secka returned to legal practice in Banjul and remains active in public life.

NATIONAL RECONCILIATION PARTY (NRP). New opposition party formed by Fajara hotelier **Hammat Bah,** to contest presidential and parliamentary elections in 1996–1997. It differs little in its policies from the **United Democratic Party (UDP),** but the attempts to unite the parties failed. Unlike the UDP leader **Ousainu Darboe,** Hammat Bah has a parliamentary seat and so has been able to continue his attacks on government policy in the National Assembly.

NENYO. The caste to which the **Wolof** assigned artisans and various craft workers. Smiths, leatherworkers, woodworkers, and *gewels,* or praise singers, belong to this caste.

NEW TOWN. A district of **Bathurst** situated inland from **Portuguese Town.**

NEWS MEDIA. *Newspapers:* Newspapers in The Gambia date back to the last quarter of the 19th century. The earliest newspaper was *The Bathurst Times,* which appeared fleetingly in 1871. In the 1880s *The Bathurst Intelligencer* and *The Bathurst Observer and West Africa Gazette* were published in the Gambian capital, but, after these, there seems to have been a considerable gap before the appearance of **Edward Francis Small's** *Gambia Outlook and Senegambia Reporter,* launched in 1922 and published with breaks until his death in 1958. After World War II, a number of other newspapers appeared. These played an important part in criticizing the colonial government and in advancing the cause of the new political movements that appeared in the 1950s. *The Vanguard,* edited by Melville Jones, was an outspoken critic of colonial administration during the run-up to independence. The radical tradition was maintained by William Dixon-Colley's *Nation,* which appeared, with growing irregularity, from the 1950s to the 1990s. Another leading newspaper was *The Gambia Echo,* which survived into the early 1970s and was supportive of the **United Party (UP),** its last editor being the UP MP for **Banjul** Central.

Many of the newspapers that appeared from the 1960s to the early 1990s were little more than a few pages of duplicated text, but in the early 1990s there was a return to properly printed newspapers, the most important being *The Point* and *The Daily Observer,* the latter being the first daily newspaper in The Gambia. The **People's Progressive Party (PPP)** had its own newspaper, *The Gambia Times,* in the 1980s, but it collapsed before the coup which swept away the PPP. The **People's Democratic Organisation for Independence and Socialism (PDOIS)** established, and continues to publish, its own cyclostyled newspaper, *Foroyaa,* when the movement was launched in the mid-1980s. PDOIS leaders were believed to be behind the clandestine and freely distributed occasional publication, *The Voice of the Future,* which attacked the PPP government in the strongest terms from the late 1970s until the 1981 coup attempt.

Altogether, there have been a dozen newspapers in The Gambia since

World War II, many of them poorly produced and written and subject to intermittent publication. Several have had political affiliations, and most have taken a critical stance towards government, a tradition laid down in the late colonial period. The colonial administration, the PPP government, and the **Armed Forces Provisional Ruling Council (AFPRC)/Alliance for Patriotic Re-orientation and Construction (APRC)** regime have all sought to restrain the more defamatory and inflammatory publications by means of libel and sedition laws, but this has not stopped individual newspapers and journalists from courting legal prosecution or other measures (such as withholding advertisements or restricting access to newsprint or the government printing press—ironically, used to print some newspapers critical of the government). All newspapers face serious financial problems, owing to limited circulation and advertising revenue. Many journalists have also lacked the opportunity for specialist training, though some are former employees of the government information ministry, which produces its own news publication—*The Gambia News Bulletin* (now relaunched as *The Gambia Daily*).

Radio and Television: Radio developed in the 1950s with government "rediffusion" of material over a public loudspeaker system in **Bathurst.** The British government presented the country with a small radio station at independence, with only limited broadcasting hours. This has since been extended to include Community Radio Stations in three provincial centers, and there are four private radio stations: Radio Syd, Radio One FM, Citizen FM, and Sud FM (a branch of the Senegalese Dakar Sud FM), principally broadcasting popular music and advertizements. For a time during the early days of the **Senegambia Confederation,** limited air time was provided on Senegalese television for Gambian programs. President **Yahya Jammeh** launched a free national television service as part of his electoral campaign in 1996. While principally limiting itself to general information and entertainment, state-run radio and television in The Gambia has always been accused of giving unfair coverage to the government of the day during elections. Certainly a significant amount of airtime is given to the activities of the head of state and the government.

NIAMINA. One of the nine **Mandinka**-controlled kingdoms located along the south bank of the **Gambia River** in the early 19th century, located directly east and south of the river as it makes its great bend to the east. By the late 1870s, most of the traditional rulers had been driven out or had assumed a subordinate position to **Fodi Kabba.** Niamina was the most westerly extension of the Kingdom of **Fuladu,** and therefore its eastern section was a battleground between the **Marabout** forces and those of **Alfa** and **Musa Molloh.** During the 20th-century British reorganization of the **Protectorate,** Niamina was joined with the territory of the old Mandinka Kingdom of **Eropina.** This composite was placed in the **MacCarthy Island** Division, then subdivided into three districts, each under the direction of a chief.

NIANI. A north bank area which stretches from Nianiji Bolon on the west to Sandugu Bolon on the east. In the early 19th century, this large territory was divided into two **Mandinka** dominated kingdoms. In the 1830s, **Kemintang** caused considerable disturbance in the area and for a time dominated Upper Niani despite British attempts to defeat him. The ruler of Lower Niani, whose base was at Kataba, maintained excellent relations with the British in the 1840s, dating from the time when British military forces protected him from Kemintang. Despite the practice of allowing **Marabouts** a premier place in the kingdoms, Niani became a major battleground in the **Soninke-Marabout Wars.** Bounded on the west by **Ma Bah's** kingdom of **Baddibu** (Rip) and on the east by **Wuli,** which was dominated by **Bakari Sardu,** the territory was ravaged by a series of competing armies. In the 1880s, the contending forces of **Mamadou N'Dare** and **Sait Maty** continued the unrest in Niani. Niani was divided into two districts in the 20th-century British reorganization of the **Protectorate.** Upper Niani was renamed Sami. Each district was placed under the direction of a chief.

NIUMI. One of the five major north bank kingdoms controlled in the early 19th century by **Mandinka** rulers. Niumi was strategically located, fronting on the Atlantic Ocean and dominating the entrance to the **Gambia River.** Because of its geographical location, Niumi was in contact with the Europeans at an early date. In 1826, the British negotiated a treaty whereby the entire river frontage of Niumi passed to the British as the **Ceded Mile.** They immediately proceeded to build Fort Bullen in order to command the entrance to the Gambia River. Difficulties over this cession caused the **Barra or Anglo-Niumi War** of 1830–1831. During the **Soninke-Marabout Wars,** Niumi was a major battleground, as first **Ma Bah** and then his lieutenants sought to add the territory to the kingdom of **Baddibu. Amer Faal** was the most important of the **Marabouts** in Niumi. From his base at Tubab Kolon, he continued to raid through the area until a combined British and **Soninke** force took his fortified town in 1866. Thereafter there was relative peace in Niumi, largely because the British considered the security of Niumi vital for the maintenance of their authority in the Ceded Mile. In the 20th-century reorganization of the **Protectorate,** the area became a district in the Lower River Division (North Bank Division), and the ruler of Niumi was considered one of the most important chiefs of the Protectorate.

N'JIE, ALHAJI ALIEU BADARA, GMRG, GCMG, GCRG (awarded posthumously) (1904–1982). Civil servant and politician, born of a **Wolof** family in **Bathurst.** Although their names are the same, he was not related to **Ebrimah Dowda N'Jie** or **Pierre Sarr N'Jie.** He attended Methodist mission schools in Bathurst and entered the civil service in 1925. He held a number of positions and retired in 1958 as the Registrar of the Supreme Court. Although a Muslim, N'Jie opposed the **Gambia Muslim Congress's** attempt to use **religion** for political purposes, and instead helped form the **Gambia Democratic Party (GDP).** Following the demise of the GDP, he joined the **People's Progressive Party (PPP)** and headed a number of ministries before being appointed in the late 1960s as Minister of State for External Affairs and Resident Minister in Dakar. In the reshuffle of ministries after Gambia became a republic, he was made Minister of Information and, in 1971, was appointed Minister of State in the President's Office. Dropped as candidate in **Kombo** North, where he was the sitting MP, to make way for a woman candidate, he was persuaded to lead the PPP election campaign, but was killed in a helicopter crash on April 21, 1982, while traveling with the presidential entourage to Brikamaba in **MacCarthy Island** Division.

N'JIE, EBRIMAH DOWDA (?–1970). Lawyer, civil servant, and politician, and one of the founding members of the **United Party (UP).** Unlike his brother, **Pierre Sarr N'Jie,** Ebrimah tended to stay in the background. Although a member of the House of Representatives, a minister in his brother's government of 1961, and the party's Deputy Leader, he did not aspire to high office. He agreed to join in a postindependence coalition government with the **People's Progressive Party (PPP)** in early 1965 and held ministerial office for several months, until breaking with the PPP over the decision to introduce a referendum on a republic in November that year. P. S. N'Jie had earlier withdrawn his party's participation from a coalition administration. A rift in the UP in May 1970 caused the party to depose P. S. N'Jie as leader and elect Ebrimah to succeed him. However, before his leadership could really be tested, he was killed in an automobile accident on October 19, 1970.

N'JIE, PIERRE SARR (1909–1993). A **Bathurst** barrister and politician. He was born on July 17, 1909, and educated at St. Augustine's School, Bathurst. While in his early twenties, he worked in a series of government departments, including the Public Works Department. He eventually became an Assistant Clerk of the Courts. In 1943, he left for England and served briefly in the Royal Artillery. He began his legal training in 1944 at Lincoln's Inn and was called to the Bar in 1948. He returned to the Gambia and began practicing law in Bathurst. In 1951, he was defeated for an elected seat on the **Legislative Council.** Shortly afterward, he and other **Wolof** formed the **United Party (UP).** In 1954, he was elected to the Legislative Council with the highest number of votes in the poll. The following year he clashed openly with Governor **Sir Percy Wyn-Harris** and resigned from the government. His absence from government proved fortunate, since he escaped the stigma of appearing to be controlled by the British. In the elections of 1960 for an expanded House of Representatives, the UP returned six members, although the newly formed **People's Progressive Party (PPP)** showed great popular strength in the **Protectorate.** In 1961, N'Jie's rapport with the Protectorate chiefs influenced Governor **Sir Edward Henry Windley's** decision to appoint him the Gambia's first Chief Minister. However, in the 1962 elections, the UP could win only 13 seats to the PPP's 18, and P. S. N'Jie became the leader of the opposition.

The influence of the UP continued to decline after Gambian independence, despite its power base in the old **Colony** area and its coalitions with other Gambian parties. N'Jie's popularity also waned, and in May 1970 he was replaced as leader of the United Party by his brother, **Ebrimah Dowda N'Jie.** After his brother's death in 1970, the party once more chose P. S. as leader. In late 1972, his political fortunes reached a nadir when he was barred from the House of Representatives because of non-attendance. He took little active part in the 1977 general elections, seldom venturing out of his home on Buckle Street, save to go to daily Mass at the nearby Roman Catholic cathedral, and played no part in political life subsequently. An engaging but erratic personality, P. S. N'Jie, even in political decline, continued to enjoy strong support among older women voters in **Banjul.** He found it particularly difficult to adjust to the Protectorate's domination of political life after 1962 and stayed away from parliament as an unhelpful (from the UP's point of view) gesture of protest. He died on December 11, 1993.

N'JIE-SAIDY, MRS. ISATOU (1952–   ). Vice President of the Republic of The Gambia. She was born at Kuntaya, North Bank Division, on March 15, 1952. A mother of four children, N'Jie-Saidy was educated at **Armitage** High **School,** 1969–1970, and **Yundum College,** 1971–1974. She undertook graduate studies at the Delft Research Institute for Management Science, the Netherlands, receiving a Diploma in Industrial Management, in 1979; at the University of the Philippines, receiving a Certificate in Small-Scale Industrial Information Management, in 1981; and at the University of Wales, Swansea, receiving an M.Sc. Economics (Social and Economic Development) in 1989. Her varied career included periods as a schoolteacher, 1970–1976; she was Senior Business Adviser with the Indigenous Business Advisory Bureau, 1976–1983, and Departmental Executive Secretary of the Women's Bureau of the National Women's Council, 1983–1989. At the same time she served on various boards and committees, among them the Gambia College Council, the National Scholarship Advisory Board, the Royal Victoria Hospital Management Board, and the Mile Two Prison Visiting Committee. She also chaired the National Civic Education Panel, 1995–1996.

NOHOR. **Wolof** term which distinguishes a person whose father was *dema* (a witch) but whose mother was not a witch. Such people are believed to be gifted with second sight, but cannot otherwise do harm.

NYAMALO. The title given in **Mandinka** society to the lowborn caste of artisans, or praise singers, comparable to the Wolof *nenyo.*

-O-

O'CONNOR, MAJOR-GENERAL LUKE SMYTHE (1806–1873). Governor of the Gambia from 1852 to 1859 and Commander in Chief of British military forces in West Africa. Born in Dublin on April 15, 1806, O'Connor joined the 1st West India Regiment as an ensign, in 1827 and worked his way up to Major-General in 1866. His regiment was sent to West Africa in 1843, and after a posting to British Honduras he returned to Africa in 1852 as Governor of the Gambia. O'Connor recommended a forward policy to the British government in order to secure **Bathurst** and the **Colony** area from the threat of both the **Marabouts** and the **Soninke** in adjacent areas. His suggestions were not accepted, and he was forced to follow a defensive posture in regard to those leaders who threatened British hegemony. O'Connor negotiated the cession of more territory from **Suling Jatta** of **Kombo,** and this helped precipitate open conflict with **Omar of Sabaji** and **Fodi Kabba** of **Gunjur.** He sent a punitive expedition to Sabaji in 1853, but this did not end the problem, and two years later, Omar directed a major thrust at the Soninke in Kombo and their British protectors. In June 1855, O'Connor's forces were defeated and he was wounded. Only by the most strenuous efforts, and with the support of the King of **Barra** and with French reinforcements from Senegal, was he able to resume the offensive and capture Sabaji. In April 1856, O'Connor arranged a truce between the Marabouts and Soninkes in Kombo. He was responsible for major additions to the town of Bathurst; he supervised the construction of a barracks and a civil hospital, and the Albert Market dates from his tenure. After peace returned to Kombo, O'Connor resumed his practice of touring the upriver areas, attempting to secure a rapprochement with the riverine rulers in this brief lull in the fighting between traditionalists and Muslims. Returning to duties in the Caribbean, O'Connor was responsible for putting down the Morant Bay rising in Jamaica in 1865. He died in Dresden on March 24, 1873.

O'HARA, GENERAL CHARLES (1740?–1802). An officer of the Coldstream Guards who became, in 1766, the first Governor of the **Province of Senegambia,** and was also founder of O'Hara's Corps. O'Hara was the illegitimate son of an Irish peer, the second Lord Tyrawley. After a distinguished military record in Germany and Portugal, he was appointed Commandant at Goree, Senegal, in 1766, and Lieutenant-Colonel of the **Royal African Corps,** a force of three infantry companies largely made up of military delinquents, raised specifically for the defense of the territory. One company was posted to the Gambia and was stationed at James Fort. O'Hara devoted most of his energies to the problems of Senegal, leaving the Lieutenant-Governors in the Gambia to deal with the problems of trade, diplomacy with Gambian chiefs, and the threat of a revived France. Unfortunately, the Lieutenant-Governors tended to disobey orders, carry on private trade, and, in general, act without restraint. In 1775, the problem of governing the Senegambia was compounded by the cruel and arbitrary actions of Lieutenant-Governor **Matthias MacNamara.** Thus, when O'Hara ended his 11-year tour, the Province was in turmoil. Afterwards, O'Hara served in the American colonies (being present at the British surrender at Yorktown), in the West Indies, India, and the Mediterranean. He ended his career as Governor of Gibraltar. O'Hara died of the effects of earlier war wounds on February 21, 1802.

OMAR OF SABAJI (Sukuta). Little is known of his life before his arrival in the Gambia, except that he was a Mauritanian and had taken part in Abd-el-Kader's uprising against the French in Algeria in 1847, where he had acquired a modicum of military training. In the Gambia, he moved to Sabaji where, in conjunction with other **Marabouts,** he began to organize the population disaffected by the forced cession of their town to the British in 1853. He was also responsible for spreading the belief that he had the power to turn British bullets into water. Omar supported **Fodi Kabba** in his dispute with **Kombo,** which led directly to the storming of the latter's town and the death of Kombo's ruler, **Suling Jatta,** in June 1855. This, plus further disturbances at Sabaji, convinced the British Governor, **Colonel Luke S. O'Connor,** to send a small military detachment to Sabaji. This force was driven out and retreated to Jeshwang and, after O'Connor with all of his available troops, had marched to their relief, he decided to take his 260 men and attack Sabaji directly. The people of Sabaji, led by Omar, and reinforced from other towns, trapped O'Connor's troops. The British had to retreat, with a quarter of their number killed or wounded. If Omar had pressed his advantage, he could have bypassed O'Connor and marched on **Bathurst.** With reinforcements from **Barra** and Kombo, and French troops from Goree, O'Connor and the West African regiments marched to Sabaji, and after fierce fighting, took the town on July 15, 1855. Omar escaped and fled the Gambia, presumably for Senegal, and thereafter was never a factor in the **Soninke-Marabout** conflicts.

ORD, MAJOR-GENERAL SIR HARRY ST. GEORGE, CB, KCMG, GCMG (1819–1885). Major-General, Royal Engineers, and colonial Governor. Born at North Cray, Kent, on June 17, 1819, Ord enrolled at the Royal Military Academy (Woolwich) in 1835. He was sent to the West Indies, 1840–1845 and undertook special duties on the West African coast and Ascension Island in 1849–1850. He was sent to Africa again in November 1855 on a special mission to the Gold Coast. Ord was Lieutenant-Governor of the West Indian island of Dominica, 1857–1861, and became Governor of Bermuda in 1861. During a leave of absence in November 1864, Ord was appointed a Special Commissioner in connection with the Ashanti disturbances on the Gold Coast. He returned to Bermuda in November 1866. Ord became the first Governor of the Straits

Settlements (Malaya), 1867–1873, and, after a period of unemployment, was made lieutenant-governor of South Australia and Governor of Western Australia in 1878. He retired in 1879 and died on August 20, 1885.

Ord's findings, based on his visit to West Africa in 1864–1865 as a Parliamentary Commissioner investigating the position of the **British West African Settlements,** had a great bearing on official British policy toward the region. Although agreeing in the main with those critics of colonial policy who believed that these settlements were not profitable, he did not recommend their abandonment. With special reference to the Gambia and Freetown, he concluded that Britain had a moral obligation to the African people who had sought the protection of the Crown. Agreeing with Governor **G. A. K. D'Arcy,** Ord stated in his 1865 report that some way should be found to extend British protection to the troubled areas on the north bank of the **Gambia River.** The Select Committee of Parliament used Ord's report as justification for a no-expansion doctrine that became the official British policy for two decades.

ORFEUR, CHARLES (?–1745). Chief Agent of the **Royal African Company** beginning in 1718. He had joined the company only a few months earlier as a writer. His attempts to repair James Fort and to improve the Company's trade were interrupted by the appearance in of pirates in 1719. They sacked the fort, took a number of ships as prizes, and scattered the small garrison. In 1721, Orfeur handed over what was left of the garrison to the new Governor, Colonel Thomas Whitney. He was replaced in command of the trading activities by two new merchant **factors.** Orfeur continued in the Company's service in a subordinate position until 1723, when the death of his superiors once more placed him in charge of the Company's trading activities. He assisted **Captain Bartholomew Stibbs** to prepare for his upriver expedition and commanded one of the Company ships in action in 1726 against a would-be pirate. In mid-1727, he gave over supreme authority to Daniel Pepper, who proceeded to loot the Company of as much as he could. Eventually, in 1737, Orfeur was given the permanent appointment of Chief Agent in the Gambia, and he endeavored to increase the Company's profits despite increasing French competition and the resumption of the Anglo-French wars in 1743. He was killed by some of the subjects of the King of **Barra** in 1745 while on a trade mission.

ORGANIZATION FOR THE DEVELOPMENT OF THE GAMBIA RIVER BASIN/ORGANISATION POUR LE MISE EN VALEUR DU FLEUVE GAMBIE (OMVG). Established in 1978 to coordinate the development of the **Gambia River** basin in the Senegal-Gambia region, its headquarters is located at Kaolack in Senegal. OMVG membership was subsequently extended to include Guinea and Guinea-Bissau. Long-range plans for a bridge-barrage at Yelitenda in The Gambia and a hydroelectric plant at Kekriti in Senegal, together with schemes for the upper Gambia in Guinea, have failed to materialize, owing to the difficulties in raising external funding and concerns about the environmental impact of some of the proposals.

OZANNE, JOHN HENRY (?–1902). Appointed as the first **Travelling Commissioner** for the north bank of the **Gambia River** in 1893. His district began at Suara Creek and extended past Niambantang approximately 120 miles upriver. Like his counterpart, **Cyril Frederic Sitwell,** on the south bank, he traveled the entire area on foot, stopping at each major village to explain its new position in the scheme of **Protectorate** government. Later he passed on the newest regulations, which had been decided on in **Bathurst.** He also adjudicated disagreements between villages and sat with the African rulers when they heard civil or criminal cases. Considering the long history of disorders in his territory, Ozanne surprisingly found little hostility or resentment. This was due, perhaps, to the proximity of the French who were greatly disliked both by the people and by their rulers. Before he died in Bathurst on February 28, 1902. Ozanne had firmly established the basis of British rule in the northern parts of the Protectorate.

-P-

PALMER, SIR HENRY RICHMOND, KCMG, CMG, CBE (1877– 1958). Colonial Governor and scholar. Palmer was born on April 20, 1877, and educated at Oundle and Trinity College, Cambridge. He joined the Nigerian colonial service in 1904 as an Assistant Resident. After serving as Resident, Bornu, Palmer rose to become Lieutenant-Governor, Northern Nigeria. He was Governor of the Gambia, 1930–1933, and ended his colonial service as Governor of Cyprus. He also qualified as a barrister.

Palmer's Northern Nigerian background was evident in his approach to the administration of the Gambia **Protectorate.** In 1933, he issued his *Political Memoranda for the Guidance of Commissioners,* which reflected many of the concepts of **indirect rule** as enunciated by Lord Lugard and

Sir Donald Cameron. He also issued a series of ordinances in 1933 designed to regularize and standardize government and court activities in the Protectorate. In the previous year he had added a second African member to the **Legislative Council** and also appointed one of the Commissioners of the Protectorate to the Council. This was the first time the Protectorate was directly represented in the central government. In 1931, Governor Palmer also sponsored the formation of the advisory **Bathurst** Urban District Council to act as a point of contact between the people of the **Colony** and the government. This organization later developed into the Bathurst Town Council. Palmer was also an accomplished Arabic scholar and historian and, in 1931, published *The Carthaginian Voyage to West Africa in 500 B.C. together with Sultan Mohammed Bello's Account of the Origin of the Fulbe.*

PARK, MUNGO (1773–1805). Scottish physician and explorer. He was sponsored by the **Association for the Discovery of the Interior Regions of Africa** in 1795 to investigate the many rumors connected with the Niger River, and he spent some time studying **Mandinka** at Dr. Laidley's station at Karantaba before leaving the Gambia on his first expedition. After many hardships, he reached Segu and the Niger before being forced to turn back. He returned to the Gambia in September 1798 with definite proof of the existence of the great river and its direction of flow, and some knowledge of the people of the western savannah. In 1805, Park, this time sponsored by the Colonial Office, set out from the Gambia on his ill-fated second expedition. There were far too many Europeans in the large entourage, and the journey was begun during the rainy season. By the time Bamako was reached, only Park and four companions were healthy enough to continue. They constructed a raft and floated down the Niger as far as Bussa (in present-day Nigeria), where they are believed to have drowned in the rapids. Park's journal of his second expedition was later brought to the coast by one of his followers, Issaco. Park's two expeditions were the tangible beginnings of the drive by Europeans to open the interior of West Africa.

PATEY, REAR ADMIRAL, G.C.E., CMG. The Administrator of the Gambia from 1866 to 1871. He was one of the key informants for the Colonial and Foreign Offices in their attempt to exchange the Gambia for suitable territory elsewhere in Africa. He agreed with **Sir Arthur Kennedy,** his immediate supervisor, that there were few good reasons for Britain to retain the Gambia. He reported that the cost of maintaining the garrison was high and the bulk of the **groundnut** trade was already dominated by the French. The endemic warfare between **Fodi Kabba** and the **Soninke** rulers of **Kombo** fostered his belief that little could be done to improve the condition of Africans adjacent to the **Colony.** Patey's attitude was, without doubt, colored by the disastrous cholera epidemic which struck the Colony in late April 1869. Before the disease had run its course, over 1,100 citizens of **Bathurst,** out of a population of 4,000, had died. Patey was the Administrator during the height of the upriver violence attendant on the rise of **Alfa Molloh** and the collapse of **Ma Bah's** empire.

PAUL, SIR JOHN WARBURTON, GCMG, KCMG, OBE, MC (1916–). Paul was born on March 29, 1916, and educated at Weymouth College and Selwyn College, Cambridge. He was commissioned in the Royal Tank Regiment in 1937 and captured by the Germans in 1940. Released from a prisoner of war camp in 1945, he was appointed as ADC and Private Secretary to the Governor of Sierra Leone. After being called to the bar at the Middle Temple in 1947, he returned to Sierra Leone, working his way up from District Commissioner to Provincial Commissioner (1959) and Secretary to the Cabinet (1960). Paul was Governor of the Gambia, 1962–1965, and stayed on until 1966 as Governor-General. He was Governor of British Honduras, 1966–1972, and of the Bahamas, 1972–1973. On retiring from the Colonial Service he served as Deputy-Governor of the Isle of Man, 1974–1980. In the Gambia, he immediately established good relations with the then Chief Minister, **Pierre Sarr N'Jie,** and his successor, **Sir Dawda Jawara,** who became the first Prime Minister. From the first, Paul recognized that his position was transitional, and he contributed much to the framing of Gambian proposals for independence.

PEANUTS. See GROUNDNUTS.

PEOPLE'S DEMOCRATIC ORGANISATION FOR INDEPENDENCE AND SOCIALISM (PDOIS). Familiarly known as DOI, the PDOIS emerged in 1986 from a marxist pan-African socialist clandestine group (Red Star) centered on three highly principled radical intellectuals, **Sidia Jatta, Halifah Sallah,** and Sam Sarr, who were widely believed to be the publishers of the banned political periodical, *Voice of the Future.* DOI was highly critical of the moderate pro-Western policies of the **Dawda Jawara** government as well as of its domestic record. Technically a political movement rather than a party, it was not banned following the military takeover in July 1994, despite occasional clashes with the **Armed Forces Provisional Ruling Council (AFPRC).**

DOI contested general elections in 1987, 1992, and 1997, winning its first and only seat in the last-mentioned election. It was not simply the leftist ideology of DOI that cost it support; it also lacked experience of organizing electoral campaigns and was ideologically opposed to the patronage system that underlies the political process. Consequently, though it increased the number of its candidates from four in 1987, to 14 five years later, and finally to 17 in 1997, it was only in the last of these elections that it won a seat. Party spokesperson Sidia Jatta won **Wuli,** his home district, with a minority share of the vote. Elsewhere, DOI fared best in the Greater **Banjul** area; Halifah Sallah took a third of the votes in Serekunda East, still not enough to win. Jatta also stood as presidential candidate in 1992 and 1996, clearly more as a gesture than in serious expectation of defeating either Sir Dawda Jawara or **Yahya Jammeh.** Jatta was elected party leader at DOI's congress in December 1997, breaking with the movement's previous practice of collective leadership. Sallah was elected Secretary-General, and other members of the party executive were Amie Sillah, Adama Bah, Sheikh Ndow, and Sam Sarr. Notwithstanding its reputation for political integrity, and its attempt to relocate itself ideologically toward the center, DOI remains a fringe political organization. It collected less than 8 percent of the national vote in the 1997 election, but continues to provide trenchant criticism of the Jammeh government, despite the latter's self-designated radical political program, both in the National Assembly and in its newspaper, *Foroyaa.*

PEOPLE'S DEMOCRATIC PARTY (PDP). Small, moderate, short-lived political party set up by a medical doctor from **Kombo, Dr. Lamin Bojang,** to contest the 1992 general and presidential elections. Given that he had no previous political experience, Bojang did remarkably well to gain 6 percent of the presidential vote, although he came in a poor third in the parliamentary election in Kombo Central. None of the other 16 PDP candidates succeeded in winning, although the party obtained some 4.5 percent of the total vote. The party relied to an extent on defectors from the main parties as its candidates, and financial support came from a maverick **Serahuli** businessman, Solo Dabo, who had previously backed the **People's Progressive Party (PPP)** and then the **National Convention Party (NCP).** The PDP became moribund after the 1992 elections, and financial and organizational problems prevented Bojang from standing in the 1996 presidential elections. Instead, he threw in his lot with **Yahya**

Jammeh and the **Alliance for Patriotic Re-orientation and Construction (APRC).**

PEOPLE'S PROGRESSIVE ALLIANCE (PPA). See **SISAY, SHERIFF.**

PEOPLE'S PROGRESSIVE PARTY (PPP). This was originally formed by David (now **Sir Dawda) Jawara, Sanjally Bojang,** and other **Protectorate** representatives to contest the 1960 elections. The PPP evolved from the Protectorate People's Society, an organization aiming to promote the interests of provincials, and particularly **Mandinka** young men, living in the **Bathurst** area, which had been founded on December 30, 1957. First known as the **Protectorate People's Party,** reflecting its original constituency, the PPP was formally launched at **Basse,** Upper River Division, to coincide with the annual Protectorate Chiefs Conference in 1960. The word "People" was adopted to combat accusations of tribalism. Nevertheless, PPP support remained strongest in the Protectorate (subsequently renamed the Provinces) with its greatest support among the Mandinka people.

In the 1960 elections, the PPP won eight seats to the House of Representatives as against only six won by the **United Party (UP).** This was counterbalanced, however, by the eight appointed chiefs, and when the Governor, **Sir Edward Henry Windley,** decided to appoint a Chief Minister, he selected **Pierre Sarr N'Jie,** the UP leader, instead of Jawara, the PPP leader. At the next election in 1962, for an expanded House in which the chiefs' powers had been greatly reduced, the PPP won 18 of the contested seats. The PPP took the country to independence and won every election subsequently, until overthrown in the military coup of 1994. When The Gambia became a republic in 1970, its presidential candidate, Jawara, won every presidential election with a substantial majority. In the last election he contested, in 1992, he won over 58 percent of the vote, 2 percent more than President **Yahya Jammeh** obtained in the presidential election of 1996.

PPP policy was characterized by moderation in domestic policy and external relations. Relations with the British always remained good, independence was achieved with a minimum of friction, and the PPP cultivated good relations with Britain and the West in subsequent years. It also pursued good relations with the socialist bloc and most African and third world states as well, consistent with its policy of diversifying its aid partners. The PPP came to be dominated by its leader, particularly after the move to an executive presidency in 1970, and during its long period in office, several presumed challengers were either expelled from the party or demoted, and usually reappointed later. The party tended to ossify with power and incurred increasing criticism from disaffected elements from inside and outside its ranks. The **People's Progressive Alliance (PPA), National Convention Party (NCP),** and **Gambia People's Party (GPP)** were examples of the former; other attacks came from youth elements, both from inside the party and from radical elements in the wider society.

The PPP's inability to respond to mounting accusations of corruption and cronyism, together with its unshakable grip on the electoral process, led a growing number of its critics to contemplate extra-constitutional action against it. It survived a coup attempt in 1981, but succumbed to another putsch in July 1994. The new military regime abolished the PPP as one of its first political measures. Although vilified by its opponents, and particularly by the military junta, the PPP's record in maintaining an open political system was rarely surpassed in postcolonial Africa, and its economic and social performance, notwithstanding periodic exposure of corruption, again compared favorably with many better-endowed countries on the African continent.

PETERS, LENRIE (?–1968). Journalist and political activist. Born in Sierra Leone, among his children was Dr. Florence Mahoney, a distinguished Gambian educationalist and historian. Peters edited the *Gambia Echo* from December 1947 until his death in 1968. Originally an accountant with Elder Dempster, he spent most of his later years with the trading firm of S. **Madi,** ending as a director. Peters died in **Bathurst** on February 14, 1968.

PETERS, DR. LENRIE (1932–   ). Poet and surgeon born in **Bathurst** and named after his uncle. Peters was educated in secondary schools in the Gambia and Freetown and graduated from Trinity College, Cambridge. He completed medical school at University College Hospital, London, in 1959 and then studied surgery at Guildford, U.K. Later, he became a member of the Royal College of Surgeons. Returning to the Gambia, he continued the practice of medicine and became the Chief Surgeon and Director of the **Protectorate** Hospital at Bansang. Leaving the civil service, he entered private practice and runs the Westfield Clinic at **Serekunda.**

While he was still in the United Kingdom, *Poems,* his first collection of poetry, was published in 1964 by Mbari Press in Ibadan, Nigeria. The following year he published a semiautobiographical novel entitled, *The Second Round*. These two works brought him to the attention of literary England and he appeared on a number of radio programs on the BBC. His reputation as one of Africa's finest poets was enhanced by the publication of three other works: *Satellites* (1967), *Katchikali* (1971), and *Selected Poems* (1982). Peters played an important role in the transition from military to civilian rule in 1995–1996, chairing the National Consultative Commission set up in December 1995 by the **Armed Forces Provisional Ruling Council (AFPRC)** to gauge public opinion.

PORTENDIC. A trading station in Mauritania for merchants dealing in gum arabic. Theoretical British rights to trade there were surrendered by a treaty with France in 1857, in exchange for the cession of **Albreda** on the north bank of the **Gambia River.**

PORTUGUESE TOWN. One of the original small villages that made up **Bathurst** in its early days, located along the shore, north of the administrative center of the settlement. It was the business center and the most prosperous area; deriving its name, according to **Sir John Milner Gray,** from its mulatto population—known as "Portuguese"—who migrated there from St. Louis and Goree when those settlements were returned to the French in 1814. These residents constituted the largest element of the town's population in its early days and were made up of merchants and their dependents and artisans. Another theory claims the district acquired its name from settlers from the Portuguese colony of Cape Verde, who arrived in a schooner in the 19th century.

PROTECTORATE. The Protectorate of the Gambia came into being in 1889, through a policy of gradual British encroachment on riverine territory to the interior of the earlier established British **Colony** of the Gambia, centered on **Bathurst.** The need to intervene in the political affairs of the interior in the closing decades of the 19th century was brought about by the **Soninke-Marabout Wars** and by growing French interest in the region. The Anglo-French demarcation of the boundaries of the Gambia enabled the British, by 1901, to consolidate their administration of the Protectorate.

In keeping with British policy elsewhere, the Governor, **Sir Robert B. Llewelyn,** adopted the practice of **indirect rule,** whereby, as far as possible, and subject to observance of British standards and acceptance of the guidance of British officials, local administration was placed in the hands of 35 district chiefs and a larger number of village headmen. British field officers, **Travelling Commissioners,** later renamed Divisional Commissioners, were responsible for the general supervision of African rulers and, with the introduction of legal, fiscal, and administrative measures, they aimed at a gradual modernization of rural administration. The system had the merit of maintaining the British presence with the minimum of disruption and cost; its downside was that very little development took place, and power was largely in the hands of a handful of European officials and the chiefs.

Protectorate Africans were "British protected persons" rather than "British subjects," and in consequence did not enjoy the legal or constitutional rights enjoyed in the Colony proper until 1960, when a national electoral system was introduced, with a majority of elected seats in the new House of Representatives given to the Protectorate. This not only marked the end of Colony dominance of political life, but also saw the demise of the power of chiefs. Following independence, the name "Protectorate" was changed to "Provinces," to symbolically put an end to historical divisions in Gambian society. Rural administration also changed: while Divisional Commissioners were retained as agents of central government in the Provinces, six elected Area Councils were set up to take on some of the administrative and developmental responsibilities of the chiefs. Since independence in 1965, successive Gambian governments have put the Provinces at the center of their national development programs, but though all Gambians now enjoy the same legal rights, living conditions and opportunities for personal advancement remain significantly worse in rural areas, accounting for the steady migration to the **Banjul** area. See also **Ozanne, J. H; Palmer, Sir Henry Richmond; and Sitwell, Cyril Frederic.**

PROTECTORATE PEOPLE'S SOCIETY/PROTECTORATE PEOPLE'S PARTY. See PEOPLE'S PROGRESSIVE PARTY.

-Q-

QADIRIYYA. The chief Muslim *tariq,* or mystical brotherhood, in western Africa in the 19th century. Founded in Baghdad by Muhammad Abd Al Djilani (1079–1166), it was introduced into the sahelian region of West Africa in the 15th century by Muhammad Abd Al Karim Al-Maghribi. It was the first such *tariq* formed to make the doctrines of Islam more intelligible to the ordinary believer, but it lost ground to the **Tijaniyya** and **Mouride** brotherhoods in Senegambia by the end of the 19th century.

QUADRANGLE. A group of government departments arranged in a hollow square, adjacent to State House in central **Banjul.** The oldest part dates back to the early 19th century, when it was used as an army barracks.

QUIN, THOMAS F. British merchant who was described as the most substantial trader in the Gambia in the early 1860s. He had previously been in the employ of the government. Quin was one of the most vocal opponents of the two plans to exchange the Gambia for French territory. Although his fortunes in the Gambia had declined by 1875, he remained a powerful aid to the London and Manchester Chambers of Commerce in bringing pressure to bear on the government to end the negotiations with France.

-R-

RECAPTIVES. See LIBERATED AFRICANS.

REEVE, HENRY FENWICK, CMG, MICE, FRGS, FSA (1854–1920). Reeve, who was born in Kent on April 7, 1854, and educated at Melbourne University, Australia, worked for the governments of New South Wales, Victoria, Fiji, and the West Indies before being appointed as Chief Commissioner of the Anglo-French Boundary Commissions of 1895–1896 and 1898–1899, to demarcate the boundaries of the Gambia. In 1912, Reeve published a book entitled *The Gambia,* which remains a good reference work for some aspects of African migrations and European occupation. It is particularly valuable for the section written by Dr. Hopkinson on animal and plant life in the Gambia at the beginning of the twentieth century. Reeve left the Gambia for Lagos, where he served as Acting-Governor in 1902. He died on January 18, 1920.

REFFELL, JOSEPH (?–1886). Son of **Thomas Reffell** and a leader of the repatriate African community in **Bathurst.** Educated in Freetown, he found employment as a sergeant and clerk in the military store in Bathurst, until dismissed. He then worked for two different European merchants as a trader upriver, but again was dismissed. Notwithstanding all this, Reffell was provided with financial assistance from the **liberated African** community to pursue legal studies in Britain, with a view to defending their interests, but he was denied the right to practice. Not surprisingly, Reffell was a constant critic of the European merchants and the colonial administration, becoming one of the chief spokesmen for the younger generation of liberated Africans who were openly critical of British administration of the **Colony.** He was a regular correspondent for the *African Times,* which articulated the grievances of educated Africans against British rule. In the early 1870s, Reffell became one of the most important Gambian leaders in the struggle against Britain's proposal to exchange the Gambia for French territory elsewhere. In his later years he turned to **agriculture** and attempted to begin a cooperative farming system utilizing modern Western methods to produce tropical products for export.

REFFELL, THOMAS (1794–1849). A Christian **recaptive** Igbo who, in the 1820s, was resettled in **Bathurst** from Sierra Leone. His surname was taken from the European manager of the **Liberated African** Department in Sierra Leone. A former soldier, he became a trader and was affluent enough to afford to educate his son, **Joseph Reffell,** in Sierra Leone. He served with distinction in the volunteer militia during the **Barra War** of 1831. In 1842, he founded the Igbo Society, a voluntary association open to both men and women of Igbo descent. This was the first of the friendly societies which became major vehicles for expressing to government the opinion of important segments of Bathurst society.

RELIGION. The Gambia is an overwhelmingly Muslim society, with over 95 percent of the population professing Islam. There is a small but influential Christian minority, just over 4 percent of the populace—42,083, according to the 1993 population census—three-quarters of whom live in the Greater **Banjul** area and **Brikama.** It is hard to determine how many Gambians still adhere to traditional religions; only 836 admitted to this in the 1993 census, but this tiny number conceals the persistence of older forms of religious belief among those belonging to the two world faiths. Belief in magic is still evident, and Muslim **Marabouts** are frequently consulted about occult matters and provide charms and amulets to invoke supernatural intervention or ward off malign forces. The presence of Islam in the Senegambia region, in limited forms—principally in the form of proselytizing individual Muslim traders—dates back centuries, but it was only in the 18th and 19th centuries, and particularly as the result of the **Soninke-Marabout Wars** in the second half of the latter century, that Islam overwhelmed, though never quite wiped out, traditional African religious beliefs.

Christianity is a more recent presence. Portuguese attempts to convert Africans in the lower riverine areas in the 16th century did not survive, and it was only in first half of the 19th century that Christianity was reintroduced by Protestant and **Roman Catholic** missionaries. Among the former, the **Wesleyans** played the most important part, though **Anglicans** and, at one time, Quakers have been active too. Despite attempts to establish mission stations upriver, most Christian converts and their descendants are to be found in the area around Banjul, and the Anglican and Roman Catholic cathedrals, as well as the principal Wesleyan chapel, are located in the Gambian capital.

Notwithstanding their limited success in the religious sphere, the Christian missions in the Gambia, as elsewhere in British colonial Africa, were the principal providers of Western education, and many Muslims, later prominent in public life, were educated in Christian schools. A widely-observed characteristic of interfaith relations in The Gambia is the high degree of tolerance and cooperation between Muslims and Christians, and it is not unusual to have members of both faiths in the same family.

RENDALL, GEORGE (?–1837). Previously the acting Chief Justice of Sierra Leone, he was appointed Lieutenant-Governor of the Gambia in February 1830. He inherited the pent-up resentment of **Burungai Sonko,** the King of **Barra,** and his advisers. They felt they had been cheated by not receiving payment for the stone quarried at **Dog Island,** resented the cutting back on the king's subsidy, and most of all they felt the losses from custom duties after the cession of the **Ceded Mile.** A minor altercation between two men from Essau and the canteen operator of Fort Bullen triggered open warfare in August 1831. A motley group of soldiers, merchant sailors, and civilians decided to attack the stockaded town of Essau. They were repulsed by the townspeople with a number of casualties. The Europeans fled the scene, crossed over to **Bathurst,** and left Fort Bullen to the people of Essau. Governor Rendall's call for assistance was heeded by the French who sent troops and a warship. Their presence stabilized the situation. Burungai Sonko's forces repelled three attacks upon Essau, and by the end of the year the British had still not been able to take the town. Burungai Sonko, however, decided to make peace, and in January 1832 the **Barra War** came to an end. In 1834, Rendall was faced with another threat to British supremacy in the upper river, the actions of Chief **Kemintang.** A military expedition was sent against the chief's town of Dungasseen. This was a fiasco, and the British had to abandon three cannon in their retreat.

Perhaps the most telling failures of Rendall's tenure were the schemes to resettle **liberated Africans** in the Gambia. Large numbers were sent from Sierra Leone without proper advance planning. Some were sent to **MacCarthy Island,** others to the Ceded Mile, and others were posted outside Bathurst. With few funds and no coordination of administrative effort, there was little Rendall could do to relieve the plight of the majority of the freed slaves, and it was left to his successor to solve the problem of the liberated Africans. Rendall died in 1837 in Bathurst of yellow fever.

RICHARDS, ARTHUR FREDERICK, First Baron Milverton of Lagos and Clifton, Bristol, CMG, GCMG (1885–1978). Richards was born in Bristol on February 21, 1885, the son of a timber merchant. He was educated at Clifton College and Christ Church, Oxford. After university he entered the British colonial administration in Malaya, in 1908, and, over the next 22 years, rose to the rank of Governor of North Borneo. Singled out as a "high flyer," Richards was made Governor of the Gambia, where he served from 1933 to 1936. From the Gambia he was appointed Governor of Fiji and High Commissioner, Western Pacific, 1936–1938, and then Governor of Jamaica, 1938–1943. He returned to West Africa in 1943 as Governor of Nigeria, retiring in 1947 with a peerage. While heading the Gambian administration, Richards operated under the handicap of continued reduced revenues due to the world depression. Major developments during his short tenure were the two **Protectorate** Ordinances which clarified the major Ordinance of 1933 and established a new yard tax rate.

RICHARDS, J. D. (?–1918). Bathurst-born **Aku,** whose **liberated African** parents came from Abeokuta in western Nigeria. He was a prosperous merchant, prominent in the kola nut trade with Freetown and a senior member of the Methodist church. Richards was also Secretary of the Gambia Native Association, which championed the interests of the African community in their disputes with the colonial administration and European merchants from 1875 to the early 1880s. Despite this, he was appointed to the **Legislative Council** in March 1883, as its first African member, and there he continued to speak out against government on a number of issues.

RIP. See BADDIBU.

ROMAN CATHOLIC MISSION. The first Christian presence in the Gambia dates back to the middle of the 15th century, with the arrival of the Portuguese in the **Gambia River.** The first Christian burial, that of a sailor called Andrew, on board **Alvise da Cadamosto's** ship, took place in May 1456. The dead mariner was buried on a small island in the estuary of the river, which was named after him. St. Andrew's Island later, became the base of operations for the **Courlanders** and subsequently the British, who renamed it **James Island.** Prince Henry the Navigator sent out the Abbot of Sotto de Casa and a companion in 1549, to establish a mission to the Nomimansa (**Niumi** *mansa*)—the ruler of the coastal kingdom of Niumi, directly opposite present-day **Banjul.** The mission was not a success, although Portuguese traders subsequently established themselves in a number of riverine villages as far inland as **Barrakunda** Falls at the eastern extremity of the Gambia. These intermarried with local women to create an ostensibly Catholic community, known as "Portingales." Among their settlements were San Domingo, opposite James Island, Tankular, Kansala and **Geregia.** Churches as well as trading posts were constructed, although priests had to come from the Cape Verde Islands. By the end of the 18th century the "Portingales" had died out as a distinct community, and with them, the Catholic presence on the river.

The Catholic presence was renewed in 1823 by members of the French Sisters of Charity from Goree island in Senegal. These worked among the poor in **Bathurst,** but, as with other early Christian missions, ill-health forced them to leave. Catholic fathers from Paris established another mission in 1849–1850, and French nuns returned to Bathurst in 1883, with the arrival of three Sisters of Cluny, who were engaged principally in educational and charitable activities. Irish priests further strengthened the small Catholic presence among the urban **Wolof** and were also engaged in educational activities. St. Augustine's schools and the Roman Catholic cathedral on Hagan Street in Banjul, seat of the diocese of The Gambia, were the visible results of their endeavors. As with the Protestant missions, the Catholics are mainly confined to the area around Bathurst and eastern **Kombo.** Catholics are the largest of the Christian communities, numbering 27,200 at the end of 1995.

ROWE, SIR SAMUEL, KCMG (1835–1888). The son of a Wesleyan minister, Rowe was born in Macclesfield, Cheshire, on March 23, 1835, and qualified as a physician in 1856. He joined the Army medical staff in 1862 and was posted to Lagos. After a break to complete his medical studies in Britain in 1864–1866, he returned to West Africa, this time being posted to the Gold Coast. He served at various times in Lagos and the Gold Coast, took part in the Ashanti War of 1873–1874, and, after retiring from the Army as a brigadier-surgeon, was reemployed as an administrator by the Colonial Office. He served as Administrator of the Gambia, 1875–1877, and was promoted Governor of the **British West African Settlements**, 1877–1881. Rowe was then appointed Governor of the Gold Coast and Lagos, in which post he served from 1881 to 1884, and was reappointed as Governor of the West African Settlements in 1884. Rowe, described in an obituary as a "rough but kindly man," was a staunch imperialist who believed that both Britain and the Africans would prosper by extension of British rule into the hinterland. He opposed the schemes for exchanging the Gambia and was an implacable foe of the Colonial Office policy of surrendering to French demands in the Mellacourie, Porto Novo, and the Gambian interior. It was Rowe who planned the expedition of Administrator **Valesius Gouldsbury** into the upper Gambia. He died at Madeira on August 28, 1888, while returning home on leave.

ROYAL ADVENTURERS OF ENGLAND TRADING INTO AFRICA. A company chartered by Charles II to trade in West Africa. The glowing reports made by **Prince Rupert** were fundamental to the establishment of this Company. Despite royal support, particularly from James, Duke of York, the Adventurers did not find that trade was very profitable. The major reasons for lack of profits were trade losses incurred in the second Dutch War. In 1668, the Royal Adventurers sublet their monopoly to another trading company called the **Gambia Adventurers,** and in 1672 they relinquished it completely to the **Royal African Company.**

ROYAL AFRICAN COMPANY. An English chartered company that assumed a monopoly of trade in West Africa in 1672. Although the main area of Company concern was the Gold Coast, the Company did have a considerable investment in the Gambia. The main base in the Gambia as with previous trading companies was **James Island.** The chief **factor** of the Company was in command of a small number of soldiers and an even smaller civilian staff. In addition to James Island, the Company maintained other stations along the river. The number of these outstations varied, but there normally was trading activity on **MacCarthy Island,** near **Barrakunda** Falls, at **Bintang,** Banyon Point, and **Juffure.** At best, the profit levels were low since there were few natural products in the area and the Gambia never was an important **slave trading** entrepôt. Health conditions for servants of the Company were so poor that the trading posts were always understaffed and there was a high turnover of personnel.

Far more disastrous to the Company was the long series of European wars which pitted France against England. Local conflict with the French dated from 1681 when the French established a trading post at **Albreda** on the north bank opposite James Island. A French naval squadron forced the abandonment of James Island in 1693, and it was not reoccupied until 1698. In this latter year also, Parliament declared the West African trade open to all English merchants. The Royal African Company was still charged with the upkeep of the trade forts and could level a 10 percent duty on all goods imported to and exported from West Africa. During the War of the Spanish Succession, James Island was plundered by the French in 1704 and 1708. Only the exhaustion of the rival French company saved the Royal African Company from further depredations. The fort on James Island was rebuilt and reoccupied in 1717, but pirates sacked the island, and within four years it was necessary to send a new expedition to restore the fortunes of the Company. An attempt at sending European colonists in the 1720s proved a ghastly failure.

The period between 1730 and 1740 was the most prosperous in the long history of the Company. There was peace in Europe, the slave and gum trade was profitable, and the Company received a subsidy from Parliament. The War of the Austrian Succession ended this. Although the English destroyed Albreda, the war disturbed trade, and sickness and death forced the closing of the outstations and the near-abandonment of Fort James. In 1747, Parliament canceled its subsidy, and in 1752 the Royal African Company was finally dissolved by parliamentary action.

ROYAL AFRICAN CORPS (RAC). Formed in 1765 and composed largely of men drawn from the convict hulks in England and military offenders from other regiments, it nevertheless played an important role in the suppression of the **slave trade,** since men of the Corps served not only on land, but also on ships of the West African Patrol. At first it comprised three companies of foot soldiers and was called O'Hara's Corps, named after the first Governor of Senegambia, **Colonel Charles O'Hara.** Men of the Royal African Corps, under the command of **Captain Alexander Grant,** were responsible for occupying first **James Island** and then St. Mary's Island in 1816, and they later constructed the barracks and other public buildings in **Bathurst.** The RAC was merged with West Indian soldiers in 1840 to form the 3rd West India Regiment. Recruited from **liberated Africans** as well as from the Caribbean, its soldiers were much more resistant to tropical diseases than were European soldiers. The latter suffered appallingly—between May 1825 and July 1827, 276 of a total of 399 European soldiers landed at Bathurst died. Although white officers remained, European soldiers ceased to be recruited after 1827.

ROYAL WEST AFRICAN FRONTIER FORCE. See GAMBIA REGIMENT.

RUPERT, PRINCE, COUNT OF THE PALATINATE AND DUKE OF BAVARIA (1619–1682). Rupert was the third son of Elizabeth, Queen of Bohemia and Frederick V, Elector Palatine, and a nephew of King Charles I of England. During the English Civil War, he was one of the king's better generals. He accompanied the future Charles II into exile and took every opportunity of striking at the English Commonwealth government. One such venture concerned the Gambia when Rupert, preying on English commerce, arrived at the estuary of the **Gambia River** in February 1652. Learning of the presence of three ships of the Commonwealth, which had accompanied John Blake on a trading expedition, Rupert sailed upriver to St. Andrew's Island where he received assistance from the **Courlander** commander. He attacked Blake's ships and captured them and then sailed from the river northward to Cape Verde where one of his landing parties was captured by the **Wolof** near Rufisque. Rupert freed his men but was wounded by an arrow. He then left West Africa for the West Indies. While in the Gambia, Rupert came to believe the reports of huge gold deposits in the hinterland. Later, after the restoration, this story played an important role in the formation of the **Royal Adventurers.** Prince Rupert was one of the main sponsors of and investors in that company.

-S-

SABALLY, LIEUTENANT SANA (1994–). One of the four original planners of the July 22, 1994, army coup. A **Fulbe,** born in Kasa Kunda, near **Brikama** in the Western Division, his father was the *alkaaloo* of the village. He completed primary and part of his secondary education in Brikama, then was awarded a scholarship to **Armitage School, Janjangbure.** After working in a local supermarket he followed an elder brother into the army. Sabally was Vice Chairman of the **Armed Forces Provisional Ruling Council (AFPRC)** until accused and subsequently tried and imprisoned for seeking to overthrow **Yahya Jammeh** on January 27, 1995. Sabally was dismissed from the army, court martialed in January 1996, and given a nine-year sentence for threatening the Chairman of the AFPRC with a gun and for "inhuman treatment" of civilian detainees. Sabally was also accused of trying to delay the transition to civilian rule.

SAHO, LAMIN MUHAMMAD (1932–1993). A **Banjul Wolof,** he was educated at the Mohammedan Primary School and Methodist Boys High School, **Bathurst.** He then enrolled at Fourah Bay College, Freetown, graduating with a B.Comm. (Durham). Moving to London he read law at the University of London, 1956–1959, and was called to the bar (Middle Temple) in 1962. On his return to the Gambia he worked in government, first in the Agriculture Department from 1949 to 1950, and from 1955 as an Administrative Officer. He served as Assistant Commissioner, Central Division (now Lower River Division), 1957–1958, and was also posted to the Upper River Division. Saho was promoted to Assistant Permanent Secretary in the Agriculture Department in 1959. In 1963–1969, he had a private legal practice in Bathurst. A **People's Progressive Party (PPP)** activist, he was appointed Attorney-General in 1969 and, in 1979, he was appointed, additionally, to the newly created post of Minister of Justice. Saho was also an ex-officio member of the House of Representatives. In the general elections of 1977 he narrowly won Banjul Central for the PPP.

Saho quarrelled with **Sir Dawda Jawara** when he was refused the post of Vice President, following the demotion of **Assan Musa Camara** in 1982. He expected the vice presidency because of his key role in organizing the treason trials following the abortive coup of 1981. Saho refused the Local Government Ministry, which was offered as compensation. Never popular with Banjul voters, despite his electoral success in 1977, he was also correctly seen as a Senegalese sympathizer. He was recruited to the **Gambia People's Party (GPP)** by Camara in 1986, despite not being on good terms with him when they were both in the PPP government. Saho played no part in the electoral campaign of 1987; firstly, having been jailed in a fraud case in Britain, immediately before the election, he was barred from standing; and secondly he had a change of mind and sought to be readmitted to the PPP. Saho died on September 14, 1993.

SAIT MATY (Also known as Saër Maty) (?–1897). Son of **Ma Bah.** His mother was the niece of the **Burba Jolof.** Although a council of chiefs had selected his uncle, **Mamadou N'Dare** Bah, to succeed Ma Bah as ruler of the kingdom of **Baddibu,** Sait Maty never gave wholehearted support to Mamadou. Maty had gained considerable influence by the early 1880s because of transferred allegiance from his father and also because of his own leadership qualities. It is probable that he was the real power behind Mamadou even before the latter was badly defeated by **Biram Cisse.** In the mid-1880s, Sait Maty was involved in a series of wars with Cisse over control of the riverine areas of Baddibu. It appeared briefly in 1886 that Cisse would accept the overlordship of Sait Maty and peace would come to the north bank. However, the war continued, and in 1887, the French, fearful of an extension of the war to Saloum, decided to pacify the territory. In April 1887, the French, reinforced by the *tyeddo* of Saloum, defeated Sait Maty's forces a number of times, forcing him to flee to British protection in the **Ceded Mile.** The British, concerned with French operations so near the **Gambia River,** refused to surrender Sait Maty, and he continued to live quietly in a village near **Bathurst** until his death.

SALLAH, HALIFA BOUBACAR. See **PEOPLE'S DEMOCRATIC ORGANISATION FOR INDEPENDENCE AND SOCIALISM.**

SANYANG, KUKOI SAMBA (1953–). Self-styled marxist opponent both of the **People's Progressive Party (PPP)** and of the **Armed Forces Provisional Ruling Council (AFPRC)/Alliance for Patriotic Re-orientation and Construction (APRC).** Born in December 1953 into a **Roman Catholic Jola** family from the **Casamance** then living in Wassadu in the **Foni** East district, he was originally called Dominique Savao Sanyang. Sanyang is reported to have attended a Catholic seminary at Ngasobil, near Ziguinchor in the Casmance region of Senegal, for two or three years and then transferred to St. Augustine's High School, **Banjul.** He worked for a time in an electrician's workshop and gained his first taste of radical politics in the Black Scorpions, a militant youth organization frequently in conflict with the authorities in the capital.

After this, Sanyang is believed to have left The Gambia to study in the United States and to visit the former Soviet Union. He returned home before the 1972 elections, but, not qualifying on residential grounds to stand himself, he sponsored his brother, Momodou L. Sanyang, as an independent candidate against the PPP in Foni East. His brother was defeated and lost his deposit. Following the elections, Kukoi Sanyang is believed to have traveled overseas again, returning in time to meet the six-month residential requirement for the 1977 elections. This time he got himself adopted as a candidate for the **National Convention Party (NCP)** in the same Foni East constituency. He too was badly defeated, winning only 708 votes to his PPP opponent's 4,532.

Following this second political reverse, Sanyang disappeared from view and is believed to have traveled abroad again and become further radicalized in his political views. Returning to The Gambia around May 1981, he joined the then outlawed **Gambia Socialist Revolutionary Party (GSRP)** and, together with disaffected elements within the **Gambia Field Force,** organized the unsuccessful coup of July 30, 1981. When the Senegalese army intervened to put down the insurrection, Sanyang fled to Guinea-Bissau, and, from there, the government deported him to Cuba. He later returned to Africa to continue his opposition to the Gambian government. At one stage he resided in Libya, where he recruited supporters from among Gambians working there. From Libya he moved to Burkina Faso and was involved with the Charles Taylor armed faction in the Liberian civil war. The overthrow of the PPP in 1994 did not end Sanyang's opposition to the Gambian government. Supporters of his were involved in an attack on the army barracks at **Farafenni** in November 1996.

SARDU, BAKARI. Ruler of Bondu in the 1860s and 1870s. He had received a French education, was awarded the Legion of Honor, and, throughout his career, was very careful not to alienate the French. He became vitally involved with the upper river areas of the Gambia, to check the ambitions of his fellow rulers and also for economic gain. In 1866, he led a major invasion through **Wuli** that briefly threatened **MacCarthy Island.** This operation forced the British to abandon their policy of retreat and to send troops to the island. In the 1870s, Bakari Sardu formed an unofficial **Fulbe** coalition with **Alfa Ibrahima** of **Futa Jallon** and **Alfa Molloh.** In that period his forces made almost annual raids into the Gambia. Sardu, depending on the circumstances, would ally himself either with **Soninke** or **Marabout** factions in the Gambia.

SATEE-TIYO. Figuratively, this title means owner of the land. The *satee-tiyo* was the village head, also called an ***alkaaloo*** at times. He was normally the eldest member of the lineage that was recognized as having titular rights to the office.

SEAGRAM, HENRY F. First Governor of the independent **Colony** of the Gambia in 1843. He died of fever only a few months after assuming the office and before he could significantly effect any changes in the Colony.

SEEFOO (SEYFU) (pl.: ***SEEFOOLU***). **Mandinka** word meaning chief or ruler, possibly derived from the French word, "chef." This was the title used by the British for the 35 district chiefs of the modern **Protectorate** and continues in use today.

SELECT COMMITTEE OF PARLIAMENT (1842). The Committee was formed primarily as a response to the activities of George MacLean, President of the Council of Merchants at Cape Coast and Governor of the Gold Coast Colony. The Committee called into question the approach of the British government in all of itsWest African areas of interest. As a result of its recommendations, the Crown assumed direct control over the Gold Coast, and the decision was taken to allow each British territory to have its own administration without reference to a Governor-in-Chief. The first Governor of the Gambia under these new regulations was Captain **Henry F. Seagram.**

SELECT COMMITTEE OF PARLIAMENT (1865). The Committee was created because of parliamentary pressure to reduce the cost of administering the empire. The Committee based its recommendations largely upon the report of **Colonel H. St. George Ord.** It enunciated the doctrine of no territorial expansion in Africa, which remained the dominant official philosophy for over 20 years. The Colonial Office, following the report of the Committee, ordered the abandonment of **MacCarthy Island.** British presence in the vicinity of MacCarthy Island was left to a **factor** who was also a trader in the upper river areas. He had no official authority and had to operate without benefit of British troops. More important for the Gambia, the Select Committee recommended that all British West African possessions be placed once again under the direct control of a Governor-in-Chief, resident in Freetown. This was effected by 1866. In 1874, Lagos and the Gold Coast were removed from such control, but it was not until 1888 that the Gambia regained its administrative autonomy. The chief executive officer resident in the Gambia was called an Administrator.

SENEGAL, CLOSER ASSOCIATION WITH. This relates to the official attempts towards, as well as private views concerned with, political, social, and economic unification of the Senegambia. Serious consideration was given to this question by the British even before the constitutional advances of the 1960s. The British and Senegalese did not want to appear to force the Gambia into an unwanted association, but joining the two areas seemed an obvious solution to the perceived economic nonviability of the Gambia, and it would rectify the arbitrary division established by the **Anglo-French Convention of 1889.** For the Senegalese, a union would put an end to large-scale smuggling (principally by Senegalese nationals) of cheaper goods from the Gambia into Senegal. In 1961, an interministerial committee was created by President **Leopold Senghor** and **Pierre Sarr N'Jie,** Chief Minister of the Gambia, to examine ways toward a practical union of the two territories.

A United Nations report (the Van Moek Report: 1964), while favoring some form of ultimate political union in order to promote the economic development of both countries, proposed three options—total integration of The Gambia into an enlarged Senegal, favored by Dakar; a loose federation, not unlike the eventual Confederation, proposed by the Gambia government; and a compromise "association," which would allow for a more leisurely progression towards closer union. Senegal, still recovering from the abrupt collapse of the Mali Federation, formed between itself and the former French Soudan (1959–1960), was not inclined to force the pace; while Gambians, on the threshold of national independence, were in no mood to be absorbed by their larger neighbor. The third option was the one adopted. The Gambia became independent but immediately signed a defense agreement with Senegal, and a formal Treaty of Association was agreed to in 1967, which led to the setting up of an Inter-State Ministerial Committee, served by a Senegalo-Gambian Secretariat, charged with promoting further functional cooperation between the two states. Between 1965 and 1982, some 30 collaborative agreements were signed, and the **Organization for the Development of the Gambia River Basin (OMVG)** was created.

Closer relations were precipitated by the attempted coup d'etat in The Gambia in July 1981. The defense agreement with Senegal was invoked, and Senegalese forces entered The Gambia and put down the rebellion. The price of military assistance was the agreement by the Gambian government to enter into closer relations with Senegal. Still refusing union, the Gambian leadership opted for a confederal relationship. The **Senegambia Confederation** came into being in February 1982, and over the next eight years a number of protocols were signed, aimed at promoting closer integration between the two countries. Fundamental differences over the long-term objective of the Confederation—the Senegalese viewing it as a means to total union, and the Gambians regarding it in more limited and pragmatic terms—inevitably led to friction, and the relationship came to an end in December 1989.

Following the dissolution of the Confederation, relations between the former partners became strained, despite their signing a new Treaty of Friendship in 1991, which emphasized the "special relationship" between them. This agreement was very similar to the Treaty of Association of 1967, the position most acceptable to The Gambia, and it allowed for annual meetings of the two heads of state and the creation of a new joint commission to handle matters of common concern. Periodic Senegalese border closures and harassment of Gambian travellers were explained away as anti-smuggling measures by the Dakar authorities, but were believed by most Gambians to be motivated by pique and a desire to make things economically difficult for the **Banjul** government, since cross-border trade with Senegal and other neighboring countries was vital to the Gambian economy.

The military junta, when it came to power in Banjul in July 1994, made great efforts to establish good relations with Dakar, but cross-border restrictions remained to hinder **Armed Forces Provisional Ruling Council (AFPRC)** and **Alliance for Patriotic Re-orientation and Construction (APRC)** plans to turn The Gambia into a regional entrepôt. The worsening military situation in Senegal's southern region, the **Casamance**, where **Jola** separatists in the Movement of Democratic Forces of the Casamance (MFDC) continued to defy the Dakar government, caused suspicion of Gambian leader **Yahya Jammeh's** intentions, given his Jola background, and at the same time made it necessary for the Senegalese authorities to develop a working relationship with Banjul in order to try and contain the situation.

SENEGAL COMPANY. A short-lived but important commercial Company established by the French in 1672 as a successor to Jean-Baptiste Colbert's grandiose **West Indies Company.** In 1677, a French fleet captured Goree from the Dutch, and this became the main base of operations for the Company. In the next few years, the Company, in conjunction with French naval vessels, harassed the shipping of the **Royal African Company** and attempted to supplant the English on the **Gambia River. Factors** were established at a number of locations south of Cape Verde, a punitive expedition was mounted against Saloum, and, in 1681, the first trading station at **Albreda** was established, opposite **James Island.** The outbreak of war in 1689 reversed the fortunes of the Company, and they gave up their monopoly, first to the **Guinea Company,** and finally in 1696 to the Royal Senegal Company.

SENEGAMBIA CONFEDERATION. This was the culmination of two decades of discussion and cooperative agreements between The Gambia and **Senegal.** It was precipitated by the Gambian crisis of July 30, 1981, which made the Gambian government dependent on Senegalese security forces to restore it to power and ensure its immediate survival. The Treaty of Confederation was a surprisingly brief and simple document. Approved by the two national parliaments in December 1981, the Confederation came into being on February 1, 1982. While stressing the sovereignty of the two member states, the Treaty provided for closer union between The Gambia and Senegal, by means of an open-ended series of protocols. The fundamental contradiction in the Treaty would eventually cause the collapse of the Confederation.

Four basic objectives were set out in the original agreement: (1) the setting up of common political and administrative institutions; namely, a president and a vice president (the heads of state of Senegal and The Gambia, respectively), a council of ministers (five Senegalese and four Gambians), a confederal assembly elected indirectly by the two national parliaments (40 Senegalese and 20 Gambians), and a confederal secretariat, all funded by an annual budget paid for by the member states (two-thirds by Senegal and one-third by The Gambia); (2) the partial integration of the security forces of the two countries to create a confederal army and gendarmerie (two-thirds Senegalese, one-third Gambian) to be stationed anywhere within the Confederation; (3) the creation of an economic and monetary union between the two states; and (4) the coordination of policy in external affairs and technical fields.

In the eight years following the agreement a number of protocols were signed on common defense policies, external relations, communications, and information. The key issues of monetary and economic union were never resolved in the life of the Confederation, owing to diametrically opposed views on the appropriate extent of integration.

Senegal wished for a complete economic union, but this was unacceptable to Gambians, who feared the costs to them of such a merger. Political union was even more remote; Gambians and Senegalese again differed fundamentally over the degree of political integration. It was clear that the Senegalese saw total union of the two states as the end goal of confederation, whereas the Gambians envisaged it as a more limited agreement, designed to prop up Gambian autonomy rather than to destroy it. As a result of this fundamental disagreement over the long-term direction of the Confederation, relations between the two countries gradually soured and, by 1989, Senegalese frustration over Gambian delays in implementing economic integration and declining Gambian enthusiasm combined to bring about the suspension and then the dissolution of the Confederation in December 1989.

SENEGAMBIA, PROVINCE OF. During the Seven Years' War, 1756–1763, the British occupied and garrisoned the Senegambia. At the conclusion of the war, administration of the area was vested in a **Company of Merchants.** Revived French activity and the weakness of the Company caused a reversion of the territory to the Crown in 1765 under the name Province of Senegambia. The government system was based on that of an American colony with a Governor, Council, and Chief Justice. The first Governor was **Colonel Charles O'Hara,** who also commanded three companies of troops known as O'Hara's Corps, later renamed the **Royal African Corps.** O'Hara's 11-year tenure of office was marked by continued difficulties with French traders on the **Gambia River** and even more vexing problems of controlling the actions of the Lieutenant-Governors and their troops at **James Island.**

Matthias MacNamara, who had exercised almost independent command in the Gambia, succeeded O'Hara as Governor and almost immediately became embroiled with **Captain Joseph Wall,** his lieutenant in the Gambia. This struggle, which culminated in MacNamara's removal, weakened the entire government of the province at a time when the French had decided to aid the American Revolution. MacNamara's successor died in August 1778, and only an ensign was in command at St. Louis in January 1779 when a French fleet appeared and seized the station. The following month, the French forced the surrender of James Island and razed the fort there. Later in the year, a British squadron occupied Goree, but found James Fort to be in no condition to be re-garrisoned, and no further attempts were made to occupy any territory in the Gambia during the war. The Treaty of Versailles in 1783 returned all of the Province of Senegambia to France with the exception of the Gambia River and James Island, which were retained by the British.

SENGHOR, LEOPOLD SEDAR (1906–   ). Philosopher, poet, and politician. He was President of the Republic of Senegal, from 1960 to 1980, and a strong advocate of pan-African unity. After the collapse of the Mali Federation, Senegal's short-lived union with the former colony of French Soudan (1959–1960), Senghor sought closer union between his country and The Gambia. Although favoring a complete merger of the two countries, Senghor reluctantly recognized that Gambian public opinion was not prepared to accept complete integration in 1965 and agreed instead to a Treaty of Association in 1967, hoping this would be the beginning of a process of closer cooperation with The Gambia leading to eventual union. Senghor's policy was continued under his successor, **Abdou Diouf.**

SENHORAS. As conditions on the Senegambian coast ruled out permanent European settlement, European traders came unaccompanied and formed attachments to local African women in St. Louis and Goree. These women were known as *senhoras.* Following the return of these settlements to the French in 1814, a number of traders and their families moved to **Bathurst.** When the traders finally returned to Europe, in the late 18th and early 19th centuries, they left their businesses to their partners and the children of their relationships. A number of *senhoras* became important traders upriver as a consequence.

SERAHULI. Inhabitants of part of the area which once was the ancient kingdom of **Wuli.** The ancestors of the Serahuli have been identified as the founders of the ancient empire of Ghana. Today they form the largest population block in the extreme upper river areas of The Gambia. They are mixtures of **Mandinka,** Berber, and **Fulbe.** Serahulis were well known as long-distance traders before the coming of the Europeans, though most are farmers, despite the poverty of the soil. The Serahuli have in the past suffered greatly from food shortages, and the **hungry season** was an ever-present factor in their lives until the end of the 1950s. In the course of the **Soninke-Marabout Wars** of the 19th century, many Serahuli became mercenaries willing to serve in the armies of either side.

SEREKUNDA (SARE JOBE KUNDA). The most populous and fastest-growing urban concentration in The Gambia. Part of Kanifing municipal authority, it is located some 12 miles from **Banjul** on the adjacent mainland. It was originally a small village, but by 1983 Kanifing, at the center of which is Serekunda, had a population of 228,214, over five times that of Banjul. Principally a residential area, it is also a major market center and there is some light industry.

SERER (SERERE). According to their traditions, the Serer were an agricultural people who resided in **Futa Toro** when a series of invasions by the **Fulbe** drove them southward. Long association with **Wolof,** Fulbe, and **Mandinka** has produced in the Serer a complex admixture. The Serer speak a language classified by Joseph H. Greenberg as belonging to the northern sub-group of the Niger-Kordofanian family and closely akin to Pulaar, the language of the Fulbe and Tukulor. The Serer are to be found in the Sine and Saloum regions of Senegal, but they are also found in adjacent districts of The Gambia. Two neighboring peoples, the Serer

N'Dieghem and the Niominka, are considered branches of the Serer although they speak different dialects and had simpler political systems.

The main group of Serer was referred to by early European travellers as "Barbesins," meaning people of the *Bur* Sine. After the mid-19th century the two Serer kingdoms, Sine and Saloum, occupied very strategic locations, blocking the southward expansion of the French and also the ambitions of **Ma Bah** of **Baddibu.** In both states, **groundnut** cultivation became very important for the Serer peasants as well as for the French merchants. The Serer had a complex social and political organization in both of their kingdoms. The *burs* or kings, chosen from the *guelowar* (matrilineage of the Mandinka founders of their states), secure in the prosperity of their farming villages, could command very large armies (*tyeddos*). The Bur Sine and the Sine *tyeddos* were responsible for the defeat and death of Ma Bah in 1867, which ended all chances for a unified Muslim polity in the Senegambia.

SIMOTTO MORO (?–1881). A **Torodbe Fulbe,** a Muslim teacher, and a resident in **Fuladu** in the 1860s who had gathered around him a group of disciples. He appeared to **Alfa** and **Musa Molloh** as a threat to their complete control of Fuladu. Before they could act against him, he moved with his followers across the **Gambia River** to **Wuli** and there established the heavily fortified town of Toubacouta, which in a short time became a center for trade and learning in the upper river area. Disaffected **Fulbe** from Fuladu reinforced Simotto Moro's power and, until his death in 1881, Toubacouta was safe from attack from Fuladu.

SINGHATEH, ALHAJI SIR FARIMANG, GCMG (1912–1977). Born in **Georgetown,** he was descended from a long line of **Mandinka** traders from **Wuli.** Singhateh was educated locally at Georgetown through adoption by a British Divisional Commissioner's wife. In 1935, he volunteered to become a medical overseer at **Kerewan;** later he became a Medical Probationer attached to the Royal Army Medical Corps (RAMC) in various parts of the Gambia during World War II. In 1950, Singhateh qualified as a government pharmacist. He retired in 1963 and established his famous pharmacy at **Farafenni.** He was Chairman of the **Protectorate** People's Society, and he and his wife, she perhaps more so than he, were supporters of the Protectorate People's Party, which became the **People's Progressive Party (PPP)** in 1959. Singhateh dropped his political connections in 1964 on his appointment to the Public Service Commission. He was appointed Governor General, following **Sir John Warburton**

Paul's departure in 1966. When an executive presidency was created in April 1970, Singhateh retired. He was also a devout member and President of the local **Ahmadiyya** movement. He died on May 19, 1977.

SINGHATEH, EDWARD DAVID (CAPTAIN Rtd.) (1965–   ). Secretary of State for Presidential Affairs and responsible for the National Assembly, the Civil Service, and the Enivronment. One of four junior army officers who engineered the military coup of July 22, 1994. Born in **Banjul** in 1965 of an English mother and a Gambian father, he was educated at St. Augustine's and at Gambia High School, Banjul, where he completed his secondary education. Singhateh worked with the Civil Aviation Department as an electronic technician before entering the Gambia National Army (GNA) as an officer cadet in January 1991. He received further military training in the United States in 1991 and was commissioned as a second lieutenant in January 1992. Singhateh was Defense Minister in the **Armed Forces Provisional Ruling Council (AFPRC)** until promoted to Deputy Chairman after the **Sabally/Hydara** plot of January 27, 1995. He left the army to take up a ministerial post following the return to civilian rule. Singhateh is widely regarded as President **Yahya Jammeh's** right-hand man.

SISAY, SHERIFF (1935–1989). Politician. Born at Kudang, **MacCarthy Island** Division, he was a son of Sekuba Sisay, **Mandinka** chief of Niamina District in 1927–1952. Sisay was educated in Koranic schools and spent eight years at **Armitage School, Georgetown.** In 1957, he became a clerk in the Education Department, and was a founding member of the **People's Progressive Party (PPP),** becoming its first Secretary General in 1959, a post he held until he broke with the party in 1968. In the 1960 elections, Sisay was one of the nine PPP members elected to the House of Assembly, and he was appointed a minister without portfolio in the **Executive Council.** In March 1961, with the other PPP members, he resigned because the Governor, **Sir Edward Henry Windley,** appointed **Pierre Sarr N'Jie** of the **United Party (UP)** as Chief Minister. However, the 1962 elections gave the PPP a definite majority. Sisay became the Finance Minister and was normally recognized as the number two man in the government. As Finance Minister, Sisay framed a series of budgets that reflected Gambia's modest economic position, but did allow for needed development and growth.

   In September 1968, Sisay was expelled from the party, following a quarrel over his move from the Finance Ministry to Foreign Affairs, a move he regarded as a demotion, particularly given his senior standing in the PPP. Three other dismissed ministers also left the PPP—**Kebbah A. H. Kah, Paul Louis Baldeh,** and Yusupha Samba—and, with Sisay, they formed the People's Progressive Alliance (PPA), in October 1968, which joined the UP in opposition. The PPA, initially, campaigned vigorously against the government's proposal for a republic in 1970, seeing it as a move to strengthen Prime Minister **Dawda Jawara's** power, but just before voting took place in April, the PPA began to fall apart. Sisay disbanded the party after the referendum and, in 1972, was allowed to rejoin the PPP in the name of national unity. After a period as Governor of the Gambia Central Bank, in late 1982 Sisay rejoined the government as Minister of Trade and Finance, where he remained until ill-health intervened. Sisay died on March 4, 1989.

SITWELL, CYRIL FREDERIC (?–1900). Appointed the first **Travelling Commissioner** for the south bank areas of the **Protectorate** in January 1893. He was thus the first permanent British official in all the troubled areas from **Kombo** to **Niamina.** With his partner, **J. H. Ozanne,** the north bank Commissioner, he represented the Crown to the peoples of approximately 150 miles of riverine territory. Since he had no military or police escort, he required considerable tact in informing the chiefs and the people of their new status and of the laws and ordinances of the **Colony,** which now applied to them. He also tried to act as a neutral judge in any dispute that arose between villages or chiefdoms. Although more Travelling Commissioners were appointed in the late 1890s, their tasks were made even more difficult by the enactment of the Protectorate Ordinance of 1894, the Yard Tax Ordinance, and the Public Lands Ordinance of 1897.

In 1899, a long-standing dispute over rice land between the **Soninke** of Jataba and the **Marabouts** of Sankandi flared up. Sitwell adjudicated the matter and decided in favor of Jataba. The Marabouts of Sankandi, mostly followers of **Fodi Kabba,** refused to abide by the decision. Sitwell, accompanied by his replacement, Frederic Edgar Silva, 11 African constables, and **Mansa Koto,** the chief of Battelling, proceeded to Sankandi in June 1900 to enforce the land decision. On June 14, after a brief discussion, Sitwell's group proceeded to the center of the town, an argument developed, and some of the Marabouts opened fire. Sitwell, Silva, Mansa Koto, and six constables were killed. The violence done to Sitwell's party convinced both the British and French governments that the interior regions had to be pacified and led to the joint military expedition of 1901.

SLAVE TRADE. Slavery was an indigenous institution among all the peoples of the Gambia. It was converted by the Atlantic slave trade into a mutually profitable business for both Africans and Europeans. The Portuguese in their earliest voyages captured slaves, but slave-trading did not become important until the 16th century and the development of plantation economies in the Western hemisphere. The earliest English and French traders to the Gambia were more concerned with gum, gold, and ivory, and **Richard Jobson** in the 17th century indignantly refused to trade in slaves. However, by the 18th century, traffic in slaves was the most important business of the **Royal African Company.** Even then the Gambia was not considered a good region in which to purchase slaves, most of the trading taking place on the coasts of the Gold Coast, Dahomey, and western Nigeria. There are no reliable figures for the numbers transported from the Gambia. In peak years perhaps as many as 2,000 were sold, but, according to **Francis Moore,** the average during the first quarter of the 18th century was 1,000 per year. British abolition in 1807 dealt a major blow to the slave trade, but slave ships continued to operate in the Gambia region for decades afterwards, and individual rulers such as **Fodi Kabba** continued to trade in slaves throughout the 19th century. One of the major reasons for the occupation of **Bathurst** was the British desire to block the trade in slaves from the **Gambia River.**

SMALL, EDWARD FRANCIS, OBE (1891–1958). Journalist, trade unionist and politician. Born in **Bathurst** in January 1891, the son of a well-regarded **Aku** Methodist tailor, Small was an unusually able pupil and won a government scholarship to study at the Methodist Boys' High School in Freetown, Sierra Leone. He returned home in 1912 and worked as a clerk in the Public Works Department for a time. He then took up a teaching post at the Methodist Boys' High School in Bathurst and envisaged training as a Methodist minister. Sent upriver to Ballanghar as a probationary mission agent in 1917, he clashed with a local European trader. The incident, trivial in itself, escalated when Small denounced the local British administrator and then the Methodist church for siding with the trader and recalling him. He was dismissed for insubordination, and this series of events appears to have radicalized him politically.

While working upriver at **Kaur,** in 1919, Small was instrumental in founding the Gambia Native Defensive Union (NDU), formed among like-minded young educated Bathurst Aku. In 1919–1920, Small converted the GNDU into the local branch of the inter-territorial **National Congress of British West Africa (NCBWA)** and represented the

Gambia at the founding of the NCBWA in Accra in March 1920. As secretary of the Gambia NCBWA, Small championed African rights and frequently criticized government in his newly-established newspaper, *The Gambia Outlook and Senegambia Reporter,* the first newspaper since the demise of *The Bathurst Observer* in the late 1880s.

Undeterred by the demise of the Gambia NCBWA, and the intermittent appearance of his newspaper, in 1929 Small founded the Gambia Planters' Syndicate (later renamed the Gambia Farmers' Co-operative Marketing Association) to fight for improved **groundnut** prices, and also founded the first trade union in the Gambia, the **Bathurst Trade Union (BTU).** In the same year he organized one of the most successful strikes in colonial Africa before Word War II. He also helped bring into existence the important Gambia Trade Union Ordinance of 1932. His trade union and anticolonial activities led him to establish links with socialist and communist organizations in Britain and Europe, and he even attended a communist-organized anticolonial conference in Germany. It is unlikely that his links with international communism were other than tactical, although the government was convinced he was a Bolshevik agitator, describing him in official correspondence as a "link subversive."

The peripatetic Small continued his political career in Bathurst in the mid-1930s through the **Bathurst Rate Payers Association,** of which he was Chairman. However, by the late 1930s, he gradually mellowed in his attitude toward the government, and his strong pro-Allied stance at the commencement of Word War II persuaded the colonial administration to appoint him toward the **Legislative Council** in 1942. Following postwar constitutional reforms, Small won the first direct election to the Legislative Council in 1947, representing Bathurst. During this time he was also active in the anticommunist world trade union movement, obtaining a seat on the general executive council of the International Confederation of Free Trade Unions, a position he held from 1945 until his death in January 1958. In 1951, he was defeated for reelection to the Legislative Council by **Ibrahima Momodou Garba-Jahumpa** and **John Colley Faye.** Governor **Sir Percy Wyn-Harris** reappointed him to the Legislative Council in 1954 and recommended him for the OBE. "Pa" Small is properly regarded as the "father" of modern politics in The Gambia and a pioneer in several areas of public service.

SOLDIER TOWN. That part of **Bathurst** located at the center of the settlement, inland from the **Government House** and MacCarthy Square.

This was the area where most of the discharged soldiers resided in the early 19th century.

SOLIDARITY PARTY. A short-lived organization set up in 1962 by **Sanjally Bojang's** faction of the **People's Progressive Party (PPP)** to try and bring about a "common front" of all Gambian political parties.

SONINKE. A term which literally means giver of libations. In the upper Senegal River area, it is a name given to a people who are also called Sarakolle by the French and **Serahuli** by the British. It is also a term applied to the ancient rulers of the West African empire of Ghana. In the Gambia in the 19th century, this term applied to the traditionalist faction in the religious conflicts of the 19th century. To the **Marabouts,** the term had pejorative connotations, meaning pagans or unbelievers.

SONINKE-MARABOUT WARS. A series of conflicts that began in the early 1850s between Islamic usurpers and their converts, known as **Marabouts,** and those Gambian defenders of traditional political and religious interests, collectively referred to as **Soninke** (givers of libations, drinkers of alcohol, or unbelievers). At one time or another, these conflicts affected all the riverine areas of the Gambia and did not come to an end until 1901, with the European occupation of the Senegambian hinterland.

The wars were triggered by the religious upheavals to the east in the middle Niger area, which created expansionist Muslim states led by religious reformers such as **Al Hajj Umar Tall,** who founded the Tukulor empire, and Usuman dan Fodio, founder of the Sokoto Caliphate in what is today northern Nigeria and neighboring territory. Inspired by these examples, individuals, moved by a combination of religious zeal and personal ambition, launched a series of local wars in the Senegambian region aimed at replacing the traditional states with personal theocratic empires. The first outbreak of fighting took place in **Kombo;** in 1853–1855, **Fodi Kabba** of **Gunjur** and his ally, **Omar of Sabaji** overran much of western Kombo and even inflicted an initial defeat on the British at **Bathurst.** Although the British prevented the Marabouts taking Bathurst, they were unable or unwilling to save their Soninke allies, and by 1875, the latter had been forced to become Muslim under the suzerainty of the Marabout leaders, Fodi Kabba and **Fodi Silla.**

In the 1860s Fodi Kabba and his allies extended their activities to the **Foni** and **Jarra** districts, where they again defeated the Soninke, except for the **Jola,** who stubbornly defended their independence. Fodi Kabba's advance to the east was not checked until he encountered, in eastern Jarra, the forces of another expanding Marabout state, that of the **Fulbe** rulers, **Alfa Molloh** and his son **Musa Molloh.** The Mollohs also claimed to be waging a jihad on the middle Gambia, but it became evident by the 1870s that the pursuit of power and booty was their principal driving force.

Only in the north bank district of **Baddibu** did any Marabout leader display unambiguous religious motivation. **Ma Bah,** who seized power in Baddibu in 1861, was a **Tijaniyya** member and reformer bent on converting his Soninke neighbors by conquest. He met with a measure of success in **Niumi,** but this brought him into conflict with the British. An attempt to extend the war to the south of the **Gambia River** in **Kiang** met with a decisive defeat at the hands of the local Soninkes. Ma Bah also failed in his attempt to extend his power north into the **Serer** kingdom of Sine. In a pivotal battle in 1867, Ma Bah's forces were crushed, and he himself was killed by the army of the *Bur* Sine, **Coumba N'Doffene Diouf.** His death led to the fragmentation of his state, as his brother and his son, **Mamadou N'Dare** Bah and **Sait Maty** Bah, and a senior lieutenant, **Biram Cisse,** fought over the succession. Their internecine fighting allowed the French and British to take over the region.

Fighting continued between the warring forces until the British and French decided to occupy the Senegambian interior in the closing decades of the 19th century. Despite trying to play the European powers against each other, in the end all the Marabout leaders were forced to yield to them or die fighting. Musa Molloh made his peace with the British, which left him as a client ruler in **Fuladu,** until repeated complaints about his misrule led to his deportation to Sierra Leone after World War I, though he was allowed back in 1923, with his powers largely stripped from him. Fodi Silla, after gaining British recognition as ruler of Western Kombo, was forcefully deposed in 1894 for continuing to engage in slave raiding and threatening Anglo-French boundary commission survey work. After crossing to the French-controlled **Casamance,** he was deported to St. Louis by the French.

Fodi Kabba also retreated to the Casamance in 1892, following clashes with the British, and from there he continued to raid into Gambian territory. Following the killing of two British officials at Sankandi in Kiang, by a local Marabout chief, **Dari Bana Dabo,** a follower of Kabba, the British and French, aided by Musa Molloh, decided to put an end to his activities. He was killed during the taking of his stronghold at Medina in March 1901. Although European military intervention and political expansion put an end to the fighting and the depredations of the Marabouts, the wars destroyed the power of the Soninke rulers and led to most of their former subjects being converted to Islam. For further details of the Soninke-Marabout Wars, see **FAAL, AMER; BOJANG, TOMANI; D'ARCY, G. A. K.; JATTA, SULING;** and **O'CONNOR, LUKE S.**

SONKO, BURUNGAI. He became the ruler of **Barra (Niumi)** in 1823 and three years later signed a convention with **Captain Alexander Grant** giving the British control of the **Ceded Mile,** upon which they constructed Fort Bullen. During the next five years, the king came to regret the loss of his customs revenues and, pressured by under-chiefs, adopted an anti-British attitude. Because of actions against **Bathurst** traders in Niumi, the British suspended their annual payments to the king. His attitude and the foolishness of European and African traders in Bathurst led to the **Barra War.** A slight incident in August 1831, between two intoxicated subjects of the king and the canteen keeper at Fort Bullen, led to an attempt to take the nearby village of Essau, seat of the King of Niumi, by a motley assortment of Bathurst citizens and soldiers. They were repulsed with severe losses, and the British abandoned Barra to the king. Governor **George Rendall,** fearing collaboration between Sonko and the King of **Kombo,** pleaded for assistance from the French at Goree. With French help, a further futile attempt was made to take Essau. Later, even after reinforcements had arrived from Sierra Leone, the British were unable to capture the town. The king's subjects had, nevertheless, suffered heavily from the war, and Burungai Sonko made peace in January 1832, reconfirming the Ceded Mile Treaty.

SOUTHORN, LADY BELLA. Sister of Leonard Woolf, sister-in-law of the novelist Virginia Woolf, and wife of Governor **Sir Wilfrid Thomas Southorn.** Lady Southorn was also an author of considerable distinction, who wrote many articles concerning the Gambia. In 1952 she published an interesting, informative extended essay on Gambian history, society, and politics, entitled *The Gambia: The Story of the Groundnut Colony.*

SOUTHORN, SIR WILFRID THOMAS, KCMG, CMG, KBE (1879–1957). Southorn was born on August 4, 1879, and educated at Warwick School and Corpus Christi, Oxford. He served in the Ceylon civil service from 1903 to 1926, rising to be Principal Collector of Customs and Chairman, Ports Authority. He was then appointed Colonial Secretary, Hong Kong, in which post he served from 1926 to 1932. His first and only colonial governorship was that of the Gambia in 1936–1942. Between 1942 and 1946 he served as a Colonial Civil Service Liaison Officer. Any plans Southorn had for major improvements either for the **Colony** or for the **Protectorate** in the Gambia had to be framed within the context of revenues severely constricted by the poverty of the dependency and the effects of the world depression. After 1939, the economy of the Gambia improved substantially, as the Gambia became an important staging area during World War II. The period between 1940 and 1942 was particularly tense because the Gambia was surrounded on three sides by Senegal, whose government was controlled by Vichy France. Southorn died on March 15, 1957.

STIBBS, CAPTAIN BARTHOLOMEW. Sent to the Gambia by the **Royal African Company** in 1723 with the specific purpose of searching for the legendary upriver gold mines mentioned by **Prince Rupert** and **Colonel John Vermuyden.** He reached **Barrakunda** Falls in February 1724, and proceeded approximately 60 miles above them before turning back. Stibbs reported that he found no minerals and considered Vermuyden's report to be a myth. His negative report discouraged the Company from further exploration. Captain Stibbs's expedition has been recorded in **Francis Moore's** *Travels into the Inland Parts of Africa.* Stibbs later returned to the Gambia as a merchant of the Company and played a role in the affairs of 1729–1730 when some disaffected Europeans on **James Island** threatened to revolt and blow up the fort.

STIEL, OTTO. The third chief agent of the **Duchy of Courland** in the Gambia. He was appointed in 1653 and spent six years in the area trying to improve trade and diplomatic relations with the mid-river Gambians. However, his successes were compromised by European disturbances. Courlander ships were seized both by the Dutch and the English in their commercial war. The Dutch at Goree did not want trade competition in the Senegambia from interlopers, and they twice captured the fort on St. Andrew's Island. Stiel was made prisoner each time. His release was forced the first time by the actions of a French privateer in Swedish employ and the second time by forces loyal to the King of **Barra.** The capture of James, Duke of Courland, by the Swedes following a dynastic dispute, and the subsequent agreement reached by Courland and England in 1664, which gave St. Andrew's Island to the British, undercut all of Stiel's work in the Gambia.

STONE CIRCLES. Megaliths still of unknown origin found in western Africa from the southern Sahara in the north to Guinea-Bissau in the south. Most of them are located in Senegal. All except two of the circles in The Gambia are on the north bank of the river. They are composed of 10 to 20 standing laterite stones which vary in height from two to eight feet. These stones are arranged in circles between 10 and 20 feet in diameter. In some locations there is a complex of circles. Wassu has 11 circles and Ker-Batch has nine. The stones were cut from neighboring hillsides, and some of the larger stones weigh as much as 10 tons. Their transportation to the circle sites involved a considerable labor force and complex organization. Professional and amateur excavations indicate that in some cases the area within the circle was used as a burial place. Some skeletons and many artifacts have been uncovered. Present-day Gambians living in the vicinity of the circles have no clear notion of their origin or use. Radiocarbon dating dates them back to A.D. 640–860, though who constructed them remains unknown.

STRANGE FARMERS. Landless men who migrated seasonally to the Gambia from neighboring countries to help with planting and harvesting crops. During the **Soninke-Marabout Wars,** they served an additional function as mercenaries. During the 20th century, the strange farmers would make their own contracts with village headmen and be assigned to work for specific farmers in a village. They were assigned portions of land to work for themselves in their free time and would also normally be required to grow a part of the additional food supply needed for their sustenance. The pressure upon available food supplies in the Gambia after 1945 caused the colonial government and the chiefs to take steps to limit the immigration of these foreigners into the Gambia.

SUMA. Among the **Mandinka** kingdoms, certain village leaders had more authority over a larger area of land than other *alkaaloolu.* These leaders were called *suma.* In **Baddibu, Jarra, Niumi, Kiang,** and **Kombo** the kingship rotated between *suma* lineages.

SUMAKUNDA. The lineage in direct line of succession to the kingship in **Mandinka** kingdoms.

-T-

TALL, AL HAJJ UMAR (c1790–1863). The *khalifa* of the **Tijaniyya** *tariq* in the western Sudan and founder of the Tukulor empire. Born and educated in the **Futa Toro,** he later travelled widely and made a five-year pilgrimage to Mecca. In North Africa, he came under the influence of Ibn Muhammad al Tijani, founder of the Tijaniyya *sufi* brotherhood. Umar later lived in Hausaland where he married one of the daughters of Sultan Bello of Sokoto. In 1838, he left Hausaland and established a religious and military base at Dinguiray. By 1852, his following was large enough to declare a jihad against the Bambara, and he conquered Kaarta. In the decade after 1852, Umar's followers conquered Segu and Macina, and gained control of the upper Senegal River area. In 1863, Umar's prestige was at its zenith with the capture of Timbuktu. In the same year he was killed suppressing a revolt in Macina. He bequeathed a huge but heterogeneous empire to his son, Ahmadu. Umar's teaching and example of conquering the territories of unbelievers had a great influence upon Muslim teachers in the Senegambia. **Ma Bah** and **Alfa Molloh** both had direct connections with the Tijaniyya movement.

TANCROWALL. A Portuguese settlement sited in the vicinity of the modern village of Tankular. There was a church with a priest in residence there as late as 1730. The **Royal African Company** briefly had a factory at Tancrowall in the 1730s.

TARIQ (pl. **TURUKH**). Islamic religious confraternity comprising those individuals who subscribe to a common spiritual "path" under the guidance of a sheikh. The two most celebrated *tariq* brotherhoods in West Africa were the **Qadiriyya,** reflecting the attitudes of the more conservative Muslim teachers, and the **Tijaniyya,** founded by Ibn Muhammad al Tijani in 1781.

THOMAS, SERGEANT G. J. (?–1935). Policeman and Administrator. He was sent by Administrator **Sir Gilbert Carter** to **Baddibu** in 1885 to attempt to bring an end to the fighting between the forces of **Mamadou N'-Dare, Sait Maty,** and **Biram Cisse.** In 1889, he was appointed manager of British **Kombo,** and he later took part in the Toniataba expedition of 1892 and that of Sankandi in 1901. He retired in 1903.

THOMPSON, GEORGE. Explorer and servant of the British **Guinea Company** sent to the **Gambia River** in 1618. Despite the massacre of a number of his men by the Portuguese, Thompson was optimistic that contact with the upper river would produce a wealth of gold. In 1619, with a few companions, he reached Tenda above **Barrakunda** Falls. Thompson wanted to proceed further into the hinterland, but the others refused. In the ensuing quarrel, Thompson was killed. All his discoveries and observations perished with him since he had committed nothing to writing. It was left for **Richard Jobson** the following year to retrace Thompson's journey and record his findings for his superiors in London.

TIJANIYYA. A Muslim (*sufi*) brotherhood, or *tariq*, founded at Ain Mahdi in Morocco in 1781 by Ibn Muhammad al Tijani (1735–1815). Its doctrine and practices were noted for being relatively uncomplicated, and so they were taken up by ordinary people. The brotherhood spread to West Africa even during its founder's lifetime, but received considerable impetus from the conversion of the Tukulor leader **Al Hajj Umar Tall** during his pilgrimage to Mecca in 1852. Tall was declared *khalifa* of the western Sudan and within a decade had created a large, heterogenous empire which stretched from the middle Senegal River area to beyond Timbuktu. Tijaniyya teachers were at the forefront of the **Soninke-Marabout Wars** in the Gambia. **Ma Bah** of **Baddibu** and **Alfa Molloh** both had Tijaniyya connections. Many Gambians today owe allegiance to one of the two principal branches of the Tijaniyya located in Senegal—the Niass family of Kaolack and the Sy family of Tivouane. Both enjoy a following in **Banjul**, but Niass followers are also found in North Bank Division, the district nearest Kaolack. There are a number of subordinate Gambian **Marabouts** who belong to the Tijaniyya sect, but none has a national standing or is as publicly involved in political life as is the case in Senegal.

TOMANI (TUMANA). One of the nine **Mandinka** kingdoms located along the south bank of the **Gambia River** in the early 19th century. It stretched from a point opposite Sami Creek to Tubakuta. The Mandinka ruling dynasty was overthrown by **Alfa Molloh** in the late 1860s and was incorporated into the new state of **Fuladu.** In the 20th-century reorganization of Gambian chiefdoms, the area which was Tomani became the District of Fuladu East.

TORODBE FULBE. A sub-group of the **Fulbe** with a reputation as Islamic scholars. Although fewer in number than the other Fulbe groups, they had a profound impact on the history of the upper Gambia since most Torodbe were Muslims, and their standing gave them the opportunity to influence other Muslim groups at the beginning of the **Soninke-Marabout** conflicts.

TOURAY, YANKUBA (LIEUTENANT Rtd.) (1966–). Secretary of State for Land, Youth and Sports. He was born at Njabakunda, North Bank

Division, and educated at the Muslim High School, **Banjul,** after which he enlisted in the **Gambia National Army** as a noncommissioned officer. Commissioned and promoted to lieutenant in 1991, Touray became an administrative officer at the Army Training School in **Farafenni,** North Bank Division, in 1994. He was appointed to the **Armed Forces Provisional Ruling Council (AFPRC)** after the army coup of July 1994 and made Minister (and subsequently Secretary of State) for Local Government and Lands in the same year. He took up his present post in March 1998.

TOURE, FODI SILLA. See **FODI SILLA.**

TRAVELLING COMMISSIONERS. By the 1890s the British were consolidating their position on the middle and upper reaches of the Gambia. As part of this process it was decided, in 1893, to appoint two officials, known as Travelling Commissioners, to represent the Gambian administration on either side of the **Gambia River** to a distance of approximately 150 miles inland from **Bathurst.** They were charged to explain British policy to local rulers and later to adjudicate in local disputes and gradually get local chiefs to accept British administrative and judicial practices. Initially, they had no force at their disposal and relied very much on their tact and understanding of local societies. After the establishment of the **Protectorate,** the number of Travelling Commissioners was increased to five, each covering a more restricted district—North Bank, **MacCarthy Island,** Upper River, South Bank, and **Kombo-Foni.** The word "Travelling" was later dropped, and provincial administrators were known simply as Divisional Commissioners. These supervised the activities of district chiefs and village heads and implemented government policy. **J. H. Ozanne** (North Bank) and **Cyril Frederic Sitwell** (South Bank) were the first two Travelling Commissioners. Divisional Commissioners continue to be the agents of the Gambian central government in the provinces.

TREGASKIS, THE REV. BENJAMIN. Superintendent of the **Wesleyan Mission** in Sierra Leone and the Gambia from 1864 to 1870. He held a district meeting in **Bathurst** in early 1871, which passed a resolution condemning any transfer of the Gambia to France, thus joining the Wesleyans with the bulk of the business community in opposition to Colonial Office policy.

TUBAB (tubabo in **Mandinka**). **Wolof** term for a European or white person; in general use throughout the Senegambia. By extension it can also refer to anyone who dresses or lives in a Western manner.

TYEDDO. Warriors in service to a **Wolof** or **Serer** king or chief, selected from the *jam* or slave caste. They were also known as slaves of the crown.

-U-

UNITED DEMOCRATIC PARTY (UDP). Main new opposition party to emerge during transition to civilian rule in 1996–1997, following the banning of the three major existing political parties. Led by lawyer and civil rights campaigner, **Ousainu Darboe,** the UDP is a middle of the road party championing human rights and economic liberalism. Many of its supporters are from the banned parties. Darboe came in second to the **Alliance for Patriotic Re-orientation and Construction (APRC)** candidate, **Yahya Jammeh,** in the September 1996 presidential elections, obtaining a creditable 39 percent of the vote. The UDP also came second in the general elections of January 1997, winning 37 percent of the vote (the highest percentage gained by an opposition party since 1962) but only seven of the 45 seats in the National Assembly. UDP strength is concentrated in former **National Convention Party (NPC)** areas, such as Bakau and the **Baddibus** and the **Kiang** and **Jarra** districts of Lower River Division, although it also won one of the **Niamina** seats in Central River Division. It won over 40 percent of the vote in a further 10 constituencies. The UDP claimed, like other opposition parties, that the elections were not fair and that it should have won a majority of seats.

UNITED PARTY (UP). Formed in October 1951, after the failure of **Pierre Sarr N'Jie,** a **Bathurst** barrister, to be elected to the **Legislative Council.** The United Party was a party which from the first showed great strength in the **Colony** area, particularly among the **Wolof.** The party was successful in returning N'Jie to the Legislative Council with the largest number of votes in the poll in the elections of 1954. The following year, N'Jie was forced to resign from the government after being found guilty by an official enquiry of having made improper allegations about the police. This only served to further his reputation among the electorate. The UP thus escaped the stigma attached to the older parties of being tools of the British administration.

Despite his party coming second to the newly-established **People's Progressive Party (PPP)** in the previous year's general elections, UP leader P. S. N'Jie was invited by the new Governor, **Sir Edward Henry Windley,** to become the country's first Chief Minister in 1961. A PPP boycott of the Cabinet forced fresh elections in 1962, and, although the UP increased its parliamentary strength from six to 13, the PPP did even better, winning 18 seats, compared with eight in 1960. N'Jie was replaced by **Dawda Jawara** and a PPP government.

Even though it had lost the crucial last election before Gambian independence, the UP had every hope of returning to power. In the 1962 elections it had easily seen off the PPP attempt to penetrate its Bathurst stronghold, save for the solitary victory of ex-**Democratic Congress Alliance (DCA)** M.P., **Alieu Badara N'Jie** and at the same time taken the struggle to its political enemy in the **Protectorate,** where it won a string of seats from the North Bank Division to the eastern extremity of the country. P. S. N'Jie not only appealed for the support of fellow-Wolof upriver, he also presented the UP as the champion of other non-**Mandinka** peoples, most notably the **Fula** and **Serahuli** in the **MacCarthy Island** and Upper River Divisions, against what the UP claimed was imminent Mandinka domination. Offered the opportunity to join in a coalition government by the PPP on the eve of independence, P. S. N'Jie turned it down, still believing he and his party had every chance of returning to power. The UP scored a notable success in November 1965, when it spearheaded a successful national opposition to the referendum on a republic.

Yet, within a few years the UP went into rapid decline, brought about by a combination of poor party leadership (P. S. N'Jie was replaced briefly as party leader in 1970 by his brother, **Ebrimah Dowda N'Jie,** until the latter's tragic death the same year), the lack of a credible alternative political program, and the effective use of political patronage by Dawda Jawara to coax a number of UP provincial MPs over to the PPP. The results of the general election of 1966 confirmed the UP's inability to retain its support; in a 32-strong House its ranks were now depleted to nine (including joint candidates with **Ibrahima Momodou Garba-Jahumpa's** Congress Party), and its share of the vote fell to one-third. Further carpet-crossing took place before the 1972 elections, leaving the UP with only three MPs after the polls. The lowest point in the fortunes of the UP came when the House of Representatives barred P. S. N'Jie for repeated non-attendance. He increasingly withdrew from active political life, and those of his lieutenants still politically active entered into a tactical alliance, first with the ephemeral **National Liberation Party (NLP)** in 1977 and then with the **National Convention Party (NCP)** in subsequent elections, with the remnants of UP supporters in the provinces being urged to vote NCP, while NCP supporters in the **Banjul** area voted UP. Although this enabled the UP to recover two seats temporarily, further defections continued, and the death of P. S. N'Jie in December 1993 marked the end of the UP, which had always been his personal political instrument. As if to underscore the UP's demise, the military junta did not bother to include it among those political parties banned after the 1994 army coup.

USIDIMARE, ANTONIOTTO. A Genoese sea captain in the employ of the Portuguese. In 1455, he was commissioned by Prince Henry of Portugal to explore the coastline south of Cape Verde. In early 1456, he was joined off Cape Verde by the ship commanded by **Alvise da Cadamosto.** The two led the first European explorations of the estuary of the **Gambia River.** In a second exploration, they were escorted inland approximately 60 miles and spent over two weeks conversing and trading with Gambian rulers. Leaving the Gambia River, Usidimare proceeded to sail southward as far south as Cape Mesurado before returning to Portugal.

USTICK, STEPHEN. A **factor** assigned to **James Island** by **Major Robert Holmes** in 1661. Left in command of 29 men in the fort, he twice resisted the attempts of **Peter Justobaque,** chief factor of the **(Dutch) West Indies Company,** to seize all the recently acquired British strongholds in the Gambia.

-V-

VALANTINE, LOUIS FRANCIS (1908–?). A civil servant and High Commissioner to Britain, born in 1908 in **Bathurst.** He was educated at Methodist Boys High School and later Fourah Bay College where he received a B.A. in 1930. Three years later he entered the civil service and became a senior administrator in 1949, serving in a number of departments. In 1960, he was appointed Postmaster-General and two years later became the first Gambian Chairman of the Public Service Commission. He was Joint Secretary of the Senegalo-Gambian Inter-Ministerial Commission in 1961. He became the first Gambian High Commissioner to Britain in February 1965.

VAN DER PLAS, CHARLES OLKE. Dutch administrator, United Nations official, and creator and head of the Gambian Department of Community Development. He first came to the Gambia in 1954 to make a survey of Gambian economic and political problems for the United Nations. He returned to the Gambia in 1963 and convinced the government to establish the Department of Community Development with minimal financing, locating his headquarters at Massembi.

VERMUYDEN, COLONEL JOHN. A servant of the **Royal Adventurers** who in December 1661 left **Elephant Island** on an extended exploration of the upper river areas. His later report claimed that his expedition penetrated further into the interior than had **Richard Jobson.** He claimed to have passed Jobson's Tenda, the confluence of the Neriko River, and to have penetrated beyond the Niololokoba River before being halted in April 1662 by rapids. Vermuyden reported that at this point he had discovered a great amount of gold. He told **Prince Rupert** of this discovery and explained that he did not bring out great quantities for fear of his companions. In 1725, **Captain Bartholomew Stibbs** retraced Vermuyden's journey without discovering the slightest indication of the fabled gold deposits.

VISION 2020 (The Gambia Incorporated). Development policy statement of the **Armed Forces Provisional Ruling Council (AFPRC)/Alliance for Patriotic Re-orientation and Construction (APRC),** published in May 1996. It set out the long-term objectives of the Gambian government in respect of development strategies and sectoral contributions. Vision 2020 aims "To transform The Gambia into a financial center, a tourist paradise, a trading, export-oriented agricultural and manufacturing nation, thriving on free market policies and a vibrant private sector, sustained by a well-educated, trained, skilled, healthy, self-reliant and enterprising population, and guaranteeing a well-balanced eco-system and a decent standard of living for one and all, under a system of government based on the consent of the citizenry." The adoption of the word "incorporated" stresses the primacy of private enterprise in the transformation process.

VOUS. Neighborhood social and political youth clubs in **Banjul.** The Kent Street Vous, founded around 1967, a noted opponent of the **People's Progressive Party (PPP)** government, produced its own journal and nurtured a number of leading Gambian radicals. It has been suggested that the word derives from *rendezvous.*

-W-

WAFFA-OGOO, MRS. SUSAN (1960–). Secretary of State for Tourism and Culture. Born on October 4, 1960. She graduated with a B.A.

in Library Studies and English Literature from Loughborough University of Technology, England, in 1987. Prior to her appointment as Minister (and subsequently Secretary of State) for Tourism and Culture in 1994, Waffa-Ogoo worked as a librarian and part-time lecturer at Gambia College.

WALL, CAPTAIN JOSEPH. An Irishman who had served in the Royal Marines and in the East India Company forces before joining O'Hara's Corps in the Senegambia in 1773. After Colonel **Charles O'Hara's** departure in late 1775, Wall served briefly as Governor of the Senegambia until displaced by **Matthias MacNamara.** He was then posted to **James Island** as Lieutenant-Governor of the Gambia; here his independent actions and harsh rule caused difficulty with the garrison. He was imprisoned by MacNamara and spent 10 months in confinement in James Fort before being brought to trial. In a celebrated case in 1777, Governor MacNamara's allegations against Wall were dismissed: subsequently Wall won two civil cases against the Governor, and the Council of Trade dismissed MacNamara. Wall returned to the Senegambia and later, while Governor at Goree, had three soldiers flogged to death. He fled to Europe, and 20 years later was captured, tried for murder, and executed.

WALLIKUNDA RICE SCHEME. An attempt on the part of the **Colonial Development Corporation** to utilize modern technology to develop profitably through irrigation of 3,400 acres of rice fields. In the early 1950s, the Corporation sent 60 construction workers complete with drag lines and bulldozers to construct irrigation channels, sluices, and a pumping station at Wallikunda. Only 200 acres were ever planted, and the yield was very low, no more than could be obtained by using traditional methods. The Corporation abandoned the scheme in 1954, except for a small portion of the land that was retained as an experimental station. This ill-conceived venture was even more expensive than the fiasco of the **Yundum Egg Project** and cost the Colonial Development Corporation £1,115,000.

WESLEYAN MISSION. Its activities in the Gambia date from February 1821, when, at the request of the Governor of the **British West African Settlements, Sir Charles MacCarthy,** Wesleyan Mission House in London despatched John Morgan and his wife, together with John Baker, to establish a Christian presence. The first attempt at establishing a station at Mandinari in **Kombo** was a failure; the local ruler refused to grant the mission a plot of land, and the ill-health of Morgan and Brown forced them to return to **Bathurst** in 1824. They were also refused land to establish a base at Kataba in **Niumi,** and Tendaba, farther up the river, was regarded as too politically unsettled. The Wesleyan mission in Bathurst proved to be a success, however, and numbers of staff and African converts gradually increased. A mission house and school were started in 1825 and, in 1834, the present Wesleyan Church was built for the 250-member congregation. In 1838, the Wesleyans took over 600 acres of land on **MacCarthy Island** and began a model farm and agricultural school there. In the early 19th century, the Wesleyans were particularly effective working with **liberated Africans.** Much of the responsibility for education in the **Colony** and **Protectorate** in the early 20th century was assumed by the Wesleyans. In addition to primary schools in Bathurst, they operated a Girls High School and a Boys High School and were involved after 1947 in helping to operate the Bathurst School of Science. In the late 1950s, the two Methodist High Schools were joined to form the present Gambia High School.

WEST INDIES COMPANY (Dutch). It was created by the States-General in 1617 to promote Dutch overseas trade. In 1621, the Company obtained the Island of Goree for its base of operations to challenge French supremacy in Senegambian trade. The Company almost annually sent small ships from Goree to trade along the **Gambia River,** but the profit from such ventures was quite low. In the 1650s, the Company at first cooperated with the Duke of Courland in his Gambia trading venture, but by 1660 they had seized St. Andrew's island from him. Although the island was given back to the Duke's representatives, it was obvious that the Dutch intended to have it as a base for their Gambian operations. They were forestalled in this by the actions of **Robert Holmes** of the English **Royal Adventurers,** whose forces took the island in March 1661 and renamed it **James Island.** Holmes, in charge of another expedition, captured Goree from the Dutch in early 1664, but this station was lost later in the year when the Dutch Admiral Michiel de Ruyter in command of 13 ships arrived in West Africa. De Ruyter, however, bypassed the English possessions in the Gambia. The Dutch company thereafter enjoyed a decade of relative supremacy in the Senegal region. However, the onset of the French Wars in Europe ended the Dutch interlude in Senegambia. In 1677, the French Admiral Jean d'Estrées captured Goree and then drove the Dutch from all their coastal factories. After this, the Dutch Company never attempted to challenge France or Britain in the Senegambia.

WEST INDIES COMPANY (French). A short-lived company created in 1664 by the all-powerful Minister, Jean-Baptiste Colbert. In a grandiose gesture, he gave the Company monopolistic rights along the shores of the Atlantic Ocean from Canada to the Cape of Good Hope. His scheme for wresting trade from the enemies of France by means of this Company collapsed in 1672. Trading rights in West Africa were then assigned to the **Senegal Company.**

WINDLEY, SIR EDWARD HENRY, KCMG, CMG, KCVO (1909–1972). Windley was born on March 19, 1909, the son of a white Rhodesian father and a French aristocrat mother, the Vicomtesse de Toustain. He was educated at Repton and at Cambridge University. Windley spent most of his career in Kenya, rising from District Officer in 1931, through Provincial Commissioner in 1948, to Chief Native Commissioner and Minister for African Affairs in 1953. He ended his colonial career as Governor of the Gambia, 1958–1962. Windley was responsible for introducing the new Constitution, which provided for a greatly expanded House of Assembly and allowed the elective principle to be applied to the **Protectorate** in 1960. He made the decision to appoint Gambians to ministerial positions in the government based upon the results of the election, and in 1961 appointed **Pierre Sarr N'Jie,** leader of the **United Party (UP),** as Chief Minister. Windley, influenced perhaps by his own French background, favored the proposed union of the Gambia with Senegal. After retiring from the colonial service he became a businessman and died in an air crash in Australia on January 5, 1972.

WOLOF. One of the most important people of the Senegambia. While they form a majority of the population of Senegal (with heaviest concentrations in Walo, Cayor, **Jolof,** and parts of Baol, Sine, and Saloum), in the Gambiathey constitute just over 16 percent of the population, 130,546 (1993). They are found mainly in upper and lower Saloum districts and in the northern sections of **Niani,** Sami, **Niumi, Jokadu,** and in restricted areas of upper **Baddibu. Banjul** is also predominantly a Wolof town, but the Wolof of Banjul have a different origin from those of the **Protectorate** since the ancestors of the Banjul group came from St Louis and Goree in Senegal, immediately after the founding of Bathurst.

The Wolof language has been classified by Joseph H. Greenberg as belonging to the northern sub-group of the Niger-Kordofanian family of languages and is a lingua franca spoken widely in present-day Senegambia. Wolof social organization is extremely complex, based upon a tripartite division of the society into freeborn, low-caste members, and slaves. Although many present-day Wolof are involved in trading and other occupations associated with modern urban life, most Wolof are farmers and live in villages. The land is divided into small plots assigned to individuals who practice subsistence **agriculture.** Their major cash crop in both Senegal and the Gambia is **groundnuts.**

Historically, the Wolof states of the Senegambia were Jolof, Walo, Baol, and Cayor, whose rulers (*burba, temy,* or *damel*) controlled their people through a complex bureaucracy combined with armed force. Those kingdoms played an important role in temporarily checking the southward and eastward advance of the French in the two decades after 1855, but were among the first territories incorporated into the French empire during the "scramble." The Wolof in the area of the Gambia Protectorate had not established strong central polities before the **Soninke-Marabout Wars** and were politically dependent upon **Mandinka** or **Serer** overlords.

WRIGHT, SIR ANDREW BARKWORTH, KCMG, CMG, CBE, MC (1895–1971). Born on November, 30, 1895, in Knowle, Dorset, the son of an Anglican clergyman, Wright was educated at Haileybury and at Jesus College, Cambridge. He served in the Suffolk Regiment during World War I, being awarded the Military Cross. He joined the civil administration of Cyprus in 1922, rising to be Colonial Secretary of Cyprus in 1937. Wright re-enlisted in World War II, leaving with the rank of Lieutenant-Colonel to become Colonial Secretary of Trinidad, 1943–1946. He served as Governor of the Gambia, 1946–1949 and returned to Cyprus as Governor from 1949 to 1954. Although Wright was not involved in the planning, it was during his tenure of office that the **Colonial Development Corporation** made and implemented its decision to invest in the disastrous **Yundum Egg Project** and the marginal experimental rice farm at **Wallikunda.** Wright had to frame his budgets with the knowledge that much of the financing for continued improvements in the economic and social sphere envisaged by the British government in the period immediately after World War II would not be forthcoming. Wright died on March 24, 1971.

WULI. Located in the extreme upper river area, in the 19th century it was one of the five north bank kingdoms controlled by the **Mandinka.** Founded in the 14th century by migrants from the **Mali empire,** it had become independent by the time Portuguese traders arrived in the mid-15th century. **Soninke** traders travelling between the Gambia, Senegal, and the Niger River region made Wuli a major trading area during the long period of the Atlantic **slave trade.** Throughout the **Soninke-Marabout Wars,** the rulers of Wuli maintained a loose client relationship with **Bakari Sardu,** the ruler of Bondu, who used the territory as a corridor and staging ground for his raids into the Gambia. Despite a number of attempts, **Musa Molloh** of **Fuladu** was never able to add Wuli to his extensive kingdom. The rulers of Wuli cooperated fully with the various Boundary Commissions in the 1890s, and **Yarbutenda,** one of its river towns, became the terminal point for describing the arc defining the eastern boundary of the Gambia. Most of the kingdom was incorporated into the Gambia by the British, although the northern portion became a part of Senegal. The international frontier dividing the kingdom and the construction of the railway in Senegal ruined Wuli's economic position, and most of what had become a poor, sparsely populated area became a chiefly district in the 20th century reorganization of the **Protectorate.**

WYN-HARRIS, SIR PERCY, MBE, CMG, KCMG (1903–1979). Colonial administrator, mountaineer, and yachtsman. Wyn-Harris was born in London on August 24, 1903, the son of a company director. Educated at Gresham's College and Caius College, Cambridge, he joined the colonial service in Kenya in 1929, rising to the rank of Chief Native Commissioner. He became Governor of the Gambia in 1949 and, unusually, served for two terms of office. Although he retired in 1958, Wyn-Harris continued to undertake official duties—in 1959, he was a member of the Devlin Commission of Enquiry into the Nyasaland disturbances; in 1960–1961, he was British Administrator of the Northern Cameroons during the UN plebiscite. A keen mountaineer—he was the second person known to have climbed Mount Kenya—he took a prominent part in the British Everest expeditions of 1933 and 1936.

His period in office coincided with the growth in nationalist sentiment in West Africa, and three political parties—the **Gambia Democratic Party (GDP),** the **Gambia Muslim Congress (GMC)** and the **United Party (UP)**—were formed in the Gambia to contest the elections for the **Legislative Council** in 1951 and 1954, a significant innovation introduced by Wyn-Harris. He also permitted the leaders of the three parties to hold quasi-ministerial office to enable them to gain experience of government. His clashes with **Pierre Sarr N'Jie** in 1955 lost him popularity with the **Bathurst** populace. A stickler for hard work, Wyn-Harris was never happier than when on tour upriver, and he took a particular interest in trying to improve conditions in the **Protectorate.** Despite these efforts and the modest but significant constitutional advancement that he introduced for the **Colony,** Wyn-Harris had so alienated the Bathurst element that rather than depart the country in the usual blaze of public ceremony, he quietly slipped across the border to Senegal and made his way to Britain from there. In retirement, Wyn-Harris (he only adopted the hyphenate, "Wyn" in 1954—apparently he was named "Wynne" on his birth certificate) took up yachting, sailing solo to The Gambia as part of a circumnavigation of the world. He died in Petersfield, England, on February 25, 1979, having lived a life "packed with Welsh pugnacity and vigour," as one obituarist wrote.

-Y-

YAMYAMAKUNDA. The site of one of the major **Royal African Company** factories along the **Gambia River.** It was located on the south bank approximately two miles northeast of the present village of Sankulekunda. The earlier factory was completely rebuilt by **Francis Moore** in the 1730s when he was a **factor** there.

YARBUTENDA. A town in the upper river district of **Kantora.** According to the **Anglo-French Convention of 1889,** Yarbutenda was to be the key to defining the eastern boundary of the Gambia. The boundary was to be the arc of a radius of 10 kilometers drawn with its center at Yarbutenda. The survey commission of 1891 discovered that the maps of the Gambia were incorrect, as there were two sites that might be the town mentioned in the Convention. Despite further agreements between the French and British in 1898 and 1901, the eastern boundary was never satisfactorily determined on the ground.

YUNDUM. A small town in **Kombo,** which during the **Soninke-Marabout Wars** was allied with the British. Because of this and because the chiefs of the town were **Soninke,** it was an objective for **Fodi Kabba, Fodi Silla,** and their followers. In the late 1940s, it was the site of the disastrous egg scheme sponsored by the British **Colonial Development Corporation.** Some of the scheme's abandoned concrete buildings were incorporated into the fabric of the Gambia Teachers Training College. During World War II, the Allies situated an airfield at Yundum, and this has since become Gambia's international airport. See also **Yundum College; Yundum Egg Project.**

YUNDUM COLLEGE. Prior to 1949, all Gambian teachers received their training in Sierra Leone or the Gold Coast. In that year a training center was opened at **Georgetown,** which offered a one-year course. Most of the buildings of the defunct egg scheme were acquired from the **Colonial Development Corporation (CDC),** and the Teachers Training College was moved to **Yundum** in 1952. In the following year, the course was opened to women, and in 1954 the program was lengthened to two years. Beginning in 1955, major improvements were made to the buildings, and the administration of the college was separated from the Board of Education and placed under a Board of Governors. Yundum students and ex-students were to play a significant part in radical protest against the **People's Progressive Party (PPP)** government. When the College, renamed Gambia College, was relocated a short distance away, its former buildings were converted into the **Gambia National Army (GNA)** barracks.

YUNDUM EGG PROJECT. A plan put into effect by the **Colonial Development Corporation (CDC)** in late 1948, designed to make the Gambia a major exporter of eggs and dressed chickens. An initial appropriation of £500,000 was made, and an American poultry expert, Millard Phillips, was appointed Field Director. The plan was to clear the bush and timber and sell the wood and plant the prepared land with cereal crops so that no feed need be imported for the birds. Permanent poultry houses were built to accommodate enough chickens to provide at maximum production 20 million eggs and one million pounds of poultry meat per year. The project was plagued from the start by over-optimistic estimates by the officials of the CDC and the field staff who ignored the advice of Governor **Sir Andrew Wright** and his staff. Timber from the cleared site was not of export quality, and the CDC had difficulty even selling it for firewood. By October 1950, crop reports showed an average grain yield of only 207 pounds per acre as compared with estimates of 900 pounds per acre. The poultry, expensive Rhode Island Reds, proved highly susceptible to fowl pest and died by the thousands. By the time the Board of Directors of the Corporation agreed in February 1951 to close the project, it had cost, in direct appropriations, £910,000.

Appendix 1

Chief Executives, 1829–1999

Governors and Administrators

1829	Lt.-Col. Alexander Findlay	Lieut-Governor
1830	George Rendall	Lieut-Governor
1840	Sir Henry F. Huntley	Lieut-Governor
1843	Captain Henry Seagram, R.N.	Governor
1843	Cdr. E. Norcott, RN	Governor
1844	Cdr. G. Fitzgerald, R.N.	Governor
1847	Sir Richard MacDonnell	Governor
1852	Sir Arthur Kennedy	Governor
1852	Col. Luke S. O'Connor	Governor
1859	Col. G. A. K. D'Arcy	Governor
1866	Adm. C. G. E. Patey	Administrator
1871	T. F. Callaghan	Administrator
1873	Sir Cornelius H. Kortright	Administrator
1875	Sir Samuel Rowe	Administrator
1877	Surgeon Major Valerius Gouldsbury	Administrator
1884	Sir C. Alfred Moloney	Administrator
1886	Sir John S. Hay	Administrator
1888	Sir Gilbert T. Carter	Administrator
1891	Sir Robert B. Llewelyn	Administrator
1901	Sir George C. Denton	Governor
1911	Lt.-Col. Sir Henry Galway	Governor
1914	Sir Edward J. Cameron	Governor
1920	Captain Sir Cecil H. Armitage	Governor
1927	Sir John Middleton	Governor
1928	Sir Edward Denham	Governor
1930	Sir H. Richmond Palmer	Governor
1933	Sir Arthur Richards	Governor

1936	Sir W. Thomas Southorn	Governor
1942	Sir Hilary Blood	Governor
1947	Sir Andrew B. Wright	Governor
1949	Sir Percy Wyn-Harris	Governor
1957	Sir Edward Windley	Governor
1962	Sir John Paul	Governor (Governor-General after independence in 1965)
1996–1970	Alhaji Sir Farimang Singhateh	Governor-General

Gambian Chief Executives

1961	Pierre S. N'Jie (UP)	Chief Minister
1962	Sir Dawda K. Jawara (PPP)	Prime Minister
1970	Sir Dawda K. Jawara (PPP)	President
1994	Lt. Yahya. Jammeh	Chairman, AFPRC
1996	Col. (retd.) Yahya Jammeh	President

Appendix 2

Gambian Parliamentary Election Results, 1960–1997*

1960	1962	1966	1972
PPP 9	PPP 18	PPP 23	PPP 28
UP 4	UP 13	UP 4	UP 3
DCA 1	DCA 1	UP/CP 5	IND 1
IND 5	IND 0		

1977	1982	1987	1992
PPP 27**	PPP 27	PPP 31	PPP 25
NCP 5	NCP 3	NCP 5	NCP 6
UP 2	UP 0	GPP 0	GPP 2
NLP 0	IND 5	PDOIS 0	PDP 0
IND 0	PDOIS 0		

1997
APRC 33
UDP 7
NRP 2
PDOIS 1
IND 2

*The number of seats increased from 32 to 45 during the period. In addition there are a number of nominated members, currently four (as well as the Speaker), and five chiefs, elected separately from among the district chiefs.
**Jokadu constituency election postponed: PPP won by-election.

Appendix 3

Gambian Presidential Election Results, 1972–1997

1972

Sir D. K. Jawara (PPP)*
P. H. Coker (UP)

1977

Sir D. K. Jawara (PPP)*
S. M. Dibba (NCP).

1982

Sir D. K. Jawara (PPP)	72.44%
S. M. Dibba (NCP)	27.56%

1987

Sir D. K. Jawara (PPP)	59.65%
S. M. Dibba (NCP)	27.43%
A. M. Camara (GPP)	13.52%

1992

Sir D. K. Jawara (PPP)	58.4%
S. M. Dibba (NCP)	22.0%
A. M. Camara (GPP)	8.1%
Dr. L. Bojang (PDP)	6.0%
S. Jatta (PDOIS)	5.2%

1997

Y. Jammeh (APRC)	56.0%
O. Darboe (UDP)	39.2%
S. Jatta (PDOIS)	2.7%
H. M. K. Bah (GRP)	2.1%

*President elected indirectly by elected MPs.

Appendix 4

Results of Referenda for a Republic

November 1965

Yes   61,568
No   31,921
Fell short of two-thirds majority by 758 votes.

April 1970

Yes   84,968
No   35,638

Met voting requirements.

Appendix 5

Gambian Population Statistics*

1963	315,486
1973	493,499
1983	687,817
1993	1,038,145

*Official census returns.

Appendix 6

Gambian Population: Ethnic Distribution*

	1973	1983	1993
Mandinka/Jahanka	186,241	251,997	353,840
Fula**/Tukolor	79,994	117,092	168,284
Wolof	69,291	84,404	130,546
Jola/Karoninka	41,988	64,494	95,262
Serahuli	38,478	51,137	79,690
Serer	9,229	15,511	24,710
Aku	4,386	5,032	16,550
Manjago	5,596	10,741	7,458
Bambara	1,722	3,035	6,194
Others/Not Stated	3,791	13,796	13,601

*Official census returns.
**"Fula," not "Fulbe," is the form normally used in present day Gambia and is the variant used in the censuses.

Bibliography

Since the publication of the second edition of this work, there has been a very substantial increase in the number of publications on postcolonial Gambia, mainly in the form of articles in scholarly journals, newspapers, and news magazines, and in government publications and other official reports and studies. There are still few monographs on The Gambia, though there is a growing number of unpublished theses. Some are available in photostat and microfiche format from University Microfilms, Ann Arbor, Michigan. Given this embarrassment of riches, the bibliography has had to be selective—identifying only the most relevant publications on the most important subjects.

Those seeking further bibliographical information can do no better than consult Professor David Gamble's four major volumes of Gambian bibliography, amounting to nearly 10,000 items, spanning every conceivable subject and covering several languages, African and European, from the earliest historical references to 1987. All scholars of The Gambia are indebted to Professor Gamble for his lifelong dedication to Gambian bibliography. No other country has been so well served in this respect by a single scholar.

The two major repositories of Gambian documentation are the British Public Record Office, Kew, London, and the Gambia National Archives in the Quadrangle, Banjul. The latter holds a variety of published sources, including newspapers, as well as original official correspondence and reports. Both operate the 30-year rule on accessing confidential documents. Another collection is to be found at the Gambia National Library in Banjul. Official documents relating to censuses, economic and social matters, and planning, which have not been placed in the National Archives, may be consulted at the appropriate government ministries in Banjul. Some early Gambian newspapers are held at the British Library Newspaper depository in Colindale, north London.

General

Bibliographies and Travel Guides

Bibliographies

Gamble, David P. *Gambia Government Serial Publications of the Colonial Period: A Provisional List.* San Francisco, Calif.: David P. Gamble, 1982.
———. *A General Bibliography of The Gambia up to 31st December 1977. Supplement I.* San Francisco, Calif.: David P. Gamble, 1987 (Gambian Studies, no. 18).
———. *A General Bibliography of The Gambia. Supplement II. 1978–1982.* San Francisco, Calif.: David P. Gamble, 1987 (Gambian Studies, no. 19).
———. *The Gambia.* London: Clio Press, World Bibliographical Series vol. 91, 1988.
———. *A General Bibliography of The Gambia. Supplement III. 1983–1987.* San Francisco, Calif.: David P. Gamble, 1990 (Gambian Studies, no. 24).
Gamble, David P., and Louise Sperling. *A General Bibliography of The Gambia (up to 31 December 1977).* Boston: G. K. Hall, 1979.
National Bibliography of the Gambia. Banjul: National Library, 1978–.

Travel Guides and Reference Works

Africa Contemporary Record. New York: Africana Publishing. Annual.
Africa South of the Sahara. London: Europa Publications. Annual.
Fletcher, Andria, and Mitnee Duque Gosswiller. *The Gambia.* Covina, Calif.: Classic Publications, 1977.
The Gambia: The Land and the People/Le Sénégal: La terre et les hommes. Dakar, Senegal: Les Nouvelles Editions Africaines, 1986.
Newton, Alex. *West Africa: A Travel Survival Kit.* London: Lonely Planet, 1981 and reissues.
Tomkinson, Michael. *The Gambia: A Holiday Guide.* London: Michael Thompson, 1983.

Maps

Map: The Gambia. Scale 1:250,000. Tolworth, England: Directorate of Overseas Surveys for The Gambia Government, 1980 (Series D.O.S. 615. Edition 1-D.O.S. 1980).

William R. Stanley. *Tourist Map of The Gambia*. Banjul: Ministry of Tourism, 1979.

Dictionaries and Grammars

Faye, J. C., and M. A. Sillah. *The Orthography of Gambian Languages—Wolof and Mandinka*. Bathurst: 1956.

Gamble, David P. *Elementary Mandinka*. San Francisco, Calif.: David P. Gamble, 1987.

———. *Intermediate Gambian Mandinka-English Dictionary*. San Francisco, Calif: David P. Gamble, 1987.

———. *Intermediate Mandinka*. San Francisco, Calif.: David P. Gamble, 1987.

Gamble, David P., and M. Baldeh. *Gambian Fula-English Dictionary*. San Francisco, Calif.: David P. Gamble, 1981.

Gamble, David P., Linda K. Salmon, and Mary Umah Baldeh. *Firdu-Fula Grammar* (Gambian dialect). San Francisco, Calif.: David P. Gamble, 1981.

Nussbaum, Loren V. *Dakar Wolof: A Basic Course*. Washington, D.C.: Center for Applied Linguistics, 1970.

Rowlands, E. C. *A Grammar of Gambian Mandinka*. London: SOAS, 1959.

Sapir, J. David. *A Grammar of Diola-Fogny*. Cambridge: Cambridge University Press, 1965.

Tarawale, B., et al. *Mandinka English Dictionary*. Banjul: National Literacy Advisory Committee, 1980.

History

Archaeology

Beale, P. O. *The Anglo-Gambian Stone Circles Expedition, 1964–65: A Report Presented to the Prime Minister of The Gambia*. Bathurst: Government Printer, 1966.

———. "The Stone Circles of The Gambia and Senegal." *Tarikh* 2, 2 (1968): 1–11.

Evans, Deric. "Stonehenges of West Africa." *Country Life* 157 (16 January 1975): 134–135.

Palmer, Sir Henry Richmond. "Stone Circles in the Gambian Valley." *Journal of the Royal Anthropological Institute* 69 (1939): 273–283.

Parker, Henry. "Stone Circles in Gambia." *Journal of the Royal Anthropological Institute* 53 (1923): 173–228.

Exploration and Travel

15th and 16th Centuries

Asseline, David. *Les antiquités et chroniques de la ville de Dieppe.* 2 vols. Dieppe: 1874.
Hakluyt, Richard. *Principal Navigations of the English Nation.* 5 vols. London: Hakluyt Society, 1927 (see especially vol. 4, 285 and vol. 5, 44–52).
Monod, Theodore, ed. *Description de la côte occidentale d'Afrique par Valentin Fernandes (1506–1510).* Paris: 1938.
The Voyages of Cadamosto and other Documents on Western Africa in the Second Half of the 15th Century. Translated and edited by Gerald Roe Crone. London: Hakluyt Society, 1937.

17th Century

Barbot, Jean A. *Description of the Coasts of North and South Guinea.* London: n.p., 1732. The first edition of this work was prepared in the 1680s. See especially 70 ff.
Cultru, Prosper. *Premier Voyage de Sieur de la Courbe.* Paris: Larose, 1913.
Jobson, Richard. *The Golden Trade.* London: Penguin Press, 1932.
Le Maire, M. *Voyage to the Canaries, Cape Verd and the Coast of Africa under the Command of M. Dancourt, 1682.* Edinburgh: privately printed, 1887 (see especially 35–60).
Perrot, Nicolas. *L'Afrique de Marmol—de la traduction de Nicolas Perrot.* 3 vols. Paris: Billaine, 1667 (see vol. 3, 70–90).
Rochefort, Jannequin de. *Voyage de Libye au Royaume Genega.* Paris: n.p., 1643.
Stibbs, Capt. B. *Journal of a Voyage up the Gambia.* Printed in Francis Moore, *Travels in the Inland Part of Africa.* London: Edward Cave, 1738.
Thevenot, Melchisedech. *Mémoires du voyage aux Indes Orientales du Général Beaulieu.* Paris: n.p., 1672.
Warburton, Eliot. *Memoirs of Prince Rupert and the Cavaliers.* 3 vols. London: Bentley, 1849 (see: vol. 3 for a reproduction of Colonel Vermuyden's account of a voyage to the Gambia in 1760).

18th Century

Adanson, Michael. *A Voyage to Senegal, the Isle of Goree and the River Gambia.* Translated from the French. London: Nourse, 1759 (see 156–172).

Astley, Thomas. *A New General Collection of Voyages and Travels.* 4 vols. London: Thomas Astley, 1745. Vols. 1 and 2 contain many of the older travel accounts—Cadamosto, Barbot, de Rochefort, Le Maire, and others.

Blagdon, Francis. *Modern Discoveries.* London: n.p., 1802. Vols. 3 and 4 contain S. M. X. Golberry. *Fragmens d'un voyage en Afrique (1785–1787).*

Churchill, Awsham, and John Churchill. *A Collection of Voyages.* London: 1704. Contains older accounts such as those of Courbe and Barbot.

Golberry, Silvanius Meinrad Xavier. *Fragmens d'un voyage en Afrique (1785–1787).* 2 vols. Paris: Treuttel and Wurtz, 1802. English translation, *Travels in Africa.* 2 vols. London: Ridgway, 1803.

Labat, Jean Baptiste. *Nouvelle relation de l'Afrique Occidentale.* 5 vols. Paris: Cavelier, 1728 (see vol. 1, 304–307; vol. 4, 256–264, 367–380; vol. 5, 2–22, 307–324).

Moore, Francis. *Travels in the Inland Part of Africa.* London: Edward Cave, 1738.

Park, Mungo. *Travels in the Interior Districts of Africa.* 2 vols. London: Murray, 1816.

Smith, William. *A New Voyage to Guinea.* London: Nourse, 1744. Reprint: London: Cass, 1967 (see 32 ff. for a description of Smith's visit to the Gambia in 1726–1727).

Walckenaer, Baron Charles Athanase. *Histoire générale des voyages, ou nouvelles collections des relations de voyages par mer et par terre en différentes parties de l'Afrique.* 21 vols. Paris: Lefèvre, 1826–1831.

19th Century

Alexander, James E. *Narrative of a Voyage of Observation Among the Colonies of West Africa.* 2 vols. London: 1853 (see vol. 1, 70–72).

Bowdich, T. E. *Excursions in Madeira and Porto Santa, to which is added . . . "A description of the English Settlements on the River Gambia" by Mrs. Bowdich.* London: Whittaker, 1825.

[Burton, Sir Richard F.] "An F.R.G.S." *Wanderings in West Africa from Liverpool to Fernando Po.* 2 vols. London: Tinsley Bros., 1863 (see vol. 1, 143–190).

Ellis, A. B. *The Land of Fetish*. London: Chapman and Hall, 1883 (see 1–34).

Gaunt, Mary. *Alone in West Africa*. London: Werner Laurie, 1912 (see 13–47).

Gray, Major William. *Travels in Western Africa in the Years 1819, 19, 20, and 21 from the River Gambia, thru Woolli, Bondoo, Galam, Kassan, Kaarta and Foolidoo to the River Niger*. London: Murray, 1825 (see 25–80; 365–368).

Hewett, Captain J. F. Napier. *European Settlements on the West Coast of Africa*. London: Chapman and Hall, 1862. Reprint: New York: Negro U.P., 1969 (see 534–77, 202–289).

Huntley, Captain Sir Henry. *Seven Years' Service on the Slave Coast of Western Africa*. 2 vols. London: Newby, 1850.

Mitchinson, A. W. *The Expiring Continent, A Narrative of Travel in the Senegambia, etc.* London: Allen, 1881.

Mollien, G. T. *Travels in the Interior of Africa to the Sources of the Senegal and Gambia in the Year 1818*. Edited by T. E. Bowdich. London: Colburn, 1820.

Poole, T. E. *Life, Scenery & Customs in Sierra Leone and the Gambia*. 2 vols. London: Bentley, 1850 (see vol. 2, 70–85, 138–140, and 205 ff.).

Rançon, A. *Dans la Haute-Gambie. Voyage d'exploration scientifique, 1891–1892*. Paris: Société d'Editions Scientifiques, 1894.

Reade, W. Winwood. *Savage Africa*. London: Smith, Elder, 1864 (see chapters 30–33).

Whitford, John. *Trading Life in Western and Central Africa*. London: Porcupine, 1877 (see 18–22).

Wilson, J. L. *Western Africa, Its History Conditions and Prospects*. London: 1856.

Wood, J. Dobson. *To West Africa and Back: An Account of a Trip to Gambia and the Canary Islands*. London: n.p., 1894.

20th Century

Crowder, Michael. *Pagans and Politicians*. London: Hutchinson, 1959 (see 34–43).

Hardinge, R. *Gambia and Beyond*. London: Blackie, 1934.

Hempstone, Smith. *Africa, Angry Young Giant*. New York: 1961 (see 359–392). Published in England as *The New Africa*. London: Faber and Faber, 1961.

Hodson, H. "Golden Gambia." *Travel*, January 1957, 52–54.

Huxley, Elspeth. *Four Guineas*. London: Chatto and Windus, 1954 (see 1–45).

MacColl, R. "Gambia, The Colony Nobody Knows." *Atlantic,* May 1962, 108–112.

Phillips, R. H. "Up River through the Gambia." *Crown Colonist* 3 (1933): 249–250.

Porter, Sibyl. "Gambia Journey." *West African Review,* April 1952, 330–332.

Rice, Berkely. "Enter Gambia, Laughing." *Harper's,* October 1966, 74–78.

———. *Enter Gambia: The Birth of an Improbable Nation.* Boston: Houghton Mifflin, 1967.

Van der Plas, C. O. "Discovering the Gambia." *United Nations Review,* December 1958, 15–19.

Willis, Colin. *White Traveller in Black Africa.* London: Dobson, 1951 (see Chapter 10).

Historical Publications

Archer, F. Bisset. *The Gambia Colony and Protectorate.* London: St. Bride's Press, 1906.

Armitage, Capt. C. H. "The Gambia Colony and Protectorate." *Journal of the Royal Society of Arts,* 22 June 1928, 811–818.

Blackburne, Kenneth W. *Lasting Legacy: A Story of British Colonialism.* London: Johnson, 1976 (see 56–75).

Blake, J. W. *European Beginnings in West Africa.* London: Longmans, Green, 1937. Reprint: Westport, Conn.: Greenwood Press, 1969.

Boulegue, Jean. *Les Luso-Africains de Sénégambie, XVI–XIX siècle.* Dakar: Université de Dakar, Département d'Histoire, Travaux et Documents, 1, 1972.

Brooks, George. "Peanuts and Colonialism. Consequences of the Commercialization of Peanuts in West Africa, 1830–70." *Journal of African History* 16, 1 (1975).

Cultru, Prosper. *Les origines de l'Afrique occidentale: Histoire du Sénégal du XVe siècle à 1870.* Paris: Larose, 1910.

Currey, E. Hamilton. "Boat Actions and River Fights—The Baddiboo War." *United Services Magazine* 49 (1914): 124–133.

Curtin, Philip D. *Economic Change in Precolonial Africa: Senegambia in the Era of the Slave Trade.* 2 vols. Madison: University of Wisconsin Press, 1975.

Davies, K. G. *The Royal African Company.* London: Longmans, Green, 1957. Reprint: New York: Octagon Press, 1975.

Deschamps, Hubert. *Le Sénégal et la Gambie.* Paris: Presses Universitaires de France, 1964.

Diederich, Heinrich. *Herzog Jakobs von Kurland Kolonien an der Westkuste von Afrika.* Miltau: 1890.

Eckert, Walter. *Kurland unter dem Einfluss des Merkantilismus, 1551–1682.* Riga: Löffler, 1927 (see 113–191).

Faal, Dawda. *A History of The Gambia AD 1000–1965.* Banjul: D. Faal, 1997.

Fitzgerald, H. E. *The Gambia and Its Proposed Cession to France.* London: Unwin, 1875.

Gailey, Harry A. *A History of the Gambia.* London: Routledge & Kegan Paul, 1964.

Galloway, Winifred Faye. *A History of Wuli from the Thirteenth to the Nineteenth Century.* Ann Arbor, Mich.: University Microfilms, 1975.

————. *James Island: A Background with Historical Notes on Juffure, Albreda, San Domingo, Dog Island.* Banjul: Oral History and Antiquities Division, for The Gambia National Monuments and Relics Commission, 1978.

Grant, D. *The Fortunate Slave: An Illustration of African Slavery in the Early Eighteenth Century.* London: Oxford University Press, 1968 (an account of Job ben Solomon).

Gray, Sir John M. "Zimmerman's 18th Century Gambia Journey." *African Affairs* 58, 230 (February 1959): 65–74.

————. *A History of the Gambia.* Cambridge: Cambridge University Press, 1940. Reprint: London: Cass, 1966.

Hamlyn, W. T. *A Short History of the Gambia.* Bathurst: Government Printer, 1931.

Harden, D. B. "The Phoenicians on the West Coast of Africa." *Antiquity* 87 (September 1948): 141–150.

Hatton, P. H. S. "The Gambia, the Colonial Office and the Opening Months of the First World War." *Journal of African History* 7, 1 (1966): 123–132.

Hurstlet, Sir Edward. *Map of Africa by Treaty.* London: 1894.

Klein, Martin. *Islam and Imperialism in Senegal.* Stanford: Stanford University Press, 1968.

Langley, M. "Gambia: Trading Post to Independent Nation." *History Today,* June 1965, 420–425.

Lawrence, A. W. *Trade Castles and Forts of West Africa.* London: Cape: 1963; Stanford, Cal.: Stanford University Press, 1964. (see especially 250–261).

Macklin, B. W. "Queens and Kings of Niumi." *Man* 35 (May 1935): 67–68.

Mahoney, F. K. "Notes on Mulattoes of the Gambia before the Mid Nineteenth Century." *Transactions of the Historical Society* [Ghana] 8 (1965): 120–129.

————. "African Leadership in Bathurst in the Nineteenth Century." *Tarikh* 2, 2 (1968): 25–38.

Martin, Evelyne. *The British West Africa Settlements 1750–1821.* London: Longmans, Green, 1927.

Mattiesen, Otto Heinz. *Die Kolonial und Überseepolitik der kurlandischen Herzöge im 17 und 18 Jahrhundert.* Stuttgart: Deutsche Ausland Museum und Institut, 1940.

Mbaeyi, P. M. "The Barra-British War of 1831: A Reconstruction of Its Origins and Importance." *Journal of the Historical Society of Nigeria* 3, 4 (June 1967): 617–631.

————. *British Military and Naval Forces in West African History 1807–1874.* New York: Nok, 1978. For Gambia references, see 23–25, 40–42, 71–78, 100–101, 112–117, 160–161, 168–171, 175–177.

Palmer, H. R. *The Carthaginian Voyage to West Africa.* Bathurst: Government Printer, 1931.

Pfeffer, Karl Heinz. *Sierra Leone and Gambia.* Bonn: Deutscher Afrika Geselleschaft: Die Lander Afrikas, Band 11, 1958.

Quinn, Charlotte A. "Maba Diakhou Ba, Scholar-Warrior of the Senegambia." *Tarikh* 2, 3 (1968.)

————. "Niumi: A Nineteenth Century Mandingo Kingdom." *Africa* 38, 4 (October 1968): 443–455.

————. "Mandingo States in Nineteenth Century Gambia." In *Papers on the Manding,* ed. Carleton T. Hodge. Bloomington, Ind.: Indiana University; The Hague: Mouton & Co., 1971.

————. "A Nineteenth Century Fulbe State." *Journal of African History* 12, 3 (1971): 427–440.

————. *Mandingo Kingdoms of the Senegambia: Traditionalism, Islam and European Expansion.* Evanston, Ill.: Northwestern University Press, 1972.

————. "Maba Diakhou and the Gambian *Jihad,* 1850–1890." In *Studies in West African Islamic History,* vol. 1, ed. John Ralph Willis. London: Cass, 1979: 233–258.

Reeve, Henry F. *The Gambia.* London: Smith, Elder, 1912.

Sabatie, A. *Le Sénégal: Sa conquête et son organisation, 1364–1925.* Paris: 1962.

Sillah, M. B. "The Demise of Kings." *West Africa,* June 6, 1983.

Southorn, Lady Bella. "James Island." *West African Review,* May 1949, 484–489, 506–507 (photographs).

————. *The Gambia.* The Story of the Groundnut Colony. London: George Allen & Unwin, 1952.

Southorn, Sir Wilfrid Thomas. "Earliest British Settlement in Africa." *Crown Colonist* 13 (1943): 391–392.

Stein, Robert. "Mortality in the Eighteenth Century Slave Trade." *Journal of African History* 21, 1 (1980).

Verdier, A. *Echange de territoire coloniale*. La Rochelle: 1876.

Weil, Peter M. "Slavery, Groundnuts, and European Capitalism in the Wuli Kingdom of Senegambia, 1820–1930." *Research in Economic Anthropology* 6 (1984): 77–119.

Wood, W. Raymond. "An Archaeological Appraisal of Early European Settlements in the Senegambia." *Journal of African History* 8, 1 (1967): 39–64.

Wright, Donald R. *The Early History of Niumi: Settlement and Foundation of a Mandinka State on the River Gambia*. Athens, Ohio: Ohio University Center for International Studies, Africa Program, 1977.

————. *Oral Traditions from The Gambia. Vol. I: Mandinka Griots*. Athens, Ohio: 1979.

————. *Oral Traditions from The Gambia. Vol. II: Family Elders*. Athens, Ohio: 1980.

————. "Uprooting Kunta Kinte: On the Perils of Relying on Encyclopedic Informants." *History in Africa* 8 (1981): 205–217 [critique of Alex Haley's research for *Roots*].

Young, Frederick, et al. *Report of the Council of the Royal Colonial Institute on the Gambia Question*. London: 1876.

Great Britain, Colonial Office and Parliamentary Papers

British Parliamentary Papers: The Gambia Papers 1845–87. Shannon: Irish University Press, 1971. Reprint.

Correspondence Relating to British and French Jurisdiction. African No 377. 1890.

Correspondence Relating to the Gambian Expedition. 1901. The details of the joint French-English expedition against Fodi Kabba and Musa Molloh.

Correspondence Relating to the Territories on the River Gambia. African No 348. 1887.

Correspondence Respecting the Affairs of the Gambia and the Proposed Exchange with France. C.1409. London: 1876.

Petitions from the Inhabitants of the Gambia, praying that the settlement be not ceded to France. C.1498. London: 1876.

A Reply of the Merchants of the Gambia to the Despatches of Sir Arthur Kennedy. West African Pamphlet No 1. 1870.

Politics and Administration

Colonial Period to Independence

General

Crowder, Michael. "Chiefs in Gambia Politics." *West Africa*, 18 October 1958, 25 October 1958.

Foon, Marion, "Operation Ping-Pong to Beat Votes Fiddlers." *Journal of African Administration* 13, 1 (January 1961): 35–37.

Gailey, Harry A. "Gambia Chiefs' Question." *West Africa,* 11 March 1961.

———. "What Next in the Gambia." *West Africa,* 22 July 1961, 29 July 1961.

———. *A History of The Gambia.* London: 1964 (184–205).

Land, Harry. "What Status for Sierra Leone and Gambia?" *New Commonwealth,* September 1960.

———. "The Gambia—Politics and Groundnuts." *New Commonwealth,* September 1962.

Langley, J. Ayo. "The Gambia Section of the National Congress of British West Africa." *Africa* 39, 4 (Oct. 1969): 382–395.

Nyang, Sulayman S. "The Historical Development of Political Parties in The Gambia." *African Research Bulletin* 5, 4 (1975).

———. *The Role of the Gambian Political Parties in National Integration.* Ann Arbor, Mich.: University Microfilms, 1981. Covers period from 1860s to 1972.

Orde, M. H. "The Development of Local Government in Rural Areas in the Gambia." *Journal of Local Administration Overseas* 4, 1 (January 1965): 51–59.

People's Progressive Party (PPP). *A Better Life for Our People: Achievements of the People's Progressive Party 1962–1979.* Banjul: n.d.

———. *The Voice of the People. The Story of the PPP, 1959–89.* Banjul: 1992.

Perfect, David. "The Political Career of Edward Francis Small." In A. Hughes, *The Gambia: Studies in Society and Politics.* Birmingham, England: Centre of West African Studies, Birmingham University African Studies Series, 3, 1991 (64–79).

Price, J. H. "Women in Politics." *Proceedings of the Nigerian Institute of Social and Economic Research* [Ibadan, Nigeria] (1959): 151–158.

Weil, Peter. M. *Mandinka Mansaya: The Role of the Mandinka in the Political System of the Gambia.* Ann Arbor, Mich.: University Microfilms, 1968.

Welch, Claude. "Gambia's David Kairaba Jawara." *Africa Report* 10, 2 (February 1965).

Articles Listed Chronologically, No Author

"The Gambia's Amiable Ambassador." [Portrait of Rev. J. C. Faye] *West Africa*, 30 August 1952.

"Government Confers with Chiefs in the Gambia," *New Commonwealth*, 6 July 1953.

"Gambia and Malta." *West Africa*, 11 January 1958.

"P.S. N'Jie." [Portrait] *West Africa*, 3 May 1958.

"Training Period for Gambian Politicians." *New Commonwealth*, June 1959.

"Universal Suffrage for the Gambia" *New Commonwealth*, October 1959.

"Politics in the Gambia." [1960 elections] *West Africa*, 21 May 1960.

"One Gambia Party Now Seeks Independence." *New Commonwealth*, September 1960.

"Gambia's Next Step." *West Africa*, 26 November 1960.

"Independence Aim in the Gambia." *New Commonwealth*, December 1960.

"Role of the Chiefs in the Gambia." *New Commonwealth*, January 1961.

"Gambia Moves Forward." *West Africa*, 1 April 1961.

"Seyfou Omar M'Baki-Portrait." *West Africa*, 8 April 1961.

"Independence for Gambia?" *West Africa*, 20 May 1961.

"Gambia Has a Chief Minister." *New Commonwealth*, May 1961.

"Man of the People." [Portrait of P. S. N'Jie] *West Africa*, 29 July 1961.

"Self-Government for the Gambia." *West Africa*, 5 August 1961.

"Independence on the Agenda." *West Africa*, 19 August 1961.

"Blow to Gambia's Ruling Party." *New Commonwealth*, December 1961.

"The Gambia Looks Forward." *West Africa*, 17 March 1962.

"Gambia on the Verge of Self-Government." *New Commonwealth*, April 1962.

"Campaigning in the Gambia." *West Africa*, 19 May 1962.

"New Men in the Gambia." *West Africa*, 9 June 1962.

"Self-Government in the Gambia." *West Africa*, 28 July 1962.

"Independence '63?" *West Africa*, 13 April 1963.

"Full Internal . . ." *West Africa*, 20 July 1963.

"Election Controversy in the Gambia." *New Commonwealth*, October 1963.

"Gambia's Critical Period." *West Africa*, 16 May 1964.

"Gambia 1962 Election Judgment." *West Africa*, 11 July 1964.

"Towards an Independent Gambia." *West Africa*, 18 July 1964.

"The Last Governor." [Portrait, Sir John Paul] *West Africa*, 22 August 1964.

"The Gambia's Number Two." [Portrait, Sheriff Sisay] *West Africa*, 31 October 1964.

"New Voice from Africa." [Dawda Jawara] *West Africa,* 13 February 1965.
"The Gambia's High Commissioner." [Louis Valantine] *West Africa,* 20
    February 1965.

*Gambia Government and British Government, Selected Ordinances
and Other Publications (listed chronologically, ordinances first;
except where otherwise stated, all are Gambian government
publications, published in Bathurst by the Government Printer)*

No 11. 1894. *Protectorate Ordinance.* The basic government ordinance that
    established indirect rule in the Protectorate, it remained in force subject
    to changes by Amendment Ordinances until 1913. However, even after
    being officially supplanted, this Ordinance remained the key to the future
    theoretical development of Protectorate Administration.
No 7. 1895. *Protectorate Yard Tax Ordinance.* First defined a yard as the ba-
    sic unit of taxation for the Protectorate and established scales of taxation.
No 6. 1896. *Protectorate Land Ordinance.* The basic ordinance that gov-
    erned all Protectorate lands, except Public Lands, until 1945. All lands
    were to be held by the Native Authorities and administered by them for
    the good of the people of a district.
No 4. 1897. *Protectorate Land (Amendment) Ordinance.* Vested the admin-
    istration of Public Lands in the Chiefs and Headmen of the Protectorate.
No 7. 1902. *Protectorate Ordinance.* Brought Fuladu, previously controlled
    by Mussa Molloh, under the Protectorate system. Also extended the system
    to British Kombo. Otherwise this Ordinance was a repeat of No 11, 1894.
No 11. 1909. *Protectorate (Amendment) Ordinance.* The most important
    amendment to No 7, 1902, gave the native tribunals jurisdiction over all
    natives of West Africa resident in a given district.
No 13. 1909. *Protectorate (Amendment) Ordinance.* Concerned the ap-
    pointment and regulation of badge messengers for the Chiefs.
No 30. 1913. *Protectorate Ordinance.* Repealed all previous Protectorate
    Ordinances and consolidated them, along with Rules and Regulations
    made by the Governor in Council, into one all-inclusive ordinance.
No 10. 1915. *Protectorate (Amendment) Ordinance.* Redefined and clarified
    the executive powers of the Chiefs, which had been defined in Ordinance
    No 30, 1913.
No 7. 1919. *Protectorate (Amendment) Ordinance.* Introduced a new office
    of Deputy Head Chief and a refined method of appointing and removing
    Protectorate officials. Also introduced a new scale of yard taxes.

No 13. 1944. *Protectorate Courts Ordinance.* Repealed Ordinance No 5, 1935, and instituted a High Court for the Protectorate with the same power as the Supreme Court of the Colony. Continued a Protectorate Court in each Division. Established two classes of Magistrates.

No 15. 1944. *Protectorate (Amendment) Ordinance.* Changed the title of certain territorial divisions and administrative areas. Added the position of Senior Commissioner.

No 10. 1945. *Native Authority (Amendment) Ordinance.* Gave Native Authorities the power to expel non-Gambians from the area of their jurisdiction.

No 11. 1945. *Protectorate (Amendment) Ordinance.* Amended Protectorate Ordinance No 2, 1935, to allow fines imposed on Native Officials to be paid to the general revenue of the Native Authority.

No 13. 1945. *Protectorate Treasuries Ordinance.* Established Authority of Group Treasuries. Established a Finance Committee to manage the Treasuries with a paid Treasury scribe. Established sources of revenue for such Treasuries, provided for budget estimates and better bookkeeping. Gave the authorities the right to impose, under certain conditions, local rates.

No 16. 1945. *Protectorate Land Ordinance.* Vested all Protectorate lands in the Authorities for each District. Established a land register and provided for leases to non-indigenes.

No 13. 1946. *Protectorate (Amendment) Ordinance.* Amended Ordinance No 2, 1935, by removing British Kombo from the Protectorate system.

No 16. 1946. *Education Ordinance.* Section No 13 gave the Native Authorities the right to open new schools under the general supervision of the Protectorate Education Officer.

No 7. 1947. *Protectorate (Amendment) Ordinance.* This brought Ordinance No 3, 1933, and Ordinance No 2, 1935, closer together by defining "Native Authority" in terms of the definition of 1933 and by substituting "Native Authority" for "Chiefs" in Section 13 of Ordinance No 2, 1935.

No 10. 1947. *Protectorate Treasuries (Validation) Ordinance.* No Proclamation had been issued putting Ordinance No 13, 1945, into effect. Since Treasuries had been established, it was necessary to enact this ordinance, making such establishments legal.

Instructions for the Travelling Commissioners of the Gambia. West African Pamphlet No 125. 1923.

Political Memoranda for the Guidance of Commissioners and Other Government Officers Working in the Protectorate. 1933.

Instructions for the Guidance of Commissioners. 1936.

Report of the Committee on the Legislative Council Franchise. Sessional Paper No 2. 1944.

Some Aspects of Local Government. Foreword by Sir Hilary Blood. 1946.
Report of the Bathurst Temporary Local Authority for the Year 1945. Sessional Paper No 9. 1946.
Hailey, Lord. *Native Administration in the British African Territories*. 4 vols. London: H.M.S.O., 1950. Vol. 3, 329–350 treats in great detail the instruments of the Gambia government up to 1951.
Consultative Committee on the Constitution. "Report. 1953." *The Gambia Gazette*. 70 (31 July 1953).
Proposed Constitutional Changes in the Gambia. Sessional Paper No 27. 1953.
Central Office of Information (London). *Constitutional Progress in the Gambia*. London: 1955.
Constitutional Development in the Gambia. Sessional Paper No 4. 1959.
Constitutional Development in the Gambia. Sessional Paper No 6. 1961.
Report of Gambian Constitutional Conference. Cmnd. 1469. London: H.M.S.O., 1961.
The Gambia Independence Conference. Cmnd.2435. London: H.M.S.O., 1964.

Independence to the Military Coup of 1994

General

Davis, D., D. Hulme, and P. Woodhouse. "Decentralisation by Default: Local Governance and the View from the Village." *Public Administration and Development* 14, 3 (1994): 253–269.
Fletcher, Andria J. *Party Politics in The Gambia*. Ann Arbor, Mich.: University Microfilms, 1978. Covers period to 1977.
Gaye, Baboucar. "Jawara's New Opposition." [interview with GPP leader, H. M. Camara] *West Africa*, 14 April 1986.
Hughes, A. "Jawara Wins Again," *West Africa*, 14, 21, and 28 April 1972.
———. "From Green Uprising to National Reconciliation: The People's Progressive Party in the Gambia 1959–1973." *Canadian Journal of African Studies* 9, 1 (1975): 61–74.
———. "Gambia Election Report." *West Africa*, 4 and 18 April 1977.
———. "The Gambian General Elections." *West Africa*, 10, 17, and 24 May 1982.
———. "The Limits of 'Consociational Democracy' in The Gambia." *Civilisations* 22, 2 and 23, 1 (1982–1983): 65–95.
———. "From Colonialism to Confederation: The Gambian Experience of Independence." In *African Islands and Enclaves*, ed. R. Cohen. Beverly Hills, Calif.: Sage Publications, 1983.

————. "Les elections gambiennes de mars 1987." *Politique africaine* 26 (1987): 121–277.

————. "The Gambia." In *Politics, Security and Development in Small States,* ed. C. Clarke and T. Payne. London: Allen and Unwin, 1987.

————. *The Gambia: Studies in Society and Politics.* Birmingham, England: Centre of West African Studies, Birmingham University African Studies Series, 3, 1991.

Manjang, Ousman. "The Gambian General Elections." *West Africa,* 10 May 1982.

————. "Gambian Liberation." *West Africa,* 26 July 1982.

Momoh, Eddie. "Jawara Wins Again." [1987 elections] *West Africa,* 16 March 1987.

Nyang, Sulayman S. "Ten Years of Gambia's Independence: A Political Analysis." *Présence africaine,* no. 104 (fourth quarter 1977): 28–45.

Sall, Ebrima. "Petite dimension et gouvernmentable: Essai d'analyse de l'edification de l'état en Gambie." Ph.D. diss., University of Paris, 1992.

Weil, Peter M. "Tradition and Opposition in Area Council Elections in the Gambia." *Journal of Asian and African Studies* 6, 2 (April 1971): 108–117.

Wiseman, J. A. "The Social and Economic Bases of Party Political Support in Serrekunda, The Gambia." *Journal of Commonwealth and Comparative Politics* 23, 1 (1985).

————. "The Gambian Presidential and Parliamentary Elections of 1987." *Electoral Studies* 6, 3 (December 1987).

————. *Democracy in Black Africa: Survival and Revival.* New York: Paragon House, 1990. See 51–64, "The Gambia."

————. "The Role of the House of Representatives in the Gambian Political System." In A. Hughes, *The Gambia: Studies in Society and Politics.* Birmingham, England: Centre of West African Studies, Birmingham University African Studies Series, 3, 1991 (80–91).

Articles Listed Chronologically, No Author

"The Gambia Goes It Alone." *West Africa,* 16, 23, 30 January, 6 February 1965.

"Newest, Smallest: Gambia Gains Independence." *Time,* 26 February 1965.

"Toward the Gambia Republic." *West Africa,* 25 September and 2 October, 1965.

"The Republic Rejected." *West Africa,* 4 December 1965.

The Gambia—May Elections." *West Africa,* 23 April 1966.
"The Gambian in Government House." [Portrait of Governor-General Sir Farimang Singhateh] *West Africa,* 30 April 1966.
"The Gambia Votes." *West Africa,* 11 June 1966.
"New Referendum on Republic." *West Africa,* 7 June 1969.
"Power in The Gambia." *West Africa,* 2 May 1970.
"Democracy at Work." *West Africa,* 15 May 1978.
"Third Opposition Party Formed." [formation of PDOIS] *West Africa,* 25 August 1986.

Gambian Government Reports

Report of the Constituency Boundaries Commission. Sessional Paper No 2. Bathurst: Government Printer, 1966.
An Act to Establish and Make Provisions for the Constitution of the Gambia. *The Gambia Gazette (Supplement)* No. 4, November 1969.

1981 Coup Attempt

Adams, James. *Secret Armies.* London: Hutchinson, 1987: 172–177.
Amnesty International Trial Observation Missions to the Republic of the Gambia (December 1980/January 1982). London: 1983.
Bakarr, S. A. *The Gambia Mourns Her Image.* Banjul: S. A. Bakaar, 1981.
———. *The Law of Treason in The Republic of The Gambia Versus Alieu Sallah and 6 Revolutionists.* Banjul: S. A. Bakaar [1982?].
Hughes, A. "Why the Gambian Coup Failed." *West Africa,* 21 October 1981, 2 November 1981.
———. "The attempted Gambian Coup d'Etat of 30 July 1981." In A. Hughes, *The Gambia: Studies in Society and Politics.* Birmingham, England: Centre of West African Studies, Birmingham University African Studies Series, 3, 1991 (92–106).
In The Gambia Court of Appeal Special Division. Criminal Appeal No 5–11/81. Taffa Camara and others. [Trial of 1981 coup plotters] Banjul: Gambia Court of Appeal [1982].
In The Gambia Court of Appeal. 2 vols. Criminal Appeal No. 29/82. [Trial of Sheriff Dibba, Pap Cheyassin O. Secka and others] [1982].
"Koro Sallah [MOJA-G leader] interview." *West Africa,* 22 and 29 March 1982.
Nyang, Sulayman, S. "The Gambia After the Rebellion." *Africa Report,* November–December 1981.

Report of the Commission to Inquire into the Conduct and Management of the External Aid Fund. Banjul: Government Printer, 1983.

"Restabilising the Gambia." *West Africa,* 10 August 1981.

Wiseman, J. A. "Revolt in The Gambia: A Pointless Tragedy." *The Round Table* 284 (1981).

————. "Attempted Coup in The Gambia: Marxist Revolution or Punk Rebellion?" *Communist Affairs* 1, 2 (1982).

1994 to the Present

General

Amnesty International. *The Gambia: Democratic Reforms without Human Rights.* 2 December 1997. London: 1997.

The Armed Forces Provisional Ruling Council's Programme of Rectification and Transition to Democratic Constitutional Rule in The Gambia. Banjul: Government Printer, 24 October 1994.

Busia, Nana Kusi Appea. "The No-Win Situation." [Two-part article on 1994 coup] *West Africa,* 30 October–5 November and 6–12 November 1995.

Dabo, B. B. "Living in Crisis." *West Africa,* 13–19 Feruary 1995.

Oat, D. R. Jr. [pseud.]. "Anatomy of a Coup." *West Africa,* 28 August–4 September 1994.

Rake, Alan. "How to Rig Elections." *New Africa,* October 1996.

Sall, E., and H. Sallah. "The Military and the Crisis of Governance: The Gambian Case." Codesria (Dakar), Eighth General Assembly, 26 June to 2 July 1995.

Whiteman, K. "The Year of Jammeh." *West Africa,* 26 December 1994–8 January 1995.

Wiseman, J. A. "Military Rule in The Gambia: An Interim Assessment." *Third World Quarterly* 17 (December 1996): 917–940.

————. "Letting Yahya Jammeh off Lightly?" *Review of African Political Economy* 72 (1997): 265–276.

————. "The Gambia: From Coup to Elections." *Journal of Democracy* 9, 2 (April 1998): 64–75.

Wiseman, J. A., and ElizabethVidler, "The July 1994 Coup d'Etat in The Gambia: The End of an Era." *The Round Table* 333 (January 1995): 63–65.

Yeebo, Zaya. *State of Fear in Paradise: The Military Coup in The Gambia and Its Implications for Democracy.* London: Africa Research and Information Bureau, 1995.

Articles Listed Chronologically, No Author

"The Coup in Banjul." *West Africa*, 1–7 August 1994.
"Who Is Yahya Jammeh?" *West Africa*, 1–7 August 1994.
"After the Coup." *West Africa*, 8–14 August 1994.
"Jammeh Counter-Attacks." *West Africa*, 10–16 October 1994.
"Sir Dawda Breaks His Silence." *West Africa*, 10–16 October 1994.
"Abortive Coup." *West Africa*, 21–27 November 1994.
"Coup Plot Foiled." *West Africa*, 6–12 February 1995.
"Towards Transition—The Report of and Recommendations of the National Consultative Committee (NCC)." *West Africa*, 13–19 February 1995.
"Gambia's Missing Millions." *New African*, January 1997.

Political Party Constitutions and Manifestos (listed chronologically)

The Gambia Muslim Congress. Party Manifesto. [Bathurst: 1959].
Constitution of the People's Progressive Party [PPP]. [Banjul: 1960?].
The Farafenni Declaration. Banjul: National Convention Party, 1976.
For Continued Peace, Progress and Prosperity. Manifesto of the People's Progressive Party [PPP]. 1987 General Elections. [Banjul: 1987].
Manifesto of the Gambian People's Party. [Banjul: 1987].
Alliance for Patriotic Re-orientation and Construction (APRC) Constitution. [Banjul: 1996].
Alliance for Patriotic Re-orientation and Construction (APRC) Manifesto. [Banjul: 1996].
The Manifesto of the United Democratic Party. [Banjul: August 1996].
Statement by Mr. A. N. M. Ousainu Darboe, the Secretary-General and Leader of the United Democratic Party (UDP), on the Occasion of the Launching of the 1996 Presidential Election Campaign. [Banjul: 9 September 1996.]

External Relations

General

Denton, Fatma E. "Foreign Policy Formulation in The Gambia, 1965–1994: Small Weak Developing States and their Foreign Policy Decisions and Choices." Ph.D. diss., University of Birmingham, England, 1998.
Gomez, Solomon. "The Gambia's External Relations: A Study in the Internal and External Factors that Influenced Foreign Policy Positions, 1965–75." Ph.D. diss., Johns Hopkins University, Baltimore, 1978.

Momen, W. C. "The Foreign Policy and Relations of The Gambia." Ph.D. diss., University of London (LSE), 1978.

Touray, Omar. "The Foreign Policy problems of Developing Microstates: The Case of the Gambia, 1975–1990." Ph.D. diss., University of Geneva, 1994.

Senegambian Relations

Bayo, Kalidu M. *Mass Orientations and Regional Integration: Environmental Variations in Gambian Orientations towards Senegambia.* Ann Arbor, Mich.: University Microfilms, 1977.

Bentsi-Enchill, Nii K. "Senegalese Presence in the Gambia." *West Africa,* 11 January 1982.

———. "Sir Dawda Explains the Confederation." *West Africa,* 18 January 1982.

———. "Senegambia Notebook." *West Africa,* 8 and 15 February 1982.

———. "Senegambia: Implementation Stage." *West Africa,* 9 August 1982.

———. "Year of Confederation." *West Africa,* 10 January 1983.

Bridges, R. C., ed. *Senegambia: Proceedings of a Colloquium at the University of Aberdeen.* Aberdeen, Scotland: 1974.

Bridges, R. C., and J. Lewis. "Beyond Francophonie: The Senegambian Confederation in Retrospect." In *State and Society in Francophone Africa since Independence,* ed. A. H. M. Kirk-Greene and Daniel Bach. London: 1995.

Coppa, Paul Joseph. "Senegambia Confederation: Prospects for Unity on the African Continent." *New York Law School* 7, 1 (Summer 1986): 66.

De Meredieu, J., and R. Aubrac. *Report to the Governments of Gambia and Senegal: Integrated Agricultural Development in the Gambia River Basin.* Rome: FAO, 1964.

Deschamps, Hubert. "Les frontières de la Sénégambie." *Revue francaise d'études politiques africaines* 80 (August 1972): 44–57.

Diene-Njie, Codou Mbassy. Gambia: *The Fall of the Old Order. Senegambia and Beyond.* Dakar: Les Editions Cheikh Anta Diop, 1996.

Diop, Momar-Coumba. *Le Sénégal et ses voisins.* Dakar: Sociétés-Espaces-Temps, 1994.

Faye, Ouseynou. "La crise casamancaise et les relations du Sénégal avec la Gambie et la Guinee-Bissau." In ibid.: 189–212.

Gaye, Baboucar. "Killing Two Birds with One Stone." *West Africa,* 9 September 1985.

Harrison-Church, Ronald J. "Gambia and Senegal: Senegambia." *Geography Magazine,* September 1966, 339–350.

———. "Senegal and Gambia: Some Problems of Association." In *Etudes de géographie tropicale offertes à Pierre Gourou.* Paris: 1972.

Hughes, A. "Senegambia Revisited or Gambian Perceptions of Integration with Senegal." In R. C. Bridges, ed., *Senegambia: Proceedings of a Colloquium at the University of Aberdeen.* Aberdeen, Scotland: 1974.

————. "The Collapse of the Senegambian Confederation." *Journal of Commonwealth and Comparative Politics* 30, 2 (July 1992): 200–222.

Janneh, Amadou S. "Dilemmas of Senegambian Integration." Ph.D. diss., University of Tennessee, Knoxville, 1990.

Omole, B. "L'éclatement de la Sénégambie." *Année africaine.* Bordeaux: CEAN, 1989.

Proctor, J. H. "The Gambia's Relations with Senegal: The Search for Partnership." *Journal of Commonwealth Political Studies* 5, 2 (1967): 143–160.

Renner, F. A. "Ethnic Affinity, Partition and Political Integration in Senegambia." In *Partitioned Africans: Ethnic Relations across Africa's International Boundaries 1884–1984,* ed. A. I. Asiwaju. London: C. Hurst, 1985.

Robson, P. "The Problem of Senegambia." *Journal of Modern African Studies* 3, 3 (October 1965): 393–407.

————. "Problems of Integration between Senegal and Gambia." In *African Integration and Disintegration,* ed. A. Hazlewood. London: 1967.

————. *Integration, Development and Equity: Economic Integration in West Africa.* London: Allen and Unwin, 1983.

"Senegambia—Maintaining Sovereignty in an Association of West African States." *Parliamentarian: Journal of the Parliaments of the Commonwealth* 67, 1 (January 1986): 14–16.

Senghor, Jeggan Colley. *Politics and the Functional Strategy to International Integration: Gambia in Senegambian Integration.* Ann Arbor, Mich.:University Microfilms, 1979.

————. *The Logical Bases for Senegambian Integration.* Banjul: Book Production and Material Resources Unit, 1985.

Van Moek, H. J., et al. *Report on the Alternatives for Association between The Gambia and Senegal.* Bathurst: Government Printer, 1964.

Welch, Claude, Jr. "Is Senegambia Any Closer?" *West Africa,* 7 March 1964, 263; 14 March 1964, 285; 21 March 1964, 313.

————. "Gambia and the U.N. Report." *West Africa,* 4 July 1964.

————. *Dream of Unity.* Ithaca, N.Y.: 1966.

Articles Listed Chronologically, No Author.

"Gambia's Links with Her Neighbours." *New Commonwealth,* January 1960, 57.

"Gambia Feels Pressure from Senegal." *New Commonwealth*, November 1960, 739.

"Gambia and Senegal Get Together." *New Commonwealth*, June 1961, 393.

"The Gambia and the OAU." *West Africa*, 5 June 1965.

"The Smuggling Problem." *West Africa*, 12 and 19 April 1969.

"Confederal Economics." *West Africa*, 20 January 1986.

"Death of Senegambia." *West Africa*, 9–15 October 1989.

Official Correspondence, Agreements, and Policy Statements (listed chronologically; except where otherwise stated, all are published in Banjul by the Government Printer)

Senegalo-Gambian Agreements (1965–1976). Senegalo-Gambian Permanent Secretariat, Banjul: [n.d.].

The Senegalo-Gambian Permanent Secretariat: Historical Background. Senegalo-Gambian Permanent Secretariat, Banjul: [n.d.].

Convention for the Creation of the Gambia River Basin Development Organisation. Banjul: 30 June 1978.

Note on Senegalo-Gambian Co-operation. Senegalo-Gambian Secretariat, Banjul: June 1979.

The Agreement Between the Republic of The Gambia and the Republic of Senegal Concerning the Establishment of the Senegambia Confederation. Dakar: 17 December 1981.

Foreign Policy Guidelines: Selected Speeches by His Excellency Alhaji Sir Dawda Kairaba Jawara, President of the Republic of The Gambia and the Honourable Minister of External Affairs, Alhaji Lamin Kiti Jabang, M.P. Banjul: Government Printer, 1982.

Protocol on the Coordination of Policy in the Field of External Relations. Banjul: 2 July 1982.

Protocol on the Financial Regulation of the Confederation. Banjul: 2 July 1982.

Protocols of the Institutions of the Confederation. Banjul: 2 July 1982.

Protocol on Confederal Defence and the Integration of the Armed Forces of the Republic of The Gambia and the Republic of Senegal for the Establishment of the Armed Forces of the Senegambian Confederation. Banjul: 12 January 1983.

Law

Bridges, Sir Philip, "A Note on the Law in The Gambia." In A. Hughes, *The Gambia: Studies in Society and Politics*. Birmingham, England: Centre of West African Studies, Birmingham University African Studies Series, 3, 1991.

The Constitution of The Republic of The Gambia. Bathurst: Government Printer, 1970.

Darboe, Momodou N. *The Interaction of Western and African Traditional Systems of Justice: The Problem of Integration.* Ann Arbor, Mich.: University Microfilms, 1982.

A Draft of a Constitution for the Second Republic of The Gambia. Banjul: Government Printer [1996].

Gray, Sir John. *Notes on Criminal Procedure in Subordinate Courts.* Bathurst: Government Printer, 1934.

Gray, Sir John, compiler. *A Revised Edition of the Ordinances of the Colony of the Gambia.* Bathurst: Government Printer, 1942.

Hopkinson, Dr. E. *Notes on the Laws of the Gambia Protectorate 1885–1923.* Bathurst: Government Printer, 1926.

Kingdon, Donald, compiler. *A Chronological Table and an Index of the Ordinances of the Colony of the Gambia, 1901–1908.* London: Waterlow, 1909.

Montagu, Algernon, and Francis Smith, compilers. *Ordinances of the Settlement on the Gambia, Passed in the Years Between the 10th August 1818 and 30 December 1885.* 3 vols. London: Eyre and Spottiswoode, 1882–1887.

Russell, Alexander, compiler. *Ordinances of the Colony of the Gambia in Force 31 July 1900, with an Appendix Containing Rules under Ordinances.* 2 vols. London: Waterlow, 1900.

Thompson, J. H., and Donald Kingdon, compilers. *The Laws of the Gambia in Force on the lst day of January 1955.* 6 vols. London: Waterlow, 1955.

Economics

General

Ahmed, I., A. Bigsten, A Munoz, and P. Vashishta. *Poverty in The Gambia.* Geneva: 1992.

Allen, C. "African Trade Unionism in Microcosm: The Gambia Labour Movement, 1929–67." In *African Perspectives,* ed. C. Allen and R. W. Johnson. Cambridge: Cambridge University Press, 1970.

Barrett, H. R., and A. W. Browne. "Environmental and Economic Sustainability: Women's Horticultural Production in The Gambia." *Geography* 76 (1991): 241–248.

Carney, Judith Ann. *The Social History of Gambian Rice Production: An Analysis of Food Security Strategies.* Ann Arbor, Mich.: University Microfilms, 1986.

——. "Peasant Women and Economic Transformation in The Gambia." *Development and Change* 23, 2 (April 1992): 67–90.

Cook, David, and Arnold Hughes. "The Politics of Economic Recovery: The Gambia's Experience of Structural Adjustment, 1985–94." *Journal of Commonwealth and Comparative Politics* 35, 1 (March 1997): 93–117.

Cooke, David G. D. "Structural Adjustment in Small States: The Case of The Gambia, 1985–1994." Ph.D. diss., University of Birmingham, England, 1995.

Dey, Jenny. "Women and Rice in The Gambia: The Impact of Irrigated Rice Development Projects on the Farming System." Ph.D. diss., University of Reading, England, 1980.

——. "Gambian Women: Unequal Partners in Rice Development Projects?" *Journal of Development Studies* 17, 3 (April 1981): 109–122.

——. "Development Planning in The Gambia: The Gap between Planners' and Farmers' Perceptions, Expectations and Objectives." *World Development* 10, 5 (1982): 377–396.

Dudgeon, G. G. *The Agricultural and Forest Products of British West Africa.* London: 1911. For the Gambia, see 1–14.

Economist Intelligence Unit. *The Gambia.* Fourth Quarter. London: EIU, 1994.

Esh, Tina, and Illith Rosenblum. "Tourism in Developing Countries — Trick or Treat? A Report from The Gambia." *Research Report no. 31.* Uppsala: The Scandinavian Institute of African Studies, 1975.

Gailey, Harry A. "Fixing the Rate for Gambia Jobs." *West Africa,* 11 February 1961.

——. "Portrait, Gambia's Labour Leader." *West Africa,* 17 May 1961.

——. "Jallow's Progress." Portrait, *West Africa,* 2 May 1964.

Gamble, David P. *Contributions to a Socio-economic Survey of The Gambia.* London: Colonial Office, 1949.

——. *Economic Conditions in Two Mandinka Villages: Kerewan and Keneba.* London: Colonial Office, 1955.

Hadjmichael, M.T., et al. "The Gambia: Economic Adjustment in a Small Open Economy." *IMF Occasional Paper 100.* Washington, D.C.: IMF, 1992.

Hamer, Alice. "Diola Women and Migration: A Case Study." In *The Uprooted of the Western Sahel: Migrants' Quest for Cash in the Senegambia,* ed. Lucie Gallistel Colvin, et. al. New York: Praeger, 1981.

Harrell-Bond, B. E., and D. Harrell-Bond. "Tourism in The Gambia." *Review of African Political Economy* no. 14 (January/April 1979): 78–90.

Haswell, Margaret R. *Economics of Agriculture in a Savannah Village.* London: HMSO, 1953.

————. *The Changing Pattern of Economic Activity in a Gambian Village.* London: HMSO, 1963.

————. *The Nature of Poverty: A Case-history of the First Quarter Century after World War II.* London: Macmillan, 1975.

————. *Energy for Subsistence.* London: Macmillan, 1981.

Hughes, A., and D. Perfect. "Trade Unionism in The Gambia." *African Affairs* 88, 349 (December 1989): 549–572.

Ivor, Thomas. "Lessons of Gambia Poultry Farm." *New Commonwealth,* August 1951, 88–89.

Jarrett, H. R. "Population and Settlement in the Gambia." *Geographic Review* 38, 4 (October 1948): 633–636.

————. "The Strange Farmers of the Gambia." *Geographical Review* 39, 4 (October 1949): 649–657.

McPherson, M. F. "The Politics of Economic Reform in The Gambia." *Development Discussion Papers No. 386.* Cambridge, Mass.: 1991: 23–24.

Manneh, Momodou S. K. *Cooperatives in The Gambia: An Examination of the Administrative Problems of the Gambia Cooperative Marketing Unions and Their Impact on National Economic Development.* Ann Arbor, Mich.: University Microfilms, 1975.

Momoh, Eddie. "Gambia Budget: Sisay's Medicine." *West Africa,* 25 July 1983.

————. "The Gambia: Struggle for Recovery." *West Africa,* 9 January 1984.

————. "Sweet and Sour." *West Africa,* 7 September 1987 [review of the Economic Recovery Program].

Perfect, D. "Organized Labour and Politics in The Gambia: 1960–85." *LABOUR, Capital and Society* 19, 2 (November 1986): 169–199.

————. "Organised Labour and Politics in The Gambia: 1921–1984." Ph.D. diss., University of Birmingham, England, 1987.

Radelet, S. "Reform without Revolt: The Political Economy of Economic Reform in The Gambia." *World Development* 20, 8 (1993): 1087–1099.

Sallah, T. M. "Economics and Politics in The Gambia." *Journal of Modern African Studies* 28, 4 (1990).

Samura, Mohammed L. O'Bai. *The Role of the Cooperative Movement in Gambia's National Development.* Ann Arbor, Mich.: University Microfilms, 1982.

Sey, Fatou. "Living with the ERP." *West Africa,* 20 October 1986.

Swindell, Kenneth. "Sera Woolies, Tillibunkas and Strange Farmers: The Development of Migrant Groundnut Farming along the Gambia River, 1848–95." *Journal of African History* 21, 1 (1980).

———. *The Strange Farmers of The Gambia: A Study in the Redistribution of African Population*. Norwich, England: Geo Books, 1982.

Vision 2020. The Gambia Incorporated. Banjul: Government Printer, May 1996.

Webb, Patrick J. R. "Of Rice and Men: The Story behind The Gambia's Decision to Dam Its River." In *The Social and Environmental Effects of Large Dams, Vol. 2*, ed. Edward Goldsmith and Nicholas Hildyard. Wadebridge, England: 1984.

Articles Listed Chronologically, No Author

"Rehousing and Townplanning in the Gambia." *West African Review*, October 1946, 1123–1124.

"Bathurst Drainage and Reclamation Work." *Crown Colonist* 17 (November 1947), 605–606.

"IICDC Statement on the Gambian Egg Scheme." *West Africa*, 21 April 1951.

"Lord Trefgarne on the Gambia Poultry Scheme." *West Africa*, 21 April 1951.

"New Act on Wages in Gambia." *International Labour Review* [Geneva] 94 (October 1966): 416.

Official Correspondence and Reports (listed chronologically; except where otherwise stated, all are published in Bathurst by the Government Printer)

Dawe, M. T. *Report on the Agricultural Conditions and Needs of the Gambia*. Bathurst: Crown Agents for the Government of the Gambia, 1921.

Brooks, A. J. *The Cultivation of Groundnuts*. Bathurst: Department of Agriculture Bulletin No 3, 1929.

Rosevear, D. R. *A Report on the Forest Conditions of the Gambia*. Banjul: Gambia National Archives, 1936. A shortened version was published as "Forest Conditions of the Gambia." *The Empire Forest Journal* 16 (1937): 217–226.

Statement of Policy on Colonial Development and Welfare. Cmd.6175. London: 1940.

Blackburne, K. W., et al. *Development and Welfare in the Gambia*. Bathurst: 1943.

Rae, C. J. *Report on Swamp Reclamation and the Improvements of Existing Rice Lands by Drainage, Irrigation, etc., in the Gambia*. Sessional Paper No 1. Bathurst: 1943.

Rodden, G. M. *A Report of Rice Cultivation in the Gambia*. Sessional Paper No 2. Bathurst: 1943.

Correspondence with the Secretary of State for the Colonies on the Replanning of Bathurst and the Development of Kombo. Sessional Paper No 1. Bathurst: 1944.

Report of a Committee Appointed to Enquire into the Conduct and Management of the River Steamer Service. Sessional Paper No 11. Bathurst: 1944.

Secretary of State's Reply to the Second Application for Assistance under C. D. W. Act for Bathurst/Kombo. Sessional Paper No 12. Bathurst: 1945.

Report of the Committee Appointed to Consider Remedial Measures to be Adopted to Deal with Overcrowding in Bathurst. Sessional Paper No 18. Bathurst: 1946.

Palmer, J. H. *Notes on Strange Farmers*. Sessional Paper No 15. Bathurst: 1946.

Report on the Gambian Egg Scheme. Cmd.8560. London: H.M.S.O., 1952.

Van der Plas, C. O. *Report of a Survey of Rice Areas in the Central Division of the Gambia Protectorate*. Bathurst: 1955.

Exploration for Petroleum Deposits in Gambia. Sessional Paper No 6. Bathurst: 1959.

Gambian Government, Development Plan, 1964–67. Sessional Paper No 10. Bathurst: 1964.

Revision of the Development Programme 1964–67. Sessional Paper No 1. Bathurst: 1966.

Gambia Government, 1967–68 to 1970–71. Sessional Paper No 4. Bathurst: 1967.

Third Development Programme 1971/72 to 1973/74. Bathurst: 1971.

Five Year Plan for Economic and Social Development 1975/76–1979/80. Banjul: 1975.

World Bank. Basic Needs in The Gambia. Washington, D.C.: World Bank, 1981.

Five Year Plan for Economic and Social Development 1981/82–1985/86. Banjul: 1982.

Tesito. Five Year Plan for Economic and Social Development 1981/82–1985/86. Banjul: 1983.

World Bank. The Gambia: Development Issues and Prospects. Report Number 5693—GM. Washington, D.C.: World Bank, 1985.

The Economic Recovery Programme. Banjul: 1986.

World Bank. The Gambia—An Assessment of Poverty. Report Number 11941—GM. Washington, D.C.: World Bank, 1993.

In addition, all Gambian government departments publish annual reports (e.g., Agriculture, Education, Labour). The President's annual address to parliament on the state of the nation is also published, as is the annual budget speech of the Minister of Finance.

ANTHROPOLOGY AND SOCIOLOGY

General

Ames, David. "The Use of a Traditional Cloth-Money Token Among the Wolof." *American Anthropologist* 57, 5 (October 1955): 1016–1024.

———. "The Economic Base of Wolof Polygyny." *Southwestern Journal of Anthropology* 2, 4 (Winter 1955): 391–403.

———. "The Selection of Mates: Courtship and Marriage Among the Wolof." *Bulletin de l'Institut français d'Afrique noire* [Dakar] Sér. B 18, 1–2 (1956): 156–168.

———. "The Dual Function of the 'Little People' of the Forest in the Lives of the Wolof." *Journal of American Folklore* 71 (January-March 1958): 23–26.

Gamble, David P. *The Wolof of the Senegambia, together with Notes on the Lebu*. London: 1967.

Haddon, A. G. *Wandering of Peoples*. London: 1911.

Jectson, Seth. "Njuli Boys: Circumcision Rites in the Gambia." *West African Review*, October 1952, 1035.

Peil, Margaret. *Cities and Suburbs: Urban Life in West Africa*. New York: Africana Publishing, 1981 [Banjul and Serekunda].

Schaffer, Matt, and Christine Cooper. *Mandinko: The Ethnography of a West African Holy Land*. New York: Holt, Rinehart and Winston, 1980.

Sonko-Godwin, Patience. *Ethnic Groups of the Senegambia*. Banjul: Sunrise Publishers Ltd., 1988.

Southhorn, Lady Bella. "The Old Woman of Fattoto." *West African Review*, July 1938, 17–18.

Weil, Peter M. "Language Distribution in the Gambia 1966–67." *African Language Review* no. 7 (1968): 101–106.

———. "The Masked Figure and Social Control: The Mandinka Case." *Africa* 41, 4 (1971): 279–293.

———. "Political Structure and Process among the Gambia Mandinka: The Village Parapolitical System." In *Papers on the Manding*, ed. Carleton T. Hodge. Bloomington, Ind.: Indiana University Press; The Hague: Mouton & Co., 1971 (249–272).

———. "The Staff of Life: Food and Fertility in a West African Society." *Africa* 46, 2 (1976).

Census Reports

Report of the Census Commissioner for Bathurst, 1944. Sessional Paper No 2. Bathurst: 1945.
Report of the Census Commissioner for the Colony, 1951. Sessional Paper No 4. Bathurst: 1952.
Report on the Census of the Population of the Gambia, April 1963. Sessional Paper No 13. Bathurst: 1965.
Population Census 1973. Provisional Report. Banjul: Central Statistics Division.
Population Census 1983. Provisional Report. Banjul: Central Statistics Division.
Population and Housing Census 1993. Provisional Report. Banjul: Central Statistics Department.

CULTURAL

The Press

General

The Daily Observer (five issues a week: independent).
Foroyaa (weekly: PDOIS).
The Gambia Daily (three times a week: state-owned).
The Gambia. News and Report (monthly: independent).
Government Gazette (occasional, official)
The Nation (would now appear to have ceased publication).
New Citizen (weekly: independent).
Newsmonth (monthly: independent).
The Point (twice weekly: independent).
Upfront (occasional: APRC).

All newspapers are published in the Banjul area. There are also occasional special interest newsletters produced by the Catholic Church and by environmental interests.

Defunct newspapers:

The African Herald.

The Bathurst Intelligencer.
The Bathurst Observer and West Africa Gazette.
The Daily News.
The Gambia Echo.
The Gambia News Bulletin.
Gambia Onward.
The Gambia Outlook.
The Gambia Outlook and Senegambia Reporter.
The Gambia Times.
The Gambia Weekly News.
The Gambian.
The Hibarr.
Kibaro.
New Gambia.
Official Gazette of the Senegambia Confederation.
The Progressive Newspaper.
The Senegambia Sun.
The Sun.
The SunTorch.
The Vanguard.
The Worker.
   Incomplete holdings of most of these are to be found at the Gambia National Archives in Banjul.

The Arts: Literature

Dibba, Ebou. *Chaff on the Wind.* London: Macmillan, 1986.
———. *Fafa.* London: Macmillan, 1989.
Peters, [Dr.] Lenrie. *Satellites.* London: Heinemann, 1967 and 1971.
———. *Katchikali.* London: Heinemann, 1971.
———. *Selected Poetry.* London: Heinemann, 1981.

The Arts: Music

Coolen, Michael T. "The Wolof *Xalam* Tradition of the Senegambia." *Ethnomusicology* 27, 3 (September 1983): 477–498.
Jatta, Sidia. "Born Musicians: Traditional Music from The Gambia." In *Repercussions: A Celebration of African-American Music,* ed. Geoffrey Haydon and Dennis Marks. London: Century, 1985 (19–29).

Jessup, Lynne. *The Mandinka Balafon: An Introduction with Notation for Teaching.* La Mesa, Calif.: Xylo Publications, 1983.

Knight, Roderic Copley. "Mandinka Drumming." *African Arts* 7, 4 (summer 1984): 24–35.

————. "Music in Africa." In *Performance Practice: Ethnomusicological Perspectives,* ed. Gerard Behague. Westport, Conn.: Greenwood Press, 1984: 53–90.

Pevar, Susan Gunn. "The Gambian Kora." *Sing Out* 25, 6 (1977): 15–17.

Religion

Ames, David. "Belief in Witches Among the Rural Wolof of the Gambia." *Africa* 29 (July 1959): 263–373.

Anderson, J. N. D. *Islamic Law in Africa.* London: 1954. See 225–248 for The Gambia.

Centenary: 100 Years of Missionary Service by the Sisters of St. Joseph of Cluny in the Gambia, 1883–1983. Banjul: Book Production and Material Resources Unit, 1983.

Biller, Sarah. *Memoir of Hannah Kilham.* London: Darton and Harvey, 1837.

Daly, John. *Four Mitres: Reminiscences on an Irrepressible Bishop: Parts 1 and 2.* Oxford: John Daly, 1983–1984.

Dickson, Mora. *The Powerful Bond: Hannah Kilham 1774–1832.* London: Dennis Dobson, 1980.

Fisher, Humphrey. "Ahmadiyya in the Gambia, French Territories and Liberia." *West Africa,* 27 January 1962, 93.

Haythornthwaite, W. "The Church in the Gambia." *East and West Review* 14 (1950): 122–125.

Morgan, John. *Reminiscences of the Founding of a Christian Mission on the Gambia.* London: Wesleyan Mission House, 1864.

Nyang, Sylayman S. "Local and National Elites and Islam in The Gambia: An African Case Study." *International Journal of Islamic and Arabic Studies* 1, 2 (1984): 57–67.

Pricket, Barbara. *Island Base: A History of the Methodist Church in The Gambia, 1821–1969* Banjul: Methodist Church Gambia, 1971.

Sanneh, Lamin O. *The Jakhanke: The History of an Islamic Clerical People of The Gambia.* London: International African Institute, 1979.

Yahuda, Patricia. "Christian Linguists in the Senegambia before 1830." Ph.D. diss., University of Aberdeen, Scotland, 1980.

About the Authors

Harry A. Gailey (B.A., M.A., Ph.D., University of California at Los Angeles) is a Professor of History and Coordinator of the African Studies Program at San Jose State University. His research in African history dates to the colonial period. A recipient of many grants and awards, he did the primary research for this work while in The Gambia on a Ford Foundation grant. Subsequently, he returned to Africa a number of times on other research projects, he also taught graduate students in Nigeria and Kenya and was a visiting lecturer for the U.S. Information Agency in The Gambia, Sierra Leone, and Somalia. He is the author of 11 books relating to modern Africa. Among these are *A History of The Gambia, A History of Africa* (3 vols.), *Lugard and the Abeokuta Uprising,* and *The Road to Aba.*

Arnold Hughes was educated at the University of Wales, Aberystwyth and Ibadan University, Nigeria. He is Professor of African Politics at the University of Birmingham and, until recently, was Director of its Centre of West African Studies. A Commonwealth Scholar in Nigeria, he has also researched widely in other parts of West Africa and, since 1972, has developed a particular interest in Gambian history and politics. He has edited or co-edited six books related to Africa, including *The Gambia: Studies in Politics and Society* and *Marxism's Retreat from Africa,* and is currently completing a monograph on the political history of The Gambia from 1816 to 1994. He has visited The Gambia over 20 times in connection with his research and conducted extensive archival research and interviews. He is also editor of *Commonwealth and Comparative Politics.*